Praise for *The Bullseye Principle*

"Effective communication is vital to business success. It is the key to real leadership and it is necessary at all levels of any enterprise. *The Bullseye Principle* is an invaluable guide to successful communication."

—Colin Stanbridge, CEO, London Chamber of Commerce and Industry

"A useful reminder for leaders and advisers of some key principles and practical approaches that will increase your impact within your organization and with your clients."

—Michael Burke, CEO Talent, Rewards, Performance, Aon

"Great insights to engage and influence people who matter the most in the moment when it matters the most, and all I need to do is to bring my best self."

—Arti Gusain, Group Leader, Leadership and Organizational Development Team, Infosys Leadership Institute

"*The Bullseye Principle* not only outlines simple tools and a 3-step process to help me connect with my audience, it also reinforces the importance of intentionality and authenticity."

—Pat Wadors, Chief Talent Officer, ServiceNow

"Love it! *The Bullseye Principle* is an excellent resource for anyone wanting to be a more engaging and influential leader."

—Kevin Kruse, Founder, LEADx.org and New York Times Bestselling Author

"*The Bullseye Principle* has empowered me to better command the attention of my audience, ensuring my message and my call to action are clearly understood."

—Jim De Maria, former Executive Director of Communication, Chicago Blackhawks

"Yet another masterpiece by Lewis and Mills . . . enthralling and captivating. I recommend this book, especially to executives who want to make their mark."

—Prachi Mishra, Learning & Development Head, Dassault India

"*The Bullseye Principle* deals with pragmatic communication strategies and tools . . . a good reference for leaders who aspire to lead transformations, persuade changes, and connect with an audience to deliver results."

—Ajinth Sreedharan, Head of North America Learning and Development, Capgemini

"The stories we tell ourselves and others make or break an organization. Lewis and Mills provide a gold standard resource here for leaders to connect with others effectively, and to simply get things done. Fabulous read."

—Han Ee Lim, CEO, Singapore Sailing

"A great read for the executive who needs a tune-up on how to have impactful conversations with their audience. The authors remind us how communication is an art in need of practice."

—Holly Buckendahl, CEO, Ronald McDonald House Charities®
Chicagoland & NW Indiana

"For years, our Executive Education clients have ranked the techniques taught by Lewis and Mills at the top of the scale. *The Bullseye Principle* is yet another 'top pick' for those who are serious about mastering communication."

—Bill Joiner, Executive Director, Business Development,
Southern Methodist University, COX Executive Education

"Relevant and timely. In an era of communication confusion, *The Bullseye Principle*, brings to light distinct communication struggles and exactly how you can improve yourself to succeed personally and professionally."

—Krysta Van Ranst, Director of Learning and Development,
Dellbrook | JKS

"*The Bullseye Principle* delivers exquisite techniques that help our leaders drive business impact and meaningful conversations that matter."

—Christina Itzkowitz, Senior Director Global Talent Management,
Charles River Laboratories

"*The Bullseye Principle* hits the mark dead center. As a former Major League Baseball player, knowing the techniques in this book would have made me a better team communicator and team leader. It definitely will aid me, post MLB, as I pursue my speaking career."

—Brian D. Barton, former Major League Baseball Player, St. Louis Cardinals

"*The Bullseye Principle* is one of the most useful and captivating books I have read in years. Simple and powerful, it cleverly links a proven methodology to help readers build executive presence and influence others simply by the way they communicate."

—Mark McNitt, Director Business Process, Ferguson Enterprises

"With an emphasis on objective and intent, Lewis and Mills have constructed a succinct technique that enables one to clearly achieve their goals through communication."

—Scott Michael Campbell, film and television actor
(*Brokeback Mountain, Flight of the Phoenix, Shameless*)

"Recent college grads, as well as more experienced workers, will find not only an entertaining read but a book that moves you from mere 'ah-ha' moments to actualizing an exciting new approach to communication and influence. Readers beware . . . there is a new you on the horizon!"

—Janine G. Tarkow, Director STRIVE Leadership Program,
University of California, San Diego

DAVID LEWIS
G. RILEY MILLS

THE BULLSEYE

PRINCIPLE

Mastering Intention-Based Communication
to Collaborate, Execute, and Succeed

WILEY

Published by John Wiley & Sons, Inc., Hoboken, New Jersey.
Published simultaneously in Canada.

For general information on our other products and services or for technical support, please contact our Customer Care Department within the United States at (800) 762–2974, outside the United States at (317) 572–3993 or fax (317) 572–4002.

Wiley publishes in a variety of print and electronic formats and by print-on-demand. Some material included with standard print versions of this book may not be included in e-books or in print-on-demand. If this book refers to media such as a CD or DVD that is not included in the version you purchased, you may download this material at http://booksupport.wiley.com. For more information about Wiley products, visit www.wiley.com.

Library of Congress Cataloging-in-Publication Data:

Names: Lewis, David H., 1970- author. | Mills, G. Riley, author.
Title: The bullseye principle : mastering intention-based communication to collaborate, execute, and succeed / David Lewis, G. Riley Mills.
Description: Hoboken : Wiley, 2018. | Includes index. |
Identifiers: LCCN 2017057632 (print) | LCCN 2018003857 (ebook) | ISBN 9781119484707 (pdf) | ISBN 9781119484677 (epub) | ISBN 9781119484714 (hardback) | ISBN 9781119484707 (ePDF)
Subjects: LCSH: Communication in management. | Leadership. | Cooperation. | BISAC: BUSINESS & ECONOMICS / Leadership.
Classification: LCC HD30.3 (ebook) | LCC HD30.3 .L486 2018 (print) | DDC 658.4/5–dc23
LC record available at https://lccn.loc.gov/2017057632

Printed in the United States of America

V10013858_091219

When an archer misses the mark . . . failure to hit the bullseye is never the fault of the target. To improve your aim, improve yourself.
—Gilbert Arland

Contents

Introduction

In order to succeed, we must first believe we can.
—Michael Korda

T ruth be told, we never intended to write the book you are now holding in your hands. After completing our first book, *The Pin Drop Principle*, we thought we had said everything we wanted to say on the subject of communication skills and becoming a more influential speaker. But in the years since its release, as we traveled the world training and coaching executives across various industries, something interesting started to happen. We began to notice distinct shifts in the way people were communicating with one another, how they were presenting information and new ways in which they were managing their teams. Communication in the corporate arena was changing and many of the old ways were no longer proving useful. One study found that people interact with their cell phones—touching, tapping, swiping—an average of 2,617 times a day.[1] Another study revealed that 67 percent of people felt that the meetings they attended at their job were generally a waste of time[2] and a third study found that 65 percent of workers wanted to receive more feedback from their managers because they were not getting what they needed.[3] We suddenly realized it was time to revisit some of the concepts we had touched upon previously and explore them in greater detail, to further the conversation and continue to untangle the intricacies of human communication and the ways in which people interact with one another.

And then the election of 2016 happened.

As a young man growing up in Queens, Donald Trump often fantasized about being an actor on the New York stage, commanding the attention of an audience and basking in the spotlight. In 2016, Trump's shocking electoral victory made the public question everything they thought they understood about how leaders are expected to behave, how messages get conveyed, and how opinions are developed. What was once thought of as effective communication seemed to momentarily get scrambled, and in some ways, redefined. We will touch upon the good, the bad, and the ugly aspects of Trump's communication in later chapters, but this, combined with groundbreaking new research on the topic of communication, created an urgency for us to embark on a more detailed exploration of modern communication with the hope of eventually sharing our findings with the public. This book is the culmination of that work.

The ability to communicate with purpose and clarity is the key to personal and professional success.

That statement is the core and founding belief behind our global communication skills training firm Pinnacle Performance Company. Those who have trained with us or read *The Pin Drop Principle* know that we approach the subject of communication from a very unique vantage point in that we both have extensive experience running businesses and managing sales teams in the corporate arena, while also having enjoyed careers as professional actors, working in television, film, and theater. It is the meshing of these two distinct skill sets—the corporate and the creative—that has formed the basis of our acclaimed, *intention-based communication*™ skills training and methodology.

For the past 15 years, we have been fortunate to train leaders and executives in nearly 50 countries, studying the way people interact with one another and noting what works, what doesn't, and where communication gets short-circuited. In the end, human beings all want to understand and be understood, but effective communication is not something that happens easily. And without a firm grasp of the elements needed to be a good communicator, there is no guarantee it will happen at all. Think about how communication impacts you on a daily basis with your boss, your clients, your peers, and even your family members. In fact, think about your life at this very moment. Wherever you are as you read this paragraph, chances are pretty good that right now, today, there is a relationship in your life, either personal or professional, that is causing you stress or anxiety. And there is also a high probability that the cause of that tension can be traced back to a problem with how the two of you are communicating with each other.

In the Pinnacle methodology, we detail how the same set of tools that actors have used for centuries to appear more confident, credible, and captivating, can just as easily be utilized by someone in the corporate environment. In the following chapters, we will delve deeper into these concepts by sharing additional principles that professional performers utilize to define their brand, show empathy, perform under pressure, and collaborate effectively with others. We will show you just how quickly and easily these techniques can be transferred to the corporate arena—helping you improve performance, re-engage with your content, and get results. Our award-winning, intention-based methodology utilizes a strategic psychological approach that incorporates the acting mindset of objective and intention to influence audience emotion to motivate behavior change. We have distilled what we call The Pinnacle Method™ down to three specific steps that we will share in Chapter 1. It is the implementation of these three steps that will serve as a foundation for the material we share throughout the rest of this book. At the end of each chapter, you will find guides called "blueprints" that we have created to help you apply the content to your own communication. These guides will not only help you lock in the learning, they can also serve as a resource whenever you need to revisit

Being good in business is the most fascinating kind of art.

—ANDY WARHOL

a specific topic—when dealing with a sudden change scenario at work, adjusting to a new role, or running a weekly status meeting.

The quote from Gilbert Arland that we include at the beginning of this book is an illuminating one. Picture an arrow whizzing through the air toward its target. That is how we view communication. It doesn't matter your role or what topic you are discussing, if the arrow that is your message does not hit its intended bullseye, you will have fallen short of the mark as a communicator. If your audience is bored during your meeting or confused during your presentation, it is your fault. The burden of engagement always lies with the speaker.

To extend the metaphor even further, if the bullseye in this image is the objective you seek with your communication and the arrow represents your message, then your intention is the way in which you *launch* that arrow—the specific adjustments you make with regard to the aim, angle, and depth of the pull—that sends your ideas out into the world. The pairing of a strong intention utilized in the pursuit of a specific objective is the secret weapon that actors and great leaders use to engage and influence and is something we will explore in greater detail shortly.

Sergey Brin and Larry Page, the brilliant computer scientists who founded Google, always believed that "hard skills" and technical expertise were the most important qualities necessary for workplace success. But in 2013, Google ran a study called Project Oxygen that shocked everyone by concluding that, among the eight most important qualities of their top employees, technical expertise actually came in dead last. The top seven characteristics of success for their teams were all "soft skills": being a good coach; communicating and listening well, having empathy toward one's colleagues, etc.[4]

In a recent Wall Street Journal survey of nearly 900 executives, more than 92 percent said skills such as communication and collaboration were "equally important" or "more important" than technical skills with regard to their workforce.[5] Unfortunately, nearly the same number of executives—89 percent—said they have a difficult time finding people with these requisite attributes.[6] One recent survey found a huge gap between the younger generation's perception of their skills and what their bosses actually thought. About 62 percent of these young workers believed their oral communication skills were good enough for them to succeed at work, but only 28 percent of their employers agreed.[7] Their ability to collaborate as part of a team was also seen differently, as 64 percent of students thought they worked well with others but only 37 percent of their bosses agreed.[8] What these numbers reveal is that communication in the corporate arena needs to be better for your teams and organizations to thrive. According to Richard Branson, the billionaire founder of Virgin Airlines, "Communication is the most important skill any leader can possess,"[9] and Warren Buffett agrees, saying, "You can improve your value by 50 percent just by learning communication skills."[10]

Scientists and experts have been studying communication for centuries to try to understand why people behave the way they do. As professional actors, we know that communication is never simply about the information being exchanged; it is also about *how* it is being communicated. In the end, it is the emotion and motivation behind your message that will compel your audience to take action. The subtle tactics and modifications an actor or speaker add to their delivery are called *intention cues*, something we will discuss in Chapter 1. According to Ken Howard, an Emmy- and Tony-award-winning actor who has also taught a course on salesmanship at Harvard, "Like an actor, the effective communicator has to have an overall objective and then play the actions to fulfill that objective. . . . At every level—in politics, diplomacy, law, education, business, social relations—effective communication is about winning people's attention, impressing them, then getting them to do what you believe they ought to do: buy the product, beat the competition, hire you."[11]

Communication, when delivered effectively, has the power to transform and deepen relationships, while ineffective communication can result in a toxic stew of anger or resentment that can lose clients, negatively impact employee morale, and ruin friendships. Sadly, when it comes to communication, most people are simply not very good at it. According to recent studies, 71 percent of those surveyed reported

Power consists in one's capacity to link his will with the purpose of others.

—WOODROW WILSON

that their managers did not spend enough time explaining goals to them.[12] Additionally, 70 percent of respondents in another survey said they would be happier and 55 percent said they would be more successful if they got along better with their bosses.[13] These numbers should be a wake-up call to anyone tasked with leading a workforce or managing a team. One popular Gallup study found that a stunning 67 percent of employees in the United States were currently "not engaged" or "actively disengaged" with their jobs[14] and that number climbs to 85 percent worldwide.[15] These disengaged employees end up costing U.S. companies an estimated $450–550 billion annually.[16] In upcoming chapters, we will delve deeper into the solutions we recommend for keeping people motivated, but clearly communication is at the forefront of these efforts.

To engage an audience and make them listen, to persuade them to take action or see something your way, your message should provide a benefit and connect directly to their own personal wants, needs, or desires. Twentieth-century Russian theater director Constantin Stanislavski, often credited as the father of modern acting, knew the importance of engagement. "Completely absorb an audience," he would say, "Making [them] not only understand but participate emotionally in . . . an experience which will not be erased by time."[17] In the following chapters, when we use the term "audience," we are referring to anyone with whom you communicate, such as peers, clients, wedding guests, or your future in-laws. Anyone you come into contact with or communicate ideas to is an audience. Viola Spolin, who revolutionized the idea of improvisational acting for twentieth-century actors, once said: "The audience is the most revered member of the theater . . . everything done is ultimately for the enjoyment of the audience. They are our guests, fellow players, and the last spoke in the wheel which can then begin to roll."[18] This same idea applies to anyone presenting information in a business setting, whether delivering a presentation to clients or running a meeting for your local PTA. Like an actor in the theater, the success of your performance will depend on how effectively you deliver your message and how well it is received by your intended audience.

"The role of public speaker has much in common with acting," said Ken Howard. "The character that you have to perfect is the best version of yourself—for that occasion and that audience. Not a phony version of yourself, just a better-prepared version."[19] In the corporate arena, the speaker's situation is similar to that of the actor's. They both have an objective they are pursuing and both employ various tactics—what we call *intentions*—to achieve that objective. The renowned acting coach Declan Donnellan takes this idea one step further, stating, "We live by acting roles, be it father, mother, teacher, or friend. Acting is a reflex, a mechanism for development and survival."[20]

In business, everyone has a role to play and an audience to influence. Our training is at the forefront of a new movement in the business world to utilize the methods of professional actors to help business leaders thrive. Schools such as MIT Sloane School of Management, Stanford Graduate School of Business, Darden School of Business at University of Virginia, Tuck School of Business at Dartmouth, Cox School of Business at Southern Methodist University, and University of Oxford and Warwick Business School in the United Kingdom have all drawn lessons from the world of theater and acting to enhance their MBA students' abilities to be strong leaders and communicators. In his groundbreaking book *Emotional Intelligence,* Daniel Goleman makes the connection between the skills of an actor and how these can be utilized for each of us in our daily lives. "People who make an excellent social impression," said Goleman, "are adept at monitoring their own expression of emotion, are keenly attuned to the ways others are reacting, and so are able to continually fine-tune their social performance, adjusting it to make sure they are having the desired effect. In that sense, they are like skilled actors."[21]

Influential leaders have been employing the principles of professional actors to improve their communication for centuries—going all the way back to 360 BC, when the actor Satyrus transformed the Athenian statesman Demosthenes into one of the most dynamic orators of all time.[22] So revered as a communicator was Demosthenes that the famed ad man David Ogilvy, widely hailed as "The Father of Advertising," cited him as the inspiration for his persuasive ad campaigns, saying, "When Aeschines spoke, they said, 'How well he speaks.' But when Demosthenes spoke, they said, 'Let us march against Philip.'"[23]

The idea of influential speakers borrowing from the actor's toolbox has a very prominent place in world history. Winston Churchill and Abraham Lincoln performed Shakespeare to help sharpen their oratorical chops. Ronald Reagan, Oprah Winfrey, Michael Strahan, Vaclav Havel, and Justin Trudeau were all actors before transitioning to leadership roles. And yet others such as Barack Obama, Bill Clinton, Angela Merkel, John F. Kennedy, Suze Orman, and Tony Robbins all studied with acting coaches to improve their presence and delivery. Even Dale Carnegie, the author of *How to Win Friends and Influence People*, started out as an actor. And there is good reason that all of these leaders have leaned on the performance methods of actors to improve their communication. Through training and practice, actors become body language detectives, human sponges, studying the way people speak, move, gesture, stand, and dress, down to the smallest detail. To some degree, the same holds true for anyone working in the corporate environment. We all make judgments about others based on how they look, what they say, and how they say it. To be trusted, we need to appear authentic and credible in the eyes of our audiences. Consequently, the more credible and believable you appear, the more trust you will engender with your audience and the more success you will inevitably achieve. Stanislavski always demanded "believable truth" from his actors, saying, "On the stage, as in real life, action, objectives, given circumstances, a sense of truth, concentration of attention, emotion, memory—should be indivisible."[24] Many of Stanislavski's methods and texts, though originally meant for actors, can serve anyone wanting to be a more influential communicator. Actors understand that communication comes from the total presence of a person and the following chapters will provide information on how to improve that as well. We all have a natural energy that runs through us and affects the way we breathe, speak, move, and listen. Much like an actor performing a scene in a play or film, when you and a coworker are talking, you're attuned to and making judgments based on their facial expressions, gestures, and tone of voice, as well as the actual words they

Intention is the key to mastery.

—ROB HANNA

are speaking. You are in motion as you try to relate to each other and you are both responding to dozens of intention cues that are happening all at once. This is the realm of the professional actor.

Jayne Benjulian, who served as the first chief speechwriter for Apple in the 1980s, understood the parallels between the performance of an actor and that of an executive in the boardroom. "Once," recalled Benjulian, "I took an Apple executive to a writing workshop to show him how actors work. He asked me: 'How do you act sincerely?' Truthfully, it's not an act. Great speakers risk being fully present in the moment."[25] Effective communication, whether during a meeting or presentation, should feel fresh and spontaneous to an audience, as if they are the first person ever to hear these words. Actors understand that nothing deflates an audience's interest level quicker than a speaker whose delivery sounds memorized or robotic. This goes for an audience watching a presentation or attending a meeting at work. You've got to engage your audience to influence behavior change and this book will help you do just that. To be clear: The goal of this book is not to teach you how to be an actor. Acting is a craft and takes years to master. Additionally, we are not asking you to become an entertainer, or magically transform into an extrovert when you are a naturally introverted person. We simply want you to be a *performer* in the sense of performance as it relates to interviews, meetings, and executive presence—bringing your best self to the moment, no matter the setting, no matter the audience.

The Bullseye Principle can be read sequentially or read in a modular way. Feel free to read the first chapter to understand our three-step process and the concepts of intention and objective and then jump to specific chapters that you find most interesting, in whatever order you choose. For those who read *The Pin Drop Principle*, the terms we use here will be familiar to you and will allow you to hit the ground running. For those who have not, we have included a glossary in the back of the book for easy reference. As you begin to consider the principles discussed in this book, carefully analyze your own communication. As with any learning process, personal development begins with self-awareness and a willingness to modify behavior to improve performance. Be honest with yourself as you begin experimenting with these concepts and charting a course forward. Don't worry about perfection; instead focus on progress. The road to becoming a more effective communicator is a journey, not a destination. Once you free yourself from the unrealistic idea of perfection, you can begin the process of true self-discovery and improvement. This is probably a good time to remind you that Martin Luther King, Jr., one of the greatest orators in history, got a C in his public speaking class as a seminary student. Only with practice and repetition can any of us hope to move toward mastery. Great speakers are made, not born. Let *The Bullseye Principle* serve as a resource that you can review and revisit as you advance in your career and continue to grow as a leader. By understanding and implementing the methodology and principles discussed in this book, improvement is not only possible, it is all but guaranteed.

Grab a highlighter and let's get started.

CHAPTER 1

Hit Your Mark
Utilizing Intention to Maximize Message Impact

Every objective must carry in itself the germs of action.
—Constantin Stanislavski

If you are a leader in the corporate arena, your role will not only require you to influence the thoughts and feelings of stakeholders inside and outside of your organization, but also to motivate their actions through your vision and ideas. This is no small feat, and it will likely happen on a daily basis, sometimes with high stakes in the balance. Great leadership is practiced one conversation at a time, and someone communicating a message must understand how they want their audience to react before being able to deliver it with impact. Actors are masters of verbal and nonverbal communication; experts at driving their messages home with intent. In this chapter, we will detail our three-step process for influential communication as well as the concepts of intention and objective (the effective communicator's secret weapon), to allow you to engage others by influencing emotions and motivating action.

THE LEGEND OF PHIL DAVISON

As of this writing, if you enter the words "worst speech of all time" into Google's search engine it will bring up over 18 million results. But the very first entry on the very first page of results is a video of a man named Phil Davison. Additionally, if you do a Google search for "worst speaker of all time" it is Phil Davison who once again comes up on the first page of results. (We will pause here for you to go watch the video on YouTube. Trust us, it's worth it.) The speech that Davison delivered brought him international infamy and was named "top political rant" of all time by the *Washington Post*. The story of Phil Davison is an interesting tale and one that offers important lessons for all of us who are tasked with influencing others with our communication.[1]

In 2010, Phil Davison was an aspiring politician in Ohio, a tall and soft-spoken man who still lived with his father in the same house where he had grown up. Davison's political career began when he walked into the Board of Elections for Stark County one day and filled out an application to run for the office of County Treasurer. Davison had been working as a local councilman at the time and decided he wanted to make a difference in his community and help people.

Davison had first become interested in the idea of public service when, as a child, a local politician had knocked on his front door, introducing himself and asking Davison's parents for their vote. Davison was intrigued by this man who had come into his house—connecting with Phil and his family on a personal level, right there at their kitchen table. Davison had listened intently to the man and decided way back then that he would pursue a similar calling himself one day. He loved the idea of meeting people, of understanding their concerns and then helping them make their lives better. During the years before the speech, Davison had been involved as a volunteer with local politics, often donating money to the local Republican party and helping out at various events and fundraisers. But mounting a campaign of his own was something that would need to wait until further down the road. For now, he was happy building relationships, making connections, and paying his dues, biding his time until the moment was right for him to run for office himself.

Then, in 2010, that moment arrived.

Davison had been working as a councilman when he was notified by a local Republican leader that there was an open position. "I thought, 'This might be my one shot,' " said Davison. Urged on by party leaders, he decided the time for him to run for office had finally arrived. The Republican party of Ohio was looking for a candidate to run for the position of Stark County Treasurer and they thought Phil would be a perfect fit. Davison learned that there were five other candidates on the ballot and all six of them had been invited to speak to a group of Republican insiders in Canton, Ohio—the very people who would decide which of the six candidates would get their endorsement and support.

Excited by the opportunity to introduce himself to local leadership, Davison went to work on his speech. He sat down at his kitchen table on a Sunday afternoon and began writing, composing a well-crafted speech that established his credibility, detailed the problems facing Ohio, and proposed a handful of clear, practical solutions that he planned to implement if elected. He threw in a relevant quote from Albert Einstein to drive the theme of his speech home and made sure the powerful phrasing and repetition in the speech would make his points more memorable. He wrote the speech in longhand and then typed it up the following day. Davison called a friend and asked him to watch while he rehearsed his speech. When he had finished the practice run, Davison was energized. The speech suddenly "came to life," he recalled, "it breathed, it moved."

The night of the speech was soon upon him and Davison felt confident and ready. He put on his best suit and headed to Canton where the influential Republican Party insiders were gathering to pick their candidate. He arrived early and did his best to mingle with the other people in attendance. The party chairman approached him and they shook hands. The chairman had placed six numbered slips of paper in a hat and invited the candidates to draw a slip to determine the order in which they would speak. Davison drew the number 6, which meant he would be speaking last, the grand finale of the night's proceedings.

The other speakers took the stage and, one by one, gave their speeches. Finally, it was Davison's turn. He set aside the microphone, judging that he would not need it. You see, something had happened prior to delivering the speech that changed the circumstances for Davison and would soon change the temperature of the room. Before taking his place amongst the other candidates, Davison had been approached by one of the local party leaders who wished him luck with his speech but informed him that party insiders had already decided which of the six candidates they would be backing in the election. "I was told, 'The vote's in and you're not getting it,' " he recalled. Davison was shocked. For years, he had given money and volunteered his time to help these people. He felt humiliated and betrayed. How could this have happened?

As Davison took the stage, he looked out into the audience and took a breath. Many of the party leaders kept their heads down, avoiding eye contact, while others sported buttons endorsing other candidates. As he unrolled his notes, Davison was overcome by emotion and he launched into the speech that would make him famous. Pacing like a caged animal, he locked in on the audience, pointing, glaring, gesticulating: "My name is Phil Davison . . . *and I will not apologize for my tone tonight!*" He delivered every word of the speech he had so carefully prepped and rehearsed. And in less than six minutes, he was done. Davison folded his notes and placed them back in his breast pocket. He took his seat and waited patiently as the votes were counted. A few minutes later, the winner was declared. Davison, alone, headed to the parking lot, got into his car and drove the 40 minutes back to his small hometown of Minerva.

The next morning Davison got up and grabbed the local newspaper to see the coverage of the election. As he read the paper at his kitchen table, the phone rang. It was a college friend, now living in New York. The friend informed Davison that the video of him giving the speech had gone viral and was burning up the Internet. Phil was dumbfounded. Why would anyone be interested in a speech by a losing politician in a local race in Ohio? He would soon find out as the telephone began to ring with one call after another: first the BBC, then *Good Morning America, Comedy Central,* CBS, ABC, NBC, and Fox. Local television reporters swarmed his front door requesting interviews. One reporter even told him: "Mr. Davison, I've been a reporter for 30 years now and I've never been as afraid to go to someone's door as I was today."

As momentum from the video continued to build, the speech popped up in the most random places: a professor in Sweden screened it for her students, college kids would watch it on repeat and then recite it word for word. A beverage company approached Davison to be the spokesman for a new Red Bull-type drink they were about to launch. And it didn't stop there—soon Hollywood came calling. Davison starred in a television commercial for Volkswagen alongside reggae legend Jimmy Cliff. That commercial, which featured a clip of Davison's famous speech, played during the Super Bowl—the most-watched television program of the year. It became a whirlwind journey toward celebrity for the aspiring politician from Minerva. Davison admitted that the sudden fame was not easy to handle. "It was embarrassing, it was exciting, it was new to me. I was scared."

And it was just about at this point in the Phil Davison saga where we enter the story.

When our first book, *The Pin Drop Principle,* was released we were frequently asked to speak at events and conferences, and as part of our presentation, we would often show the Phil Davison video because it was a perfect example of intention and objective going haywire for a speaker. The raw emotion of Davison's delivery—the ranting and pacing and pointing and glaring—did not support the message he was attempting to deliver. This mismatch made Davison appear unhinged, like a lunatic possessed by demons. The incongruence in *what* he was saying versus *how* he was saying it not only confused people, it made Davison look like he was out of control.

One day, after showing the video to a group of executives, we started to wonder what had happened to Davison after he gave that famous speech that turned him into an Internet sensation. We decided to try and locate Phil to see if we could help him develop his skills as a speaker and improve his communication style. For us, it was a chance to put our methodology to the test with what was arguably our most challenging test subject to date: the man known as "the worst speaker of all time."

After locating Phil and explaining to him who we were and what we were attempting to do, he agreed to come to Chicago. We explained our three-step process and detailed how actors and great communicators start by analyzing their audience and then identifying an objective to pursue. We explained how a speaker's body is a billboard and that every aspect of someone's communication—their posture, gestures, vocal dynamics, and movement—contain information that an audience will use to form their perception of them. And we explained that by controlling the intention cues you send out, in the manner of a great actor, you can ultimately control how an audience will feel about you.

When the coaching session was over, Davison finally understood why his speech had gone off the rails: the anger he was expressing created incongruence, or mixed messages, between what he was saying and how he was saying it. We asked him if he still remembered the words to the speech that had made him famous and if he would be willing to redo it, adjusting his intention cues this time so that they now supported the words. Davison was game so we set up a camera and started filming. As he began speaking, a transformation began to take place. Whereas the original speech made Davison look like a maniac, he now appeared relaxed, confident, and professional. He was passionate and likeable, his personality coming through in every moment. The same content now resonated in a way that it hadn't before. (To access and view this video go to www.pinper.com and click on the bullseye image in the bottom right corner of the screen.)

Since becoming famous, Davison has gone on to make appearances on television and at various conferences across the country. He is often recognized on the street or in airports. When we asked Davison how he felt about the fame and notoriety that this famous speech had brought to him, here is what he had to say: "The *Washington Post* said that 'Phil Davison's rant will never be usurped.' That's a helluva statement—it means you can't beat it! Do you know what I'm saying? 'Never be usurped.' Never. *Never*. Not 'might not be.' *Never be usurped.* And I will take that with me until the day I die and they put me in my grave. That counts for something, doesn't it?"

To this day, that speech remains the only public speech Phil Davison has ever given.

In his groundbreaking 1956 book *The Presentation of Self in Everyday Life*, psychologist Erving Goffman used imagery of the theater and the idea that human beings are "social actors"[2] to discuss communication and social interaction. He used the term "performance" to refer to any activity an individual does in front of observers, whether that be chatting with a neighbor in the front yard, facilitating a training session at work or interviewing a candidate for a job. And, like an actor on the stage, Goffman believed that during these performances an individual provides meaning to their audience by the manner in which they behave at any given moment. According to Goffman, when an individual comes in contact with other people, they modify their behavior depending on the audience and setting—much like what an actor does onstage. Goffman believed that individuals, like actors, each have a "front stage" and "back stage" persona and act differently depending on the "setting" in which their "performance" is taking place.[3] Front stage behavior is what one does when they know others are watching them, such as during a presentation at work, walking through a crowded city intersection, or running a meeting with clients. Back stage behavior is different, more private and relaxed, such as when they are at home or alone on a hike in a forest. In both behaviors, people adjust their intentional cues—their voice, dress, attitude—is an attempt to control or guide the impression that others will develop about them. The reason for this is usually to avoid embarrassment or enhance one's stature in the eyes of others. For example, a person will behave differently when meeting with the CEO in a boardroom than they would when speaking to a childhood friend over drinks. Said Goffman, "The part one individual plays is tailored to the parts played by others present."[4]

When actors train in their craft, they don't study the anatomy of the face or which muscles are used for a smile and which are used for a frown. They train themselves to access emotions through intention, knowing that when they feel a specific emotion on the *inside*, it will show on the *outside*. And what others see as a result will then impact their perception of the person. This idea transfers well to anyone in the corporate arena who is tasked with communicating a message to others. If you are presenting something that is meant to excite people but you don't personally feel excited by the proposal, that will likely be read as apathy by your audience and they may mirror back disinterest in kind. Albert Mehrabian, in his landmark study on communication, established that the congruence of your communication requires that three channels—*verbal* (what you say), *vocal* (how you say it), and *visual* (how you look)—be absolutely in sync.[5] When people take in your message, they are deciphering meaning from your delivery to determine how they should feel about what you are saying and how they should respond to it. A congruent message will help to establish trust with a listener by creating alignment and clarity between what is being said and how someone is saying it. It will also ensure consistency with your message, which is also important since studies have shown that when all three channels of communication are aligned, it is more likely that your message will be understood. When they are not, you send mixed signals to an audience that may confuse them or provide an opportunity for your message to be misinterpreted. When someone's communication is incongruent, an audience will barely listen to the message. They will be confused and focused on untangling the mixed messages rather than on the main topic. As communicators, we naturally feel the impulse to be congruent with all three channels of communication, and whenever our attitude is inconsistent with our behavior, we feel discomfort and a natural inclination to resolve it. This is important to understand when you are attempting to influence someone else with your message. If you are communicating something positive or inspiring, an audience will need to hear that reflected in your voice and see it in your body language. Your verbal communication channel communicates facts and information—a crucial element when influencing others. Your nonverbal communication communicates something different but equally important: your attitudes and emotions and how you want them to *feel* about the information. Intention is the glue that binds your verbal and nonverbal communication together. With a strong intention behind your words,

that intention will ensure congru-
ency of message and do your
communication work for you.

*The art of communication
is the language of
leadership.*

We all communicate every
day of our lives, whether we
choose to or not, and we all

—JAMES HUMES

want something as a result of the messages we are communicating. Think
about it. Your teenager throws a ball in the house and it shatters a vase—
you deliver a message. Your employee shows up late to work for the third
day in a row—you deliver a message. Your in-laws invite you to dinner
and ask how your job search is progressing—you deliver a message. In all
of these scenarios you clearly seek something from the other party and
want them to feel a certain way and take certain actions as a result of
hearing your message. The question is, how does one do this effectively?

Daniel J. O'Keefe, a professor at Northwestern University, has
defined persuasion as "a successful, intentional effort at influencing
another's mental state through communication."[6] To influence an
audience, you have to start by understanding their needs so you can
not only meet but exceed them. And not just their needs—but also their
beliefs, desires, concerns, and constraints. In fact, any aspect that will
play a factor in their decision-making process will provide you with
useful information to help customize your message. As comedian Patton
Oswalt has pointed out, "Every audience is different," so it is important
that you "make every audience *your* audience."[7]

Engagement—perhaps the most vital ingredient for effective communication—is the willing state of attentiveness an audience must be in
for you to be able to influence them. If an audience has tuned you out, it
doesn't matter how knowledgeable you are or how interesting your
information is, because little can be achieved if your audience is
distracted or asleep. As a communicator, when it comes to hitting
the mark with an audience, it is not enough that *you* understand why the
information you are presenting is important to them, your audience
must receive it with the same urgency. And that can't happen without
engagement. As Teller (born Raymond Joseph Teller), the silent half of
the magical performance duo Penn & Teller (and a former Latin teacher)

points out, a speaker "has a duty to engage." And not just engage, but "transform apathy into interest."[8] The same goes for someone in the corporate environment. Whether delivering a message to clients, detailing a new policy to team members, or updating the CEO on a recent purchase order, it is your job to not only engage them with your message, but also create a change in their knowledge, feelings, or behavior as a result of them hearing the information being shared.

In most cases, an audience in the corporate setting will be open to hearing your message—at least at the start. They want to learn, want to have better clarity or want to feel inspired by what you have to say. But it is your job to connect with them on an emotional level from the moment you enter the room until the last visual aid is displayed. If you ever wonder whether your audience is engaged or not, there is an easy way to find out: look at their faces. And not just their faces, take in their nonverbal communication. The messages they are sending back to you contain very important information. Warning signs that your audience is disengaged or bored include few questions being asked, people avoiding eye contact, blank stares, doodling, or disengaged body language such as slouching, crossed arms, or yawning. For a speaker communicating a message, eye contact is a vital tool for engagement and building rapport. If you are not staying attuned to the intentional cues being provided to you by your audience, you will likely miss fully interpreting them.

The most effective way to ensure engagement in your meetings or presentations is to create a *pattern interrupt* (or "change-up")—something you do or say that is designed to break behavior patterns or habits that can lull your audience into a state of complacency. Surprise your audience with something interesting or unexpected at frequent intervals throughout. Shift gears by changing speakers or topics. Divide your audience into groups and incorporate physical activity, if appropriate. Introduce a new visual aid or solicit feedback or opinions from people. Make your meetings and presentations a dialogue instead of a monologue. This will help you to keep the room alive. Schedule breaks to give people a chance to step away and return refreshed and ready to re-engage with your message.

CONSEQUENCES OF POOR COMMUNICATION

Think about the role you currently hold at your present company. Are there consequences that could result from poor communication? There most certainly are, and in the corporate arena, these consequences can have significant costs. Set aside hurt feelings or damaged trust, technological advances have changed the way information is shared in the workplace. Much of our communication happens through e-mail or texting, which removes body language and vocal dynamics from the equation, reducing the odds even further that your message will be received as intended. This is why emojis are so popular. When sending a written message, traditional intention cues such as facial expressions and vocal tone are not available, so an emoji serves as a visual qualifier to help express the intention behind the words and to avoid mis-interpretation by the receiver. One study found that most people who receive an article (or long e-mail) read only around 50 percent of the content unless relevance has clearly been established upfront. Another found that people are much better at communicating and interpreting tone in vocal messages than in text-based ones. In the experiment, one group of participants read statements into a tape recorder, taking either a sarcastic tone or serious tone, while another group e-mailed the same statements. When it came time to guess how accurately each of their messages would be received, both groups predicted a 78 percent success rate. Surprisingly, the partners of the participants who spoke their messages correctly identified the tone 75 percent of the time while those who read the statements on e-mail had only a 56 percent success rate.[9] These numbers are worrisome as they provide clear evidence that bulls-eyes are not being hit when it comes to our daily communication on the job. Chances are that most people can recall an instance when information was communicated from one person to another—perhaps even through various channels—and somehow ended up morphing into something entirely different than what was originally intended. Situations like this can cause stress and conflict within a team, harming relationships and even affecting the way employees view the company itself. There are many reasons why communication gets short-circuited during a meeting or presentation. Faulty technology, audience fatigue, confusing jargon, and poor acoustics can cause barriers that hinder your ability to deliver your message clearly. But in too many instances, the problem is much simpler and boils down to the fact that your personal communication was not as clear as it needed to be. Perhaps you were not fully prepared or you didn't totally understand the needs of your audience. For one reason or another, the arrow that was your message did not hit its mark.

When communication is poor between managers and their direct reports, it can have a devastating effect on morale and overall engagement within an organization. We will talk in greater detail about this subject in upcoming chapters, but according to both the Smith School of Business at Queen's University and the Gallup organization, disengagement results in a 37 percent higher absentee rate for employees, 49 percent more accidents, and 16 percent lower profitability for the company itself.[10] Specific consequences of poor communication include lack of team cohesion, unclear messaging, wasted time and resources, damaged relationships, low employee morale, higher turnover rates, lost revenue, and even injury or death. One recent example of poor communication having devastating consequences occurred when a group of teenagers took a class trip to Spain.

This past year, a young Dutch girl named Vera Mol packed her bags and joined her classmates on a trip to northern Spain. Once there, she and a group of 13 other teenagers decided to try a favorite extreme sport: bungee jumping. They gathered at the top of a 130-foot bridge and, one by one, took turns jumping. Once all of the other teens had finished the jump, night had begun to fall. As darkness filled the night sky, it was finally Vera's turn. She put on the harness and stepped to the edge of the bridge. As Vera took a deep breath, trying to calm her nerves, the Spanish instructor in charge of the jump suddenly shouted out a command to her. "No jump," he said, "It's important, no jump!" Vera, misunderstanding his pronunciation and instead reacting to the urgency in his voice, thought he had said, "Now jump!" and threw herself from the edge of the bridge. This simple misunderstanding proved fatal for the young teen. The harness Vera was wearing had not been properly secured, and she plunged to her death.[11]

One sector where communication plays a crucial role is the medical industry, where poor communication costs the U.S. healthcare system $1.7 billion a year.[12] A study by the Institute of Medicine found that up to 98,000 people die every year in the United States as a result of medical errors, and communication mistakes were the primary cause of inadvertent patient harm in over 70 percent of cases.[13] These are very troubling numbers for sure, but there is a silver lining. According to the New England Journal of Medicine, when there is proper communication between doctors and nurses, medical errors are reduced by a remarkable 30 percent.[14] We spoke to Ramesh Kaushik, a heart surgeon in New Delhi, about the role communication plays for someone in his field. According to Kaushik, who has performed more than 500 heart surgeries and transplants, "Communication is extremely essential for successful outcomes."[15] He detailed the multiple levels of communication that take place during a single surgery and how each interaction must address the individual needs and expectations of each stakeholder. "Patients need clear communication regarding their illness, the line of treatment chosen, the likely outcomes, as well as the risks involved. The patient's relatives need to know the same and also understand the role they can play in rehabilitation. Doctors who are part of the team need to be aligned on the treatment chosen and should feel as involved and committed as the lead doctor. Paramedics need to understand their critical role in providing supportive treatment that will lead to a successful outcome. All this communication effectively translates into quality patient care and an excellent patient experience."[16]

> *The difficulty lies, not in new ideas, but in escaping from the old ones.*
>
> —JOHN MAYNARD KEYNES

When an employee is working with customers, communication takes on an important role as well, offering a perfect opportunity to create a strong and positive first impression for your company. Every single interaction a customer service agent has with a customer impacts the way that the customer will feel about your company—specifically, whether they will want to do business with you and how they will speak

about you to others. But various challenges can hinder effective interactions between a customer service agent and the customer they are
attempting to assist. Think about your previous experiences and how an
interaction with a customer service agent affected your overall feelings
toward the company. The manner in which you are treated by the hotel
staff at check-in often creates the initial impression you have about
the hotel itself. The greeting you receive from the restaurant's host sets
the tone for the entire dining experience. Interactions over the phone
pose their own set of communication challenges as customer service
agents on the phone are dealing with one call after another in rapid
succession. A customer service agent who communicates through chat
adds to the challenges by regularly being required to multitask or
manage several screens or clients at a time, a fact that most customers
generally do not realize. In face-to-face customer service interactions,
there are visual and vocal cues that provide feedback to an agent in the
form of facial expressions, eye contact, and tone of voice. But none of
these are available when assisting a customer over chat, which often
causes customers to become even more frustrated.

Communication is vital for developing and strengthening the relationship between an organization and its customers. Since a customer
service agent often creates a company's first impression with a customer,
in many instances, they are the initial face of that company's brand. Every
single experience, every conversation, and every interaction that the
people in your organization have with your customers contributes to
the overall feeling your customers will have about the company itself. To
generate loyalty and trust, every single employee—from customer service
agents to management to the cleaning crew—must be attentive to the
needs of your customers and treat them with courtesy and respect. And to
be able to do this successfully, effective communication is paramount.

Anyone who leads a team or manages other people knows that at
some point they will be required to present information or deliver
feedback to others. It might happen in a boardroom, at a client site, or
even in a one-on-one setting with a subordinate. For some, having to
speak in front of a boss or client fills them with anxiety. Their heart rate
increases, their breathing becomes shallow, and they start to obsess

about mistakes they may make in the moment that could embarrass them or hurt their credibility. We will talk in upcoming chapters about how professional actors learn to manage nerves and share some techniques that you can use to manage stress and utilize it to energize your performance. While nearly every speaker or leader feels some level of anxiety before they present information in front of others, understanding the difference between good stress (called *eustress*) and bad stress (called *distress*) can make a world of difference.

The concept of "public speaking" was first developed by the ancient Greeks; however, over time, the term has become a bit outdated, weighted with negative connotations. Many people have mental scars from an experience in a high school or college speech class in which they were forced to stand up and speak in front of others and then be criticized by the entire group. In our methodology and for the purposes of this book, we'd like you to jettison the term "public speaking" from your vocabulary and replace it with a much simpler word: *communication*. This will help strip away the stigma most people have ingrained in their psyche about past experiences. Public speaking is nothing more than communicating with someone outside of your home, and it is something we all do every day of our lives. Whether it happens at a networking party, while meeting potential clients in their warehouse, or during a keynote presentation to an audience of subject matter experts, in the end, communication is simply two parties sharing and receiving messages for mutual benefit.

Aristotle's treatise, *Rhetoric,* was written in the 4th century BC and is widely regarded by rhetoricians as the single most important work on persuasion ever written. In it, Aristotle writes that a speech can be broken down to three distinct elements: *speaker, subject,* and *audience.* Think of Steve Jobs unveiling the iPhone, Winston Churchill delivering his "Blood, Toil, Tears, and Sweat" speech to Parliament, or Dave Chappelle performing stand-up comedy at Madison Square Garden. Each of these examples can be distilled down to the same three elements that Aristotle detailed nearly 2,500 years ago: Speaker. Subject. Audience.

In the years before television and the Internet, actors would travel from town to town performing on makeshift stages wherever crowds would gather. This is where the business concept of "a plank and a passion" originated, and this same idea is no different for someone presenting a new HR initiative, detailing their quarterly report to shareholders, or teaching a classroom of fifth-graders the difference between a trapezoid and a triangle. As Aristotle pointed out, we are all just speakers communicating a message to an audience. But doing so effectively is a different matter, as unexpected situations or circumstances can arise that may require a deft touch to satisfy the needs of the moment. And as anyone who has seen a boss lose their temper or a politician flub the answer to a question, when communication goes wrong, it can often go very, very wrong.

THE PERSUASION EQUATION: INTENTION AND OBJECTIVE

The methodology we detail in this book and in our trainings with executives around the globe is based on the actor's approach to communication. It follows the simple premise that whether you are pitching a product, delivering a presentation, running a meeting, or showing your neighbor how to change a flat tire, the success of your communication depends upon two things. First, you must identify an *objective*—something you want or need from your audience. And second, you must choose an *intention* that will assist you in the pursuit of that objective. We describe objective and intention like this:

Objective = What You Want
Intention = How You Are Going to Get It

The dictionary defines intention as "an aim that guides action."[17] For an actor, it is the tool that differentiates an amazing performance from a forgettable one. For a speaker, it works the same way. Intention fuels the emotion behind your words and infuses them with meaning. It provides passion and purpose to your delivery and it is this element that allows you to influence your listener and motivate them to action. Essayist Emma Hardman describes intention as the "pre-verbal firings of electricity in the brain."[18] A strong intention connects us to our overall objective—the goal we hope to accomplish with our message. Grant Halvorson, a Columbia University professor who has studied the importance of intention, found that implementing a strong intention with your communication will double the likelihood that you will achieve your goal.[19]

An important study at Case Western Reserve University became the first major scientific demonstration with regard to the ways in which intention physically manifests itself and affects the recipient receiving the information. "When you send an intention, every major physiological system in your body is mirrored in the body of the receiver," wrote Lynne McTaggart in her book *The Intention Experiment*.[20] The study also suggested that intention was more than just a change in posture or body language, but that an actual attunement of energy was needed in order to reach an audience and connect with them in any meaningful way. By putting the focus on your audience and projecting your intention toward them, it will not only bring your message into better focus, it can actually help you switch off certain neural connections, allowing you to relax and perform better in the moment. According to research done at the University of Toronto, intention can give someone a reduced sense of self-awareness and create a transpersonal experience for both the sender *and* receiver of a message.[21] This is what Stanislavski called the *communion* between a speaker and an audience—the "invisible currents which we use to communicate with one another."[22] Think of any great speech or presentation you've ever seen or heard—Kelly McGonigal, Barack Obama, Winston Churchill, Ronald Reagan, or Amy Cuddy. If you watch any of these leaders communicating at the height of their abilities, there is an electricity in their delivery that engages you so completely it borders on a transformative experience. This type of experience is what we are referring to when we talk about the power of intention for someone communicating with others. According to an article in *Scientific American*, "A body of psychological research shows that conscious, purposeful processing of our thoughts really does make a difference to what we do . . . [the] intentions we formulate to carry out specific tasks in particular circumstances . . . increase the likelihood that we will complete the planned behavior."[23]

Without a strong intention behind your words, your message will be ambiguous at best to an audience. And without clear intent you run the risk of people not knowing how to feel about your message or what to do with the information they have just heard—resulting in confusion or apathy. In a negotiation, for example, if there is ever ambiguity or lack of specificity with a detail or item, both sides will fill it in or use it to their advantage. This is why clarity and specificity are important. Essayist Emma Hardman describes the problem like this: If there is "a gap between intention and action . . . between thought and speech, between meaning and words—the gap is a black hole that words fall into."[24] The ability to communicate clearly is vital to ensure that an audience receives a message in exactly the manner it was intended. If you are not clear why your message is important to them, your audience won't be either.

In a series of experiments done at University College London, Dr. Sophie Scott used brain scanning techniques to show that when a human being listens to another person speak, they actually divide the person's message into sections and store (and remember) each part in a different part of the brain.[25] The words themselves are placed in the left temporal lobe where they are processed, but the vocal *dynamics* of the words— *how* the words are delivered—goes to the right side of the brain—the area that is also associated with music and visual images. This is why the words alone are not enough. Lack of vocal intentionality will cloud your message and leave your audience (at best) confused and (at worst) unmoved. Communicating with intention penetrates both sides of a listener's brain. Think about how a news anchor changes their vocal delivery, tone and facial expressions, when they are talking about the tragic devastation caused by a hurricane versus how they report on an inspirational story about a young girl attending space camp with dreams of becoming an astronaut. The former makes us feel sadness and empathy while the latter uplifts us.

To help you better understand how these two aspects of communication fit together, look at the phrase below, a simple framing device we call "The Persuasion Equation":

I want to _____ my audience so
                    (Intention)
that my audience will_____.
                              (Objective)

Great actors learn early on in their training that the concepts of intention and objective are essential partners in creating believable and captivating performances on stage or film. The same idea can benefit anyone who has to communicate information in the corporate arena. For any communicator, once a specific objective has been chosen and an intention activated, the pairing of these two elements will inform all aspects of one's delivery and enable a person to communicate with credibility and confidence. As Stanislavski observed, "When an actor is completely absorbed by some profoundly moving objective . . . he throws his whole being passionately into its execution."[26]

When identifying your intention, always express it as a verb—a strong action word that can activate and inform your delivery. For example, your intention might be to inspire your children to act in a certain way, or to reassure a colleague that a decision was correct. Intention helps you get to the *what* of your message. Your objective comes into clarity once you choose your intention. Let the chosen intention guide you to the bullseye of your message—whether interviewing for a job, leading a meeting, or providing feedback to a team member. Intention involves motivation and various intentional tactics you will use in the pursuit of your objective.

As a speaker moves from one intention to the next, noticeable changes should take place in eye contact, facial expressions, voice, and body language to help signify and communicate that change to the audience. We will talk about the most important intention cues for you to focus on in upcoming chapters, but each of these transitions from one intention to the next must be clear. For example, the intention at the opening of your meeting might be to *greet* your attendees, but could shift to *reassure* as you begin presenting new industry findings, and then to *excite* as you unveil the latest product you will be launching to drive holiday sales. The changes and adjustments you make in your delivery are a direct result of the intention cues you are using at any given moment. It is these intention cues—the vocal and physical manifestations of your intention—that will ensure the words and delivery match the message and help you achieve the desired result you seek with your audience.

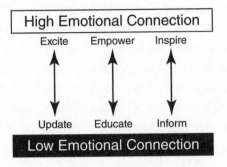

When choosing an intention, verbs that offer the opportunity for a high emotional connection are preferred versus verbs with a lower emotional connection. As you can see in the diagram above, *inform*, *educate*, and *update* have low emotional charges and are less likely to move an audience to action, while *empower*, *inspire*, and *excite* have higher emotional charges, making them better choices to motivate or influence someone. Imagine you are attending an industry conference and are in the audience for a keynote speech by a leading expert in a given field. Would you rather be *excited* by the information they are sharing or *informed* by it? *Inform, update, review,* and *report* are generally low emotion snoozers, sometimes called *treadmill verbs,* because they have no destination which means you never know when you are done. According to psychologist Ann Latham, choosing a treadmill verb is a mistake because it provides "an open invitation to talk on and on with no particular outcome in mind" and "leaves most people bored and disengaged."[27]

Outcome is not in your control. What's in your control is your effort and your intentions.

—AMIT SOOD

An objective, if properly aligned with intention, should result in a message that changes your audience's knowledge, attitude, or action with regard to the topic being presented. As a communicator, your objective is always something you need to accomplish to move your audience to action. As Stanislavski explains, "Life, people, circumstances . . . constantly put up barriers. . . . Each of these barriers presents us with the objective of getting through it . . . . Every one of the objectives you have chosen . . . calls for some degree of action."[28] In the end, without a strong intention behind your delivery—one that is specifically in line with your objective—your audience will not know how to feel about your message or what you want them to do as a result of hearing it. Conversely, a strong intention will power the arrow of your message toward the bullseye of your objective. When pursuing your objective, ask yourself the same three questions an actor asks when rehearsing a scene in a play or film:

1. *What do I want?*
2. *What is in the way of what I want?*
3. *How am I going to get what I want?*

In his book *The Actor and the Target,* Declan Donnellan writes: "The actor cannot act a verb without an [objective] . . . all an actor can play are verbs, but even more significantly, each of these verbs has to depend on a target . . . either direct or indirect, a specific thing seen or sensed, and, to some degree, *needed.*"[29] The same idea is at play when someone is communicating in the business arena. Think of a recent interaction with someone you needed to influence in which you were unsuccessful in getting what you wanted. This could be during communication with a spouse, a client, or a coworker. As you look back, is it possible that your delivery was the reason you did not get what you wanted? Were your intentions simply not communicated clearly enough at the time? Did your physical and vocal delivery not support the message?

As you begin to consider your own individual communication and how you can start to incorporate an awareness of intention and objective into it, understand this: once your objective and intention are aligned, they will often do your communication work for you. Influence involves emotion, so it is important that people feel something as a result of hearing what you have to say. A strong intention, activated properly, will inform all aspects of your communication—body language, facial expressions, vocal dynamics, and the rest. As best-selling author Simon Sinek puts it, "Our internal wiring, though complicated and messy in practice, is pretty straightforward in intention."[30]

THE PINNACLE METHOD THREE-STEP PROCESS

The simple yet essential three-step process outlined below is the framework that underpins our entire methodology. It comprises the three important steps that should be done sequentially when communicating a message to others. The three steps are:

1. *Analyze* your audience
2. *Understand* the reaction your message should elicit
3. *Modify* your delivery to achieve that result

No matter the message you are tasked with delivering—whether it is good news or bad, complicated or simple—the first step in the process of influential communication is analyzing your audience and understanding who they are and what benefit you can provide to them. Once you understand the wants and needs of your audience you can move to the second step, which is understanding how you want them to feel and, subsequently, what you want them to do as a result of hearing your message (again, this is your objective). The third step in the process is the one that professional actors do so well: modifying your vocal and visual intention cues to accomplish your objective.

Audience analysis is a complicated process but an essential place for you to start. If you ever go into a client meeting or begin a presentation without knowing with whom you are about to speak, you are walking into trouble. How can you satisfy the needs of your audience and customize your message for them if you don't know who they are? When it comes to analyzing an audience, there are many factors to consider, but for the sake of simplicity we will provide the three most important ones:

Demographic factors
The demographic make-up of your audience is the first area to analyze and this includes identifying the age, marital status, gender, education level, occupation, religion as well as cultural,

racial, and ethnic backgrounds of the various people with which you are communicating.

Psychographic factors

The second area to analyze is psychographic factors, such as any attitudes, beliefs, values, loyalties, preconceived notions, and feelings that are already in place with this audience before you even utter your first word. How much do they know about the topic or information you will be presenting? How much do they not know? If they are all experts on the topic you will need to approach the material differently than if they have no prior knowledge and the information is completely new to them.

Situational factors

Do your research ahead of time so you have a thorough understanding of the situational factors at play for your meeting or presentation: the size of the group, the time of day you will be meeting, the occasion, the length of the event, and the size of the room and seating arrangement for your listeners. Each of these elements will affect how you will deliver your information. For example, if the meeting is happening in the morning, your audience and their energy level will be different than if the group is listening to you speak at the end of the workday.

Whether defining your personal brand, running a meeting, or building a relationship with someone you have just met, understanding this simple three-step process and utilizing intention in the pursuit of a specific objective will improve your ability to engage and influence others in profound and noticeable ways. We all want something as a result of our communication and the clearer the message, the easier it will be to hit the bullseye and get what we want.

Blueprint to Bullseye—Chapter 1

Preparation Guide for Presentations

1. What topic are you presenting?

2. Who is your audience?
   a. Demographic analysis

   b. Psychographic analysis

   c. Situational analysis

3. What challenges could you face with this audience and this topic? (List three.)

4. What difficult questions might you be asked by this audience? (List three.)

5. What is the objective you hope to accomplish as a result of your audience hearing your message? (Be specific.)

6. What intentions will best help you accomplish your objective? (Choose from: excite, persuade, challenge, reassure, inspire, motivate, empower, etc.)

CHAPTER 2

Define Your Personal Brand

Establishing and Projecting Executive Presence

Personality is an unbroken series of successful gestures.
—F. Scott Fitzgerald

Personal branding is a complex idea comprising various elements, but at its core it is simply the way you project yourself to the world and, consequently, how you are seen by others. Your personal brand is not only defined by what you do and where you are headed; it is also about how you do it and why. The great dance master, Martha Graham, said: "There is a vitality, a life force, an energy, a quickening that is translated through you into action, and because there is only one of you in all of time, this expression is unique."[1] For any leader, creating a strong personal brand and projecting executive presence begins with an awareness of how you look, speak, engage, and interact with others. While there are intersections between someone's personal brand and the level of executive presence they exhibit, the two are not the same. Put simply, your personal brand is what people expect from you while executive presence is how you deliver on those expectations. To develop and maintain a strong personal brand, focus on the elements of presence detailed in this chapter and then make adjustments to your communication if elements are not aligned. As always, consistency is key to ensure the traits and behaviors people have come to expect from you are indeed what they experience. This will not only help you advance in your career, it will also allow you to develop as a leader and be more effective at influencing those around you. Presence comes from intentionality and connecting in an authentic way with others, be they peers, bosses, or clients.

In 1999, at the height of the dot-com boom, a 35-year-old former English teacher in Hangzhou, China, began to notice how the Internet was changing the way people did business. Jack Ma saw this tech boom as an opportunity with unlimited potential, so he, along with a small group of others, decided to create a company that leveraged these new technologies to help small businesses in China compete on a global scale. What began as a website helping small manufacturers sell their goods, eventually grew into the Alibaba Group, a global leader in online commerce that today boasts a value of $360 billion. For the past 18 years, Jack Ma has shaped Alibaba's global image and his personal rags-to-riches story has become an integral element of the company's brand.

Ma's success in life did not come easy. While growing up poor in communist China meant daily struggles, Ma found creative opportunities to develop his skills. One way he did this was by riding his bicycle 45 minutes each day to a hotel where international tourists would congregate. There Ma would often engage them in conversation or offer free tours of the city so he could practice his English. But as the years passed, his career trajectory seemed to lack momentum and direction. Ma had failed his college entrance exam twice and was having trouble finding employment. "I went for a job with the police," recalled Ma. "They said 'You're no good.' I even went to KFC when it came to my city. Twenty-four people went for the job. Twenty-three were accepted. I was the only guy [not hired]." At one point Ma was so desperate for work that he applied for a job at a local hotel. "My cousin and I waited for two and a half hours on a very hot summer day in order to apply for a job as a hotel waiter. After an interview, my cousin was accepted and I was rejected—the reason is he was taller and more handsome. Thirty years later, today, he is still working in that hotel, in the laundry room. And I changed my life."[2]

Ma has always positioned himself as an underdog, a fighter battling the odds, learning from each setback and failing forward. This is also reflected in the way he has positioned Alibaba as the company has expanded, fending off competition and defending itself against charges it traffics in counterfeit goods. Ma understands how branding impacts the way others view his company and see him as a leader. He knows how his inspiring personal narrative connects directly to the brand of Alibaba and, consequently, it has become a story he tells as often as he can. A born promoter, Ma is not above boosting Alibaba's brand awareness with unorthodox stunts—he once rode a motorcycle into a staff meeting and performed a Michael Jackson dance tribute for the company's 40,000 employees. More recently, he acted in a Kung Fu movie opposite action star Jet Li that was seen by over 100 million people in the first month it was released. He is also involved with various international organizations and charities, which allow him the opportunity to build relationships and extend the Alibaba brand even further. And Ma's efforts have paid off. In 2014, when Alibaba went public, it enjoyed the biggest IPO in history. Today, Jack Ma, the former English teacher who couldn't get a job serving chicken at KFC, is the richest man in China, with a net worth of over $46.6 billion.[3]

BRANDING

The concept of "personal branding"—the practice of people marketing themselves in the same manner a corporation does—first emerged in 1997, when Tom Peters, an expert in corporate branding, wrote an article for *Fast Company* suggesting individuals can be every bit as much a brand as companies such as Nike or Coke. According to Peters, by carefully defining one's personal brand, "Everyone has a chance to stand out . . . to be a brand worthy of remark."[4] Your personal brand is as much about your background, experiences, and goals as it is about your career or profession. Everything that has brought you to this moment is a part of you and will define how you act and how others will perceive you. But as it turns out, people are generally not very effective when it comes to personal branding. According to a recent article in *Forbes*, less than 15 percent of people effectively define their personal brand and only 5 percent consistently live that brand in the workplace.[5]

Your personal brand is based on how you behave and what you accomplish, as well as expectations others have about you based on their previous experiences interacting with you. The process of selling yourself is the key to persuading others to buy into your message or ideas. And, in this case, your brand is your product. None of us want to come across as phony or self-promoting—otherwise our brand will be viewed as inauthentic. Which is why establishing and then working to protect your brand through consistent and

The self is not something ready-made, but something in continuous formation through choice of action.

—JOHN DEWEY

authentic behavior is vital. It takes focus and constant, careful consideration of the choices you make.

Every experience you have had up to this moment has provided you with lessons and insights that affect the way you make decisions and behave today. When he was a child, Amazon founder and CEO Jeff Bezos (and world's richest person in 2017) spent summers on his grandparents' ranch in Texas repairing windmills. At the time, young Jeff may have preferred doing something else with his time off from school, but those experiences spent tinkering with windmills helped spark his curiosity for design and innovation. Eventually, it inspired Bezos to explore his penchant for experimentation, which led to the creation of Amazon itself, now the largest and most successful Internet retail company in the world.[6] Similarly, Steve Jobs probably had no idea that taking a calligraphy class in college would eventually inspire the typography that would one day be used in Apple computers, but it did.[7] These formative experiences not only informed the way Bezos and Jobs would go on to conduct business, they changed how we *all* now conduct business.

In his treatise *Rhetoric,* Aristotle discussed the three *means of persuasion* a speaker must utilize to influence another person: *ethos, pathos,* and *logos.*[8] Ethos speaks to the decency and character of a person or speaker. Does the person with whom I am interacting seem genuine and honest? Can I trust them? Logos goes to believability and credibility of the person's message. Do the ideas this person is putting forward seem logical and believable? Do they make sense? And pathos is the third means of persuasion. It involves passion and emotion. Does the person seem excited and engaged? Does the message they are delivering make me *feel* something? When all three means of persuasion are present and aligned, it provides a strong architecture for your personal brand. Jeff Bezos has said, "Your brand is what people say about you when you're not in the room."[9] Personal branding is where you and your career intersect, and every single interaction you have with other people will affect, positively or negatively, the feelings they develop toward you. This extends to interactions you have in person as well as online. Successful brands all make strong emotional connections with the public and the same goes for an individual developing their own personal brand.

Take a moment and think about the ways in which branding is used by celebrities and media figures. Choose two or three famous faces and try to define their personal brands in your mind. What words would you use to describe them? What feelings are generated when you see them? What have you come to expect from the way they behave and communicate with others? Think about the differences in personal branding between Jimmy Fallon, Mother Teresa, and Vladimir Putin—three influencers with decidedly different brands. As you examine each of them it is easy to understand just how much their brands are influenced by the ways they communicate and put ideas out into the world.

A positive personal brand can be valuable for anyone who works as part of a team or organization. It is what draws people toward you or, conversely, pushes them away. Beyoncé makes $50 million as a spokeswoman for Pepsi.[10] George Clooney was paid $40 million by Nespresso[11] and George Foreman made more than $200 million to put his name on a grill.[12] The reason these celebrities get paid millions of dollars to endorse products is because their personal brand is trusted and recognizable, thus giving it value. So, when it gets associated with a product, it reaps rewards for that product in the form of more sales or better name recognition. In a similar way, your personal brand also has value. The ways in which you deal with stress, manage time, and collaborate with others all contribute to your brand and affect the expectations people will have about you.

Once you establish your personal brand, maintaining and protecting that brand over time becomes an ongoing process. As Uber CEO Dara Khosrowshahi once remarked during a particularly rocky period for his company, "There is a high cost to a bad reputation."[13] Public figures who tarnished their strong personal brands through behavior inconsistent with what the public had come to expect from them include former New York congressman Anthony Weiner, a rising political star who ended his career in disgrace when convicted of sending obscene material to a minor. Cyclist Lance Armstrong won a record seven Tour de France titles before being banned for life and stripped of all titles for his role in a doping scandal. An organization that acted inconsistently with their curated image is the Catholic Church—one of the oldest and most profitable brands in history. When the church's sex-abuse scandal came to light in the 1980s, the behavior of the abusive priests was shocking to the public because it was completely unlike how a Catholic priest should behave. Repeated inconsistencies between how you want to be perceived versus how you are perceived begin to create a narrative that will change what others think of you and can redefine your brand in a negative way. One example of this took place in 2016, when Philadelphia linebacker Nigel Bradham was arrested at Miami International Airport and charged with attempting to bring a loaded gun onto an airplane. It was the professional football player's second arrest in three months. When asked to comment on the situation, Jim Schwartz, Bradham's coach, responded, "You do dumbass things, pretty soon you're going to be labeled as a dumbass."[14]

> *Brand is just a perception, but perception will match reality over time.*
>
> —ELON MUSK

It is nearly impossible to talk about branding without discussing the role it played in the 2016 election of Donald Trump. Much of the way Trump bulldozed his way into the White House was a result of his ability to connect with his audience and create a brand narrative that energized the slice of the electorate he needed to win. Before running for president, Trump had already established a global brand as a businessman and marketer, with his name on everything from golf courses to steaks. And while Donald Trump will never be considered a great orator in the mold of a Winston Churchill or Ronald Reagan, he knows how to engage an audience, build suspense, and keep people talking—all elements he learned as a television performer. As political operative Roger Stone has observed about Trump's ability to influence, "He's got a great sense of theater. He's a showman, above all."[15] The tools of his trade are emotion and identity and he uses them in a way that makes people sit up and take notice. Michael D'Antonio, a journalist and Trump biographer, puts it this way: "[Trump is] an actor who's been playing himself for his entire life, in much the same way John Wayne played himself in every role. And it's worked so well for him, playing this role of a leader and businessman, that he transitioned seamlessly into his new role as an outspoken candidate . . . enough people bought the act, and he managed to get elected."[16]

Trump's message as a candidate, and the way he delivered it, elicited strong emotional reactions from those who heard it. This was by design. Trump wanted to get people talking and he knew how to keep the cameras trained on him. "Trump didn't need policies," wrote Joe Klein in *Time*, "His attitude was the message . . . the fact that he could barely control himself was integral to what he was selling—spontaneity, authenticity, strut."[17] As his candidacy kicked off, Trump soon realized that every outrageous statement he made—no matter how offensive or ridiculous—dominated news cycles and kept his name in the headlines. By piling outrageous statement on top of outrageous statement, Trump was able to influence the media in a way that delivered him an estimated $2 billion in free advertising.[18] And because the shocking, brawling behavior Trump exhibited during the campaign was consistent with the brand he had created as a brass-knuckled businessman and television star, his base of supporters accepted it as part of the show. He knew his audience and focused his message on them like a laser beam. As Trump famously bragged, "I could stand in the middle of Fifth Avenue and shoot somebody and I wouldn't lose any voters."[19] In an article in *Politico*, Glenn Thrush described Trump's candidacy as "improvisational and impulsive . . . impelled by his branding genius and reality-TV showmanship."[20] Chris Jones, theatre critic for the *Chicago Tribune*, agreed, writing, "Trump is a brilliant performer with particular skills . . . in taking the emotional temperature of a room and filling its needs."[21] The former reality television star's freewheeling campaign style paid off. On November 8, 2016, Trump's voters delivered him the White House and the opportunity to expand his brand once again—this time on a bigger stage than he could ever have imagined.

A personal brand represents the total experience someone has or can expect when interacting with you—in meetings, on conference calls and through social media. Each and every one of us is the sum of our experiences, and just like Jack Ma or Donald Trump, every mistake we have made, every triumph we have achieved, and every lesson we have learned becomes part of who we are. Every action we take, or choose not to take, contributes to our personal brand. As the Zen Buddhist saying goes, how you do anything is how you do everything.

But a strong personal brand does not develop overnight. And just like the brands of major corporations, brands can be made and remade over time. To begin shaping your own personal brand, it is important to start by understanding how you are seen by those around you. If the brand you have created is inconsistent with the brand you envision, you may need to make adjustments to bring them into alignment. Do you want to be seen as bold but your boss thinks you are an introvert? Maybe it is time to be more forceful when advocating for your ideas. If you want to be seen as a team player but your coworkers think you are arrogant and self-involved, you could try listening more and talking less. Defining one's personal brand is not always easy. The way you see yourself versus the way others see you can often be two different things. This is why taking the time to carefully examine how you want to be seen versus how others truly see you is worth the effort. There are many elements that go into the creation and maintenance of your personal brand, including vision, style, experience, passion, purpose, values, strengths, and goals.

DEFINING YOUR PERSONAL BRAND

As an exercise, grab a pencil and paper and jot down three words you would use to describe yourself. Take your time. And be honest. Next, find someone you trust—a boss, spouse, or coworker—and ask them to provide three words they would use to describe you. Once you have their answers, compare them to the three words you used to describe yourself. Do they match? If not, how are they different? The next step in understanding your personal brand is to make a list of your core competencies—the talents and skills you possess that can provide benefit to others. Write down the ones that come to mind. And don't be humble. Which talents do you possess that could be valuable to others? Once you've finished with that, list the major experiences and accomplishments that define you to this point in your life. Awards, degrees, and promotions all count. Then write down your goals. What do you hope to accomplish this year? In five years? Ten years? These can be work-related goals or personal aspirations. What's on your bucket list? Climbing Mount Everest? Taking an acting class? Getting married? Next, write down your passions—any hobbies or activities you enjoy pursuing outside of work, such as music, travel, and exercise. How do you like to spend your leisure time? Finally, describe your values. What do you stand for? What is important to you? And what will you not tolerate under any circumstances?

CREATING A PERSONAL BRANDING STATEMENT

Now that you've taken the time to do some thorough self-analysis, use the information you've compiled on the paper to create a *personal branding statement*—no more than one or two sentences—that best describes you and the unique value you can offer to others. Think of it as a tagline or catchphrase and make it solution-oriented and unique to you. Your branding statement is not a personal mission statement or job title. Instead, it should express what you stand for, what people can expect from you, and how you will make decisions going forward. Some examples of branding statements for a teacher, a shipping manager, and a real estate agent might look like the following:

Teacher: "I help students identify their passions and talents and provide direction on how they can utilize them for future success."

Shipping manager: "I have a passion for logistics. My days are spent managing the shipping requirements of my customers to allow their businesses to grow and thrive."

Real estate agent: "I strive to be the most passionately referred agent in the real estate industry while providing excellent customer service to each and every one of my clients."

Composing a personal branding statement may take a bit of time, so don't be in a hurry. Once you've composed yours, write it down and tape it to your desk or computer so it is clearly visible. Doing this will serve as a daily reminder for you to stay committed and remain consistent in the ways you present yourself to others. Strong personal brands, much like successful corporate brands, must be developed, maintained, and protected at all costs.

THE POWER OF EXECUTIVE PRESENCE

Whether in person, on video, or even over the phone, being able to project confidence and credibility to an audience greatly enhances your ability to influence them. The concept of executive presence in business is often highly intuitive and difficult to pin down. It is a combination of many factors, such as magnetism, knowledge, passion, speaking skills, assertiveness, confidence, professional appearance, and more. All of these contribute to a person's perception of you and few people would argue that a positive executive presence will enable a person to get ahead in business. But when it comes to male and female workers, there is a divide between how they each view the importance of executive presence. In Chapter 4 we discuss the specific differences between the way female and male executives lead; for example, one recent study published in the *Harvard Business Review* found that only 45 percent of women think that executive presence helps people get ahead. And this problem is compounded by another finding from that same report: women are 41 percent less likely than men to receive feedback about their image.[22] Without honest and constructive feedback regarding one's personal brand and leadership style, how can they truly understand how they are perceived by others?

We can all think of someone with executive presence—a leader or media figure who engages an audience, displays poise under pressure, and makes it all seem effortless. Communicating with executive presence has many benefits. It can help build relationships, facilitate change, or motivate others. Think of some famous figures, past or present, that you feel exhibit executive presence. Some possible examples might include Oprah Winfrey, Jack Welch, Richard Branson, and Suze Orman. What is it about these leaders that conveys executive presence? What aspects of the ways they behave or communicate contribute to their executive presence?

ELEMENTS OF EXECUTIVE PRESENCE

Executive presence is not one trait or quality alone but a combination of traits and qualities that creates your personal distinctiveness and contributes to the overall perception others have about you. Executive presence affects how others see you, whether they listen to you, and whether they will be willing to follow you. Let's take a moment to break down the various elements that make up executive presence. As we discuss each trait in more detail, use this as an opportunity to identify which are strengths for you as well as which ones might offer opportunities for development.

Confidence

Think of any powerful world leader and you will see someone who exudes confidence in the way they communicate and interact with others. Charisma is that elusive, hard-to-define quality that combines passion and confidence and that we look for in leaders. Leaders benefit from having gravitas—the serious, dignified manner we associate with strong leaders. Additionally, the overall feeling someone has about themselves, as well as their talents and abilities, is often reflected in the way they carry themselves—how they stand, move, and speak. Interestingly though, new research has uncovered a surprising gender disparity when it comes to confidence. A study by Europe's Institute of Leadership and Management found that women in the workplace tend to have lower confidence levels than their male counterparts, with 70 percent of men having high or very high levels of self-confidence, compared to just 50 percent for women.[23] The research also explored interesting findings about the level of self-doubt men and women experience with relation to their job performance. According to research, 50 percent of women admitted to feelings of self-doubt while only 31 percent of men reported the same.[24] When it comes to projecting confidence, being prepared and knowledgeable about the information you are discussing can be your best defense against anxiety or nerves. A relaxed and comfortable communication style contributes greatly to someone's ability to appear confident and in control. Our bodies are billboards sending messages out to our audience for interpretation. If your speech and demeanor convey confidence, that is how you will be perceived by an audience.

Credibility

A person's vocabulary and the words they choose when speaking are important. Sounding uneducated or uncertain can negatively impact your executive presence and the way others will view you. One recent study found that 60 percent of executives said that sounding uneducated has a negative impact on their perception of another person.[25] Vocabulary also contributes to credibility and serves as an indicator of intelligence. It is crucial to demonstrate a depth of knowledge and grasp of subject matter when speaking to others. Words are tools of thought, so choose them carefully and use them strategically. Each word carries meaning and can elicit a specific emotional response from a listener. Words allow you to share ideas, clarify meaning, or drive action. And, in most cases, the smaller your vocabulary, the more limited your chances are for success.

When a speaker lacks knowledge or expertise in the eyes of their audience, it can have a devastating impact on the overall perception created with another person. When exhibiting executive presence, credibility leads to trust and trust is the currency with which decisions are made. Additionally, the substance of what you are presenting—the specific details and data you have chosen to include—must be accurate and should be relevant to your audience and the topic being discussed. The best way to bolster your credibility is to make sure you are knowledgeable about the subject you are presenting and adequately prepared to discuss it.

Appearance

The way we look, dress, smile, and move all contribute to the overall impression you create in the eyes of an audience. By establishing a positive first impression, you benefit from what psychologists call a *halo effect*—a cognitive bias in which the overall impression you create with another person then influences how they feel and think about your character and abilities. First impressions matter and they happen quickly. One study from the University of Glasgow's Centre for Cognitive Neuroimaging found that the brain takes just 200 milliseconds to gather most of the information it needs to determine another person's emotional state.[26] According to a study by New York University, 11 judgments happen within the first seven seconds of meeting or seeing another person, including their education level, economic level, perceived credibility/believability/competence/honesty, trustworthiness, level of sophistication, sex role identification, level of success, political background, religious background, ethnic background, and social/professional/sexual desirability.[27]

> *You can have anything you want if you dress for it.*
>
> —EDITH HEAD

Extensive research has proven the way you dress affects the way people see you and it also affects how you feel about yourself.[28] An inappropriate or unkempt appearance will undercut your credibility in the eyes of an audience. Dressing professionally shows that you take pride in your appearance. And according to a recent study from

Northwestern University, the way you dress can actually affect how well you perform at work. Researchers discovered that subjects who were required to wear lab coats during experiments actually improved their performance in tasks involving intelligence and concentration.[29] To project executive presence, you have to dress the part of an executive or leader in your given field. And like an actor in a play, the way you dress will depend on your environment and audience. If you manage a tattoo parlor you will dress differently than if you work at a law firm. Analyze your audience, understand how your manner of dress will affect them, then choose your attire accordingly.

Body Language Body language contributes to one's appearance as well. Standing (or sitting) tall and avoiding a slumped posture projects authority and confidence. Communicating from what we call a strong *home base position* will give you a solid grounding from which to communicate. A home base position is a position of openness, readiness, and availability. When standing, this means that your feet are planted, your pelvis is locked to avoid swaying or shifting and your arms hang loosely by your sides, unless gesturing. Your chest should be raised and open and your chin should be level to the ground, with eyes forward. Imagine a string at the top of your head pulling you up, elongating the spine. When presenting from a seated position sit up straight and lean slightly forward with your feet planted firmly on the ground. This will help you project confidence and mask any nervousness by grounding you in your physical space.

Nervous body language, or *pacifiers*, often show up in the form of swaying, shifting from side to side, rubbing of hands, or fidgeting with a pen or wedding ring. When a speaker is nervous or feels threatened, their natural impulse is to close off or take up less space. The more confident a person is, the more space they inhabit; the more frightened they are, the smaller they become, in an effort to hide or disappear. In truth, our brains are hardwired to equate power and confidence with the amount of space we take up. That said, there is a difference between expansive gestures and exaggerated gestures. Expansive gestures will make you look confident and engaged while exaggerated gestures will make you look overly theatrical, as if you are stretching the truth.

Confident speakers are not afraid to inhabit their space, to fill it and own it. Expansive gestures are more effective than gestures that are constrictive because they contain more information. The absence of gestures can be interpreted in negative ways. Without engaged, activated body language, you will likely be perceived as disengaged by your audience or appear uninterested in your topic. The use of movement or *spatiality* (how you use the room) can help you to project confidence and create a more intimate connection with your audience, such as crossing toward someone when answering their question. Be careful of moving too close or invading people's personal space as this can come across as intimidating or off-putting.

Eye Contact Eye contact is another critical tool for someone needing to project executive presence. Studies show that if you maintain eye contact for around 60 percent of a conversation with someone, you will come across as engaged, friendly, and trustworthy.[30] Too much direct eye contact could be intimidating and too little eye contact could make you appear as if you are avoiding their gaze. According to Katherine Schreiber and Heather Hausenblas, PhD, "Eye contact can have a memory-boosting, prosocial, and stimulating effect."[31] Connecting with your audience is critical, whether it's a large group or a single employee as it allows you to monitor how they are receiving your message. In 1885, Sir Francis Galton wrote a paper called "The Measurement of Fidget" in which he studied the body language of bored people.[32] What Galton determined was that the more bored people were, the more they would slouch, lean, and fidget, so a speaker could actually measure the level of boredom in their audience by simply observing how far from vertically upright they appeared. Attentive audiences will lean in, sit straight, and remain still as they listen to your message. This is what you are striving for, so watch the cues coming from your audience and adjust your tactics if you notice people slouching, nodding off, or fidgeting.

Smiling Smiling is also an important expression that projects executive presence. A smile, transmitted either consciously or subconsciously, is viewed across most cultures as a sign of friendliness. It also signals to others that you are relaxed and in control. If you fail to smile when meeting someone, you may be perceived in a negative light. Charles Schwab, the industrial giant who transformed wealth in America, used to tell people that his smile alone had earned him at least a million dollars.[33] Think of celebrities who are famous for their mega-watt smiles: Will Smith, Julia Roberts, Michael Jordan, Cameron Diaz, Tom Cruise. Their smiles draw people toward them and are a valuable element of their overall presence. Smiles have also been proven to affect the emotions of the people doing the smiling. Recent studies found that the mere act of smiling actually sparks biological responses in the body that trigger emotions or attitudes associated with smiling.[34]

Vocal Dynamics

New research from Yale University found that voice-only communication is often more accurate than visual cues when deciphering the intentions of another person. In a series of five experiments, individuals were asked either to interact with another person or watch an interaction between two others. In some cases, participants were able only to listen and not look; in others, they were able to look but not listen; and some participants were able to look and listen. Across all experiments, individuals who only listened to the interactions (without access to any visual cues) were able, on average, to identify more accurately the emotions being expressed by others.[35]

Constantin Stanislavski often warned his actors that "poor speech . . . conceals the thought."[36] The same is true for you when delivering a presentation or providing feedback: the burden to make your message resonate always rests with you. Every leader has a unique voice and the way they use it creates genuine feelings in the minds of their audience that contributes to presence. Using the voice effectively contributes to the clarity and impact of your message and determines to what extent you engage your audience. If your speaking volume during a meeting or presentation is too low, it shows a lack of consideration for your audience, especially those sitting toward the back of the room. If people can't hear what you are saying, you run the risk of them simply tuning you out.

A proper pace for speaking will often feel too slow to the speaker but rarely feels that way to the listener. The best way to slow down your communication is to embrace the length and frequency of pauses. Much can happen during a beat of silence, allowing an audience to ponder a question, consider a thought, or weigh an option. One misconception that people have with regard to pausing during speech is that silence might make them appear weak or uncertain. This is not the case. Often a pause can make someone seem more confident because it shows that he or she is not afraid of silence. Silence is another tool that is generally underutilized by leaders in the corporate environment. Many people make the incorrect assumption that audiences like to have information directed at them in a constant, uninterrupted stream without a break or pause. Not so. A well-placed pause can help spotlight an important piece of information, allow an audience to absorb a point, or signal that you are about to transition to a new topic. The rate at which you speak also sends signals to your audience. Speaking with a deliberate pace and applying pauses will help eliminate *verbal viruses*—the verbal fillers such as "ah" or "um"—that can damage your credibility.

Margaret Thatcher, the late prime minister of Great Britain, was nicknamed "The Iron Lady" because of the strength she projected and the fiery speeches she often gave.[37] But her ability to influence others with her communication was actually something that evolved over time. Early in her political career, Thatcher realized that voters found her speaking voice shrill and strident. Years later, Thatcher worked with the actor Sir Lawrence Olivier to lower her pitch to develop a calmer, more authoritative tone. The changes that Olivier made to Thatcher's delivery were not only astute from an actor's standpoint but, as it turns out, also scientifically supported.[38] New research from Duke University found that voters actually prefer leaders with deeper voices, because the lower tones are associated with strength, competency, and integrity.[39]

Receptivity

Being open to the ideas or opinions of others can contribute positively to executive presence and how others approach you. Good bosses realize they don't have all the answers and need input from team members to help them move a company forward. Often undervalued, accessibility and listening are important leadership skills. But active listening is not merely the act of being silent while another person is speaking, it is truly understanding what that person has said. When it comes to bosses lacking receptivity, none compare to oil tycoon Edward "Tiger Mike" Davis, also known as the "world's meanest boss."[40] As owner of the Tiger Oil Company, Edward Davis was known as a surly boss with no time for pleasantries. He especially hated having to talk to his employees in the hallways of the Tiger Oil Company headquarters, so Davis sent out the following notice to staff members, "Do not speak to me when you see me. If I want to speak to you, I will do so. I want to save my throat. I don't want to ruin it by saying hello to all of you sons-of-bitches." It is often said that people leave managers, they don't leave companies. Often undervalued, receptivity is a vital skill that not only provides benefit for business communication, but can also help you maintain healthy relationships in your personal life as well.

Manners

A basic grasp of manners may seem obvious but proper etiquette will not only help you create a positive lasting impression with an associate or client, it can also help you build and strengthen long-term relationships. How you conduct yourself at social functions, when meeting someone for the first time, and even the ways in which you recognize the achievements of others all contribute to how you are seen within your company as well as outside of it. A gesture as simple as a handshake, which has existed in some form or another for thousands of years, is a nearly universal expression when greeting someone. John F. Kennedy thought the handshake was so important he actually commissioned a study to determine the most effective handshake he should use when meeting various world leaders.[41] Your handshake is your calling card so be intentional with your use of it. Gripping someone's hand too tightly or holding the handshake for too long can make you appear controlling or dominating. Conversely, a limp handshake will communicate to the other party that you lack confidence or assertiveness. Refusing the offer of a handshake altogether, as Donald Trump did with

German chancellor Angela Merkel in a live photo op at the White House in 2017, will almost always be seen as rude or insulting.[42]

Mindfulness

According to recent studies, in any given month about a third of Americans are stressed from feeling overwhelmed.[43] Hectic schedules, pressing deadlines, and a barrage of distractions tug at our focus each day and being able to pause and reflect before responding is an important skill for a leader to possess. Mindfulness, which executives are pursuing at an increasing rate to improve their focus and well-being, is the technique or practice of generating a conscious awareness of the present moment. Studies by the American Psychological Association have found that mindfulness reduces stress, improves memory, and helps regulate fear or anxiety.[44] Mindfulness is a simple form of meditation that can allow you to gain control over unruly thoughts and behavior and stay focused when you start to feel overwhelmed or distressed. The American philosopher and psychologist William James once wrote, "The greatest weapon against stress is our ability to choose one thought over another."[45] Being able to perform under pressure while managing time and meeting deadlines is an essential aspect of executive presence. Understanding the concept of mindfulness and incorporating it into your personal and professional life can help you manage stress and get through a busy day.

> When you press the pause button on a computer it stops. When you press the pause button on a human it starts—it starts to reflect, rethink and re-imagine.
>
> —DOV SEIDMAN

One of the easiest ways to practice mindfulness is to focus on your breath. When we are born, we come into the world with full and complete breathing skills, but over time, stress and other challenges contribute to most of us breathing in a more shallow or incomplete manner. Research from Northwestern University has shown that the way in which you breathe has a direct effect on your brain and the emotions you are feeling.[46] An easy way to take control of a moment where you feel overwhelmed is to follow a simple process called *Stop-Breathe-Look-Listen*. When a moment arises and you start to feel rushed or anxious, begin by acknowledging your feelings and accept that they are valid. Next, stop whatever task you are doing at the moment and focus entirely on your breath. Inhale through your nose for five seconds and then exhale through your mouth for five. Notice everything you see and hear down to the tiniest detail, from the buzz of the air conditioner to the items of trash in the wastebasket. If you feel your attention start to drift or distractions start to pull you away from your present moment, put your focus back on your breath and let it ground you.

Conflicts at work are inevitable so the ability to handle stress and pressure is an essential skill for a leader. Personality clashes, shifting deadlines, increased competition, market fluctuations—any of these can lead to emotional situations. But according to new research from Columbia University, how you handle conflict can actually make or break your career. The researchers found that people who act too aggressively actually harm their performance while people who are perceived as too passive can hinder their ability to accomplish an objective.[47] When emotions are high, it becomes difficult to think clearly. We shift into "fight" mode and our defenses go up. When this happens, our brains get overloaded and we react emotionally before the rational part of our brain has a chance to consider the words we just spit out. This is another area where mindfulness comes in handy as there is great power in holding your tongue and letting others speak. It allows you to consider something for a moment while giving the other person the opportunity to be heard. Mindfulness has even been shown to shrink the brain's "fight-or-flight" center, the amygdala, according to research out of the University of Pittsburgh and Carnegie Mellon University.[48]

Visibility

For executives in a busy, complicated work environment, speaking up and advocating for your ideas is an important aspect of presence. To establish your value and credibility in an organization, you need to be a regular contributor in meetings and discussions at work. Find opportunities to forge connections with senior leaders and look for the chance to demonstrate your expertise when the moment arises. Every conversation you have with your boss is another opportunity to create a positive impression. Employees who rarely speak up or share their opinions in a meeting decrease their visibility by not being heard. Managers who are walled off or rarely seen in the office communicate to their workers that they are on their own.

According to a major study by LeanIn.Org and McKinsey and Co., women face a much steeper climb than men when it comes to visibility in leadership roles within an organization. Data shows that men win more promotions, better assignments, and more access to senior leaders than women do. Less than half of women feel that promotions are awarded fairly or that the best opportunities consistently go to the most deserving employees.[49] This is another reason it is important for female leaders to advocate for their ideas and not be afraid to show assertiveness by taking credit for their ideas or accomplishments. The more visible a woman becomes in the workplace, the more impact she will have with decision-makers within that organization.

Integrity

Having values by which you operate and conduct yourself is a quality that employers seek in the employees they hire. Demonstrating sound moral principles creates value with a boss or client and will increase the odds of you getting promoted or recognized. Think of the current relationship with your boss and how this person views your personal integrity. It is the same with everyone else in your life with whom you interact—clients, bosses, even your spouse. They want to be able to count on you to do what you say, when you say you will do it. Every action you take and every decision you make reveals character so it is important to demonstrate integrity in word and deed. Identify the values and beliefs you carry with you each and every day, and then demonstrate those values through your choices and behavior. Studies show that employees are 55 percent more engaged and 53 percent more focused if the leaders of their company model the desired behavior they expect from their employees.[50]

> *Authenticity is like pornography; you know it when you see it.*
>
> —MARK MCKINNON

Authenticity

The final element contributing to a strong executive presence is the ability to be seen as sincere and genuine. Research professor Brené Brown has defined authenticity as "the choice to let ourselves be seen."[51] Being authentic as a communicator also means speaking with passion about the topic or subject you are discussing. Passion is contagious; so is apathy. Passion creates a positive momentum that shows your enthusiasm for the information you are putting forward. One study out of Bentley University found that 76 percent of women and 73 percent of men surveyed saw themselves as authentic.[52]

Leaders and executives are required to make decisions every day, and each of these decisions results in consequences that contribute positively or negatively to others' perceptions of you. Each action you take, or choose not to take, becomes another brushstroke in the canvas that is your personal brand. By focusing on the elements in this chapter, you will be able to shape the image people have of you and then leverage those positive feelings to influence their emotions and actions to get what you want.

Blueprint to Bullseye—Chapter 2

Personal Branding Guide

1. List three words you would use to describe yourself.

2. List three words others would use to describe you.

3. List your personal branding statement in one to two sentences.

4. List your core competencies (talents and skills).

5. List the major life experiences that have defined you.

6. List the major accomplishments of which you are most proud.

7. Describe your passions.

8. Describe your values.

9. Describe your vision.

10. Describe your personal goals for the next one year, three years, and five years.

CHAPTER 3

Land the Job
Strategic Interviewing Techniques to Get You Hired

First, say to yourself what you would be; then do what you have to do.
—Epictetus

As the CEO of Charles Schwab, Walter Bettinger has been tasked with hiring many people over the years for his organization. When asked in a recent interview with the *New York Times* how he goes about choosing candidates, Bettinger talked about a unique method of interviewing he had devised and how it helped him better understand the character and personalities of the people he was considering hiring. "One thing I'll do sometimes is to meet someone for breakfast for the interview," explained Bettinger. "I'll get there early, pull the manager of the restaurant aside, and say, 'I want you to mess up the order of the person who's going to be joining me. It'll be okay, and I'll give a good tip, but mess up their order.' I do that because I want to see how the person responds. That will help me understand how they deal with adversity. Are they upset, are they frustrated, or are they understanding? Life is like that, and business is like that. It's just another way to get a look inside their heart rather than their head."[1]

Interviewing for a job or promotion is something almost every person will have to do in his or her lifetime. For many people, it can be an intimidating and frustrating process. Actors audition continuously as part of their job and each time they are being judged and evaluated in the moment. It can be a grueling and humbling experience, as even the most talented actors experience rejection on a relatively frequent basis. Says comedian Samantha Bee, "Part of being a performer is that failure becomes a part of your existence. Your day-to-day routine is failure, with the remote possibility of success."[2]

In this chapter, we will be discussing specific strategies and techniques to help you present yourself to a potential employer with the confidence and credibility needed to land the job. Since the interviewing process can also be stressful, we will also discuss ways to handle the speech anxiety—or *glossophobia*—that people commonly experience during the interviewing process. Actors are masters at masking their nerves and we will share just how they are able to channel their nervous energy into their performance. In researching this book, we spoke to various hiring managers and asked them to share the most common mistakes candidates make during the interview process—blunders that often end up costing them the job. We will discuss some of these potential landmines in the hope that you can avoid them in your future interviews. We will also discuss the most frequent interview questions you will be asked when interviewing and provide tips on how to successfully navigate each.

Just as casting directors all have stories about actors and auditions that did not go as planned, hiring managers also have tales of job candidates who blew their chance as a result of poor choices made during the interview process. There was the story of one candidate who brought 50 ink pens with him and proceeded to spread them all out on the table during his interview, another candidate who insisted on sitting in a yoga pose while answering questions from his interviewers, and yet another who introduced himself by his name, adding, "But you can call me Tigger. That's the nickname I gave myself."[3]

The hiring process for a manager looking for potential candidates can be a long and complicated one. The search can take weeks, months, or even years. Because of this, in most cases, the person interviewing you would love nothing more than for you to be a perfect fit for the role and organization so they can hire you and complete the hiring process. Most hiring managers are looking for a solid, competent worker who possesses the requisite attributes needed for the job and who will be pleasant to work alongside. Danny Meyer, the founder of Shake Shack, the popular fast and casual restaurant chain, talks about the two things he looks for when hiring new people. According to Meyer, 49 percent of the decision comes down to how well the person is able to do their job, the "technical magic" that the person brings to their work, while the remaining 51 percent is "who that person is while they are bringing that magic." Says Meyer, "At the end of the day, you need both. You need this blend of somebody who is great at what they do and who makes people feel great while they are doing it."[4]

Every company has their own way of interviewing candidates, some more creative than others. Facebook asks the question, "On your very best day at work, the day you come home and think you have the best job in the world, what did you do that day?"[5] The reason that Facebook asks this question is that they want to see if a candidate's drive and vision matches theirs. For years, Google was known for the difficult and strange questions posed to applicants during their interview process, such as "Why are manhole covers round?" and "How many golf balls could fit into a classic American school bus?"[6] Google has since abandoned the practice of asking brainteaser questions, but even Eric Schmidt, executive chairman of Alphabet, Google's parent company, recently struggled to answer one of Google's old interview questions when it was posed to him at a conference of entrepreneurs. The question? "You're the captain of a pirate ship and you find a chest of gold. Your crew gets to vote on how the gold is divided up. If fewer than half of the pirates agree with you, you die. How do you recommend apportioning the gold in such a way that you get a good share of the booty but still survive?"[7]

One business legend that has been passed down through generations, involved a famous business tycoon who, when giving serious consideration to a candidate, would invite the person out for a bowl of soup. If the candidate salted the soup before tasting it, this particular tycoon would not offer them the job. The reason? He did not want to hire a person who had too many assumptions built into their everyday life. He wanted people who consistently *challenged* assumptions. Whether the legend of the salted soup is true or not doesn't really matter at this point. The story is a powerful one and provides a valuable lesson that has now been passed down through generations of workers.[8]

For most people, the job search process can be an emotional experience, as there are many aspects of a person tied up in it: ego, self-worth, passion, financial need, even their identity. An interview can bring all of these aspects to the fore in a way that generates anxiety and self-doubt, which, in turn, can affect the way you present yourself to a potential boss or hiring manager. In some ways, a job interview resembles a blind date where you are attempting to impress the other person by presenting yourself in the most favorable way possible by saying the right things and behaving in the manner most likely to gain their approval.

Feeling nervous before an interview is completely understandable and very common. According to a recent study by Harris Interactive and Everest College, 92 percent of U.S. adults admit to feeling anxious about interviewing for a job.[9] Having nervous jitters before a job interview shows that you care about how you will be perceived by your interviewer. It is a result of you having an ego and worrying about your reputation as well as your desire to succeed and get hired. And while each of us reacts to stress differently, some common symptoms of speech anxiety include: increased speaking rate, flushed face, shallow breathing, stuttering speech, or a sudden loss of concentration. Other behaviors that result from nervousness are low volume, fidgeting, or giving long-winded answers to questions that could have been answered succinctly. Some people even get so nervous they say things they didn't mean to say, such as one job candidate who closed her interview by blurting out, "Thank you very much. Have a bad day!"[10]

Feeling like you are under a microscope during the interview process can be stressful, but it is helpful to remind yourself that there are different types of stress and not all stress is bad. There is good stress (called *eustress*) and bad stress (called *distress*). While eustress (the stress you experience when being challenged) can energize your delivery and infuse your interview answers with confidence and clarity, distress (the stress you feel when under threat) can have the opposite effect, causing you to panic or freeze up. As mentioned in Chapter 1, being prepared for your interview is the key to moving yourself from distress to eustress. Start by analyzing your audience (your interviewer), understand how you want them to feel as a result of interviewing you (impressed, excited), and then modify your delivery accordingly (through crisp, concise answers and a confident physical and vocal presence). The more prepared you are for your interview, the more comfortable you will be, giving yourself the space to relax into each moment and respond to your interviewer's questions instead of stressing about what you are going to say next.

One of our favorite job interview stories involves the legendary actress Shelley Winters, whose career spanned five decades and who starred in such classic movies as *The Diary of Anne Frank* and *Lolita*. Winters was in her 60s and had already won two Academy Awards when producer Irwin Allen, who was casting *The Poseidon Adventure*, asked Winters to come in and audition for a part in his film. In Hollywood, what Allen did was a major blunder. You do not ask someone of Winters' stature to audition—you simply send them the script and ask them if they want to be part of the project. But Winters was a good sport and agreed to the meeting. Wearing a goofy crushed-velvet hat, a huge overcoat, and carrying a lumpy book bag over her shoulder, she entered the casting session and sat down in a chair. Before the director could say a word, Winters opened her book bag, took out an Oscar statuette and plopped it down on his desk. After a beat, she took out a second Oscar statuette and set it on the desk next to the other one. Silence. Winters looked the director square in the eyes and barked, "Ya still want me to audition?"[11]

She got the part.

Although most of us don't have the benefit of bringing our Oscar statuettes to a job interview, Winters' story provides some important lessons about being confident in your abilities and bold during your actual interview. While it is important to project confidence during an interview, don't let your behavior or attitude veer into cockiness, which can come across negatively to an interviewer. There should be a subtle feeling of eagerness in how you answer questions but you don't want to come across as overconfident. The dangers of overconfidence include being underprepared, making unrealistic claims, or overstating your abilities. A recent study published in the *Journal of Occupational Psychology* found that a confident, comfortable vibe from someone interviewing for a job hits the bullseye for employers when they are interviewing prospective applicants. The study also revealed that job candidates who were perceived as "relaxed, interesting, strong, ambitious, mature, and pleasant" were the ones who tended to get hired.[12] You also don't want to appear overly desperate for the job, which can put off a potential employer as well. Instead, you want to create an impression in the mind of your interviewer that you would be a great asset to their organization and, if they don't take advantage of the opportunity to hire you, someone else surely will. Hollywood producer Peter Guber puts it this way: "When somebody is enthusiastic about a job opportunity—but gives off the feeling that this is not the only one they have on the table—they become more seductive in the employer's eyes. You become more desirable because it shows that you're making a conscious and thoughtful decision for the right reasons."[13] While no interviewer likes to deal with someone who spends their entire interview bragging or boasting about themselves, don't be afraid to detail your strengths and shine a light on your accomplishments or any skills you possess that make you an ideal fit for the job.

Be humble, but not too humble. Don't be invisible.

—PHARRELL WILLIAMS

Tracey Warson, Citi Private Bank North America Head, recounts one story about a job candidate who made a crucial mistake that ended up costing her the job. Recalled Warson, "One time I met with a young woman and asked her in the interview process about her compensation package and she told me what it was and then she quickly said, 'But you don't have to pay me that much.' That was just a big mistake, and I told her then, I said, 'Please promise me never to say that again.' People have got to know their own value and be confident in that."[14]

Being intentional with your communication will help you exhibit another trait that employers look for in a potential candidate: passion. Numerous studies have found that candidates who project energy and excitement are more likely to receive job offers during the interview process than those who don't.[15] And this extends not only to passion for the potential job opportunity but also personal passion about their activities and interests outside of work. Be prepared to answer questions that help the interviewer understand what makes you tick as a person and not just as a worker. When LinkedIn's Head of Recruiting, Brendan Browne, interviews someone for a job, one of the first things he does is hand them an erasable marker and directs them to a whiteboard. He then presents the candidate with the following task, asking, "What are you most passionate about? Using the whiteboard, explain to me the process of how it works."[16] Browne finds this exercise helpful because of its ambiguity and how it forces a candidate to explain something to him that they care about deeply. It reveals personality and shows whether or not the person is able to think creatively in the moment to clearly communicate a vision that is important to them.

When Burger King CEO Daniel Schwartz interviews candidates, he likes asking one question in particular: "Are you smart, or do you work hard?" Explains Schwartz, "You'd be surprised how many people tell me, 'I don't need to work hard, I'm smart.' Really? Humility is important. I like people who are passionate, who have persevered and who are clearly humble and not arrogant."[17]

As with any interaction, there are common pitfalls that can derail an effective job interview and damage your chances of getting hired. Some mistakes that hiring managers cited include: vague or general answers to questions (specificity is always best), speaking negatively about past employers (be as diplomatic as possible and avoid badmouthing anyone), asking about salary, benefits, or vacation policies too soon (leave these for later in the interview process), poor manners (etiquette matters), and failing to appreciate the interviewer's time (if you're early, you're on time). Also, it is becoming increasingly common for hiring managers to ask other decision-makers in an organization to meet potential candidates and weigh in with their thoughts and impressions. For this reason, it is important that every person you come in contact with during your interview process is treated with professionalism and respect. For example, if you treat the receptionist in the waiting room rudely or speak to them in a condescending manner, there is a good chance your behavior will be mentioned to the hiring manager once you finish your interview. According to the *Wall Street Journal*, the first impressions formed while a job applicant is waiting in the reception area before their interview factors into the hiring decision between 5 and 10 percent of the time, usually when the hiring manager is unsure whether the person is a good fit for the culture of the company.[18] Learn the receptionist's name and use it. Make eye contact. Smile. Thank them for their assistance. Your behavior with gatekeepers such as receptionists and assistants can create a positive feeling about you and your potential for the job even before you sit down with the hiring manager and can set you up for a great start.

PREPARING FOR YOUR INTERVIEW

One of the main reasons people dread interviewing for a job is that they have not done the proper homework ahead of time. Consequently, they find themselves feeling nervous, rushed or disorganized as the interview approaches, scrambling at the last minute to pull it all together. If you prepare properly for the interview, you can enjoy the actual interviewing experience and relax, knowing that your preparation has all been done ahead of time and will carry you through.

Here are some tips for proper preparation:

Do your research. Try to learn as much as you can about your potential employer. This type of research needs to take place well before your actual interview and can be done with a simple online search or by reviewing the company's website, trade journals, or industry publications that can give you greater insight into where the company is positioned in the industry. Speaking with any friends or acquaintances who presently work for the company or have worked for them in the past can also be a helpful resource. Current or former employees can provide firsthand information about the culture of the organization and what traits the hiring manager might find most valuable. They may also know the hiring manager personally and be able to give you an idea of their personality and background. This can give you a leg up on your competition and help you customize any stories or examples you may want to share during your interview. Information you want to know before your interview should include:

- Interviewer's role with the company
- Interviewer's history with the company
- CEO's name, education, history with the company
- Company's origin story (where and when it was founded, names of founders)
- Exactly what the company does and the value it provides
- The people who hold leadership positions in the company
- Any current news stories regarding the company
- Company's main clients and competitors
- Where the company is positioned in the industry

The key to strategically executing the perfect interview starts with preparation and making your unknowns known. Once you are granted the opportunity to interview, it is essential that you learn all you can about the company and job for which you are interviewing. And don't prepare by just researching the company, reread your resume or review your portfolio to ensure you remember all the important details that helped you get to this point, especially your accomplishments. The more you prepare, the more you will build confidence, and ultimately, the better you will perform in the interview. Preparation is what will enable you to stand out among the candidates.

Clothes make the man. Naked people have little or no influence on society.

—MARK TWAIN

Dress the part. The way you dress for a job interview can have a definite impact on the perception you create in the mind of your interviewer. One recent study found that being better dressed than another applicant boosts your chances of getting hired by 22 percent.[19] Try to find out what type of culture the company promotes in the workplace. Different types of jobs require different types of dress. Dress in clothing that indicates you are ready to start work today. We recommend you dress a notch up from the dress code required for the job, just to be on the safe side, but at the same time avoid overly formal clothes.

Practice your answers. Most questions that an interviewer will ask will fall into one of the following three categories: *Who are you? What can you do for me? Why should I hire you?* Try to anticipate what questions will be asked based on the information you have uncovered in your research and understand which of the three categories they fit into so you can answer accordingly. Familiarize yourself with the following questions that hiring managers commonly ask during interviews and then practice your answers to each using the guidance provided.

Question: "Tell me about yourself."

How to handle: With this question, the interviewer is creating a wide-open opportunity for you to touch on any points you wish to help them learn more about you. What you lead with is important and will reveal your priorities and your sense of self, so choose carefully. Try to turn your experiences into a concise, compelling story that reflects who you are and how and why that could provide value to their organization.

Question: "Why do you want to work for us?"

How to handle: A hiring manager asking this question is trying to understand what elements of the job you are drawn to and also how much you know about the company itself. In researching the company, start by identifying why the company is hiring for this position and use that knowledge to share specific examples from your past experiences to demonstrate why your skills align with the role.

Question: "What can you do for us that other candidates cannot?"

How to handle: This question provides you with another opportunity to highlight specific skills that you possess that align directly to the requirements of the job. If there is an accomplishment from your past that is impressive and relevant, feel free to share information on that. Again, be specific when you answer this question, tie it back to the benefit you can provide, and bring passion and confidence to your delivery.

Question: "What is your greatest strength?"

How to handle: While you may have many strengths to mention, the interviewer in posing this question is trying to determine if the strength you choose is a match for the role itself. This question lets you steer the interview where you want it to go. Whatever strength you choose to highlight—work ethic, preparation, leadership ability, communication skills—find a story or anecdote that demonstrates why this is true and then relate it back to the role for which you are being considered.

Question: "What is your greatest weakness?"

How to handle: An interviewer asking this question is looking for candor and humility in a candidate, so it is important to be honest with your answer. They also want to see how well you assume responsibility or own up to past mistakes. When answering, don't say that you have no weaknesses or that you work too hard or are a perfectionist—these "weaknesses" will come across as insincere. Instead, answer by saying, "I don't know if I would call it weakness, but there are certainly areas where I can improve," and then share a legitimate area of improvement, along with what you've done to develop your skills accordingly, such as attending a relevant training or reading a book on the topic.

Question: "Why did you leave your previous job?"

How to handle: If you left voluntarily, reference a specific characteristic that the company you are interviewing for has that your previous employer did not. If you were let go, be honest and explain the situation and own it. Explain what you learned from the experience. Phrases like "downsizing," "budget cuts," and "bad economy" are good defenses if they are true and are the reasons you are seeking this new opportunity.

Question: "What are your long-term goals?"

How to handle: This is the chance for you to show that you are an ambitious person who looks to the future and values vision. By asking this question, the interviewer is likely asking you to demonstrate your level of commitment. They want to know that you will dedicate yourself to the role and company and not start looking for another job opportunity immediately after being hired. As you answer, be careful not to focus too much on goals that don't pertain to the position for which you are interviewing. You can profess your long-term interest in the company, but outline a realistic growth strategy that is tied to the role as well as the needs and values of the organization itself.

Before any interview it can be very beneficial to do a practice session with a friend or spouse using the questions above. Like an actor doing a dress rehearsal, wear the clothes you will be wearing during the actual interview and set up chairs and a desk to simulate the environment of an office or boardroom. Film your practice sessions and then watch the playback with the person who is helping you prepare. Write down your initial impressions about what you thought you could have done better. Solicit feedback and any general impressions they have with your communication and the answers you provided. Note which of the questions gave you difficulty and then continue drilling and practicing your answers until you feel comfortable with each response. By doing this prior to the interview, you will feel more prepared and confident on the actual day.

Careers are funny things. They begin mysteriously and, just as mysteriously, they can end.

—EDWARD ALBEE

Comedian Matt Champagne once remarked, "I make a good first impression. It's every subsequent impression that I need to work on."[20] As human beings, we are hardwired to judge every person with whom we come in contact, even if we aren't consciously aware of doing so. This impulse to make snap judgments about those around us is an important evolutionary trait and has served as an essential survival mechanism for humans for centuries. And just as our ancestors made snap judgments about the people and situations they encountered, interviewers make snap judgments about job applicants. By making intentional choices that support your overall objective (to get the job), you will shape the perception you are creating in the eyes of your interviewer and increase the odds of getting hired.

One study by the University of Glasgow found that an interviewer's decision about a candidate is often set within the *first half of the first second* of the interview.[21] This means that the person being interviewed has barely uttered a word before a judgment has been made as to whether or not they will be given serious consideration for the job. Actors are used to being subject to these types of snap judgments during the audition process. *Does he look tall enough for the role? Is she too young to play a mother of three? Would he be believable as a mob boss?* Actors are trained to operate under the microscope of snap judgments so the intentional cues we use to influence the perceptions of potential decision-makers come in quite handy. And if that means looking and acting the part—dying our hair or gaining ten pounds of muscle to get the job—that's what we do. While someone in the corporate arena doesn't need to go to such extremes, it is helpful to make sure one's business attire is appropriate, any jewelry or makeup are understated, and grooming and hygiene are on point. In the end, it is about understanding the norms of the industry, knowing your audience, and dressing to impress.

The Glasgow study also revealed some interesting findings with regard to a job candidate receiving a positive snap judgment versus a negative one.[22] According to the study's findings, when the initial impression of a candidate exceeded an interviewer's expectations, that person benefited from something known as *confirmation bias*, meaning the interviewer often unconsciously confirmed their positive assessment of the candidate by rewarding that person with easier questions or fewer challenges. On the flip side, if the candidate made a negative initial impression with an interviewer, the same confirmation bias worked against them, with the interviewer making the questions harder and the challenges more difficult. This shows once again the importance of your overall presence during the opening moments of an interview. Being conscious of your intention cues is essential to moving you toward your goal of getting hired. Is it possible to recover from a less-than-stellar first impression with an interviewer? As it turns out— possible, yes. Easy? No.

According to a recent study from researchers at the University of Chicago, changing someone's initial perception of you requires considerable effort. In this study, the authors concluded, "People apparently need to commit just a few bad actions to appear . . . worse, but need to commit many good actions to appear substantively changed for the better."[23] And in an interview, committing even one or two bad actions may doom your chances. One example of this is the story of a job applicant who went to an interview and was asked by the hiring manager to tell a joke.[24] Finding himself on the spot, the man froze. The only joke he could think to tell was one he had seen on a Reddit thread the previous night about a gay dinosaur. He told the joke and laughed; the interviewer didn't. Trying to recover, the man asked the interviewer if he could tell a different joke. Unfortunately, the only other joke he could think to tell was another joke about a gay dinosaur. The manager conducting the interview stopped him halfway through the second joke and said that his boyfriend wouldn't find these jokes funny and neither did he. Needless to say, the candidate was not asked back for a second interview.

First impressions, as demonstrated by this story, can lock in an interviewer's perception of a candidate and their suitability for the job. This is why focusing on a strong start is important to establish confidence and credibility and convey high expectations for the remainder of your interview. Many candidates think their resume and experience alone will be enough to land them the job. Sadly, this is rarely the case. In fact, one recent study found that hiring managers spend only about six seconds reviewing a resume before making a decision whether or not to move forward with a candidate.[25] If you want the hiring manager to be excited by what you are sharing in an interview, your delivery should help set their anticipation levels and guide their feelings about you. If you want them to be excited you need to communicate excitement by what you say and how you say it. By assigning high expectations, it creates a positive perception that they want to be true—a confirmation bias they will feel obligated to bear out. Think about the last time someone recommended a movie to you they found highly entertaining. As you drove to the cinema, you had an expectation the movie you were about to see was going to be enjoyable and entertaining. If, 15 minutes into the movie, you found it dull and boring, this would be upsetting because it disconfirms your expectation and, thus, lets you down. The job interview process works the same way. If you demonstrate professionalism and excitement in your interactions with the hiring manager before the interview even takes place, you can leverage confirmation bias and create positive feelings with your interviewer. All of your initial interactions during the process should create a positive expectation in the hiring manager's mind. Conveying high expectations about something will lead others to automatically perceive that thing in a favorable light so as to match their expectations.

Asking questions during an interview allows it to feel more like a conversation than an interrogation. Also, at the end of most interviews, a potential employer will often ask if you have any questions for them. Asking thoughtful and relevant questions at the end of your interview is important. It not only shows you have done your homework by researching the organization and role, but it also builds rapport with the hiring manager by demonstrating genuine interest. Above all, when an interviewer asks if you have any questions for them, never say no. Here are some questions to consider asking, if given the opportunity, during an interview.

"What are three strengths or skills that are vital to this position?"

"What are some of the department's ongoing or anticipated projects?"

"What challenging aspects would I face in this role?"

"How does this company evaluate and promote its employees?"

"Can you describe the work environment at this company?"

"What industry trends do you foresee that might affect this company?"

"Is there any other information I can provide to assist in your decision?"

As we have previously discussed, being sufficiently prepared, understanding the company and role for which you are being considered, and then choosing intentions that will influence the emotions of your interviewer are crucial elements for success. When identifying the intention (or intentions) you will use to fuel your delivery, avoid treadmill verbs like *inform* and *update*. These will not elicit an emotional

The reason that you dance and sing is to make the audience feel like they are dancing and singing.

—HEATH LEDGER

reaction with your interviewer and you will likely be forgotten as soon as the next applicant comes through the door. Choose active verbs such as *excite* and *impress*. Think about what facts or information you can share to *impress* them about your previous accomplishments, *intrigue* them about interesting projects you have led, and *excite* them about the possibilities of what you could accomplish as a member of their organization. Show them you are passionate about the opportunity and let that passion be reflected in your delivery through the activation of strong and specific intentions.

And your body language and eye contact are not the only cues you can use to influence your hiring manager. As it turns out, your vocal presence also contributes greatly to the overall impression you create as well. This is why the words alone are not enough to get an interviewer excited about hiring you. Everything you say, every answer you give, and every question you ask during the interview process becomes evidence in the trial that will decide whether or not you get hired. Being able to build rapport with an interviewer and listen actively during the limited time you have with them is important. "Words are events, they do things, change things," wrote Ursula K. Le Guin in her meditation on human conversation. "They transform both speaker and hearer; they feed energy back and forth and amplify it."[26]

Often interviewers will communicate a lot of information nonverbally so you can gauge their interest levels by staying attuned to any shifts in their posture or changes in facial expressions such as smiling, leaning forward, or nodding their head in agreement when you have provided an answer to their question. There are neurons that affect the part of the brain responsible for recognizing facial expressions and reading body language and these neurons cause us to mirror what we are seeing from others in an attempt to create a bond with them. This "mirroring" reaction—what we refer to as *mirror theory*—is something psychologists call *isopraxism*.[27] Think of the automatic response you have when someone smiles at you or how you feel the impulse to yawn when the person talking to you yawns. This is how isporaxism works. In a job interview, it can be helpful to mirror any behavior or vocal cues you are noticing from your interviewer such as smiling, rate of speech, or volume levels.

NAILING THE ACTUAL INTERVIEW

Once all of the preparation has been done, it's time for the interview itself. Interviews are an excellent way for you to showcase yourself to a potential employer—to sell yourself, your skills, and your experience. During the interview, there are some telltale signs you can watch for that indicate the interview is going well, such as the hiring manager smiling and joking with you during the interview. If you and the hiring manager seem to have forged a common bond and the conversation seems natural and organic, then this is positive, as is the interview passing the extended time and the manager offering to take you on a tour of the office or headquarters. Generally, if you are not being seriously considered for the position, this will not happen. If the hiring manager introduces you to other team members or members of senior leadership, this is also good. If next steps are discussed, this is a clue that their interest in you is serious. But just as reading these positive intention cues from a hiring manager can show you how well the interview is going, there are danger signs you should look for that signal you may need to adjust your tactics to re-engage your interviewer. If the hiring manager appears disengaged or unimpressed, makes limited eye contact, frequently checks their watch, or ends the interview early, these can be signs that your answers or qualifications for the job were not satisfactory.

One instance where a lack of preparation derailed an important job interview came in the summer of 1979 when Ted Kennedy, the last surviving brother of America's storied political dynasty, was exploring a potential run for president.[28] During an interview, broadcaster Roger Mudd asked him a simple question: "Why do you want to be president?" Kennedy seemed floored by it, as if he had never considered the thought before this moment. He paused and stammered, before finally giving a stilted, technical, and passionless answer that provided little insight into his heart or true ambitions. Kennedy's campaign eventually imploded and many political analysts pointed to his fumbling response to this simple question as the beginning of the end for his presidential aspirations.

When handling interview questions, keep your answers succinct. If you can answer the interviewer's question with a simple yes or no response, do so. Unless the question requires a more detailed answer, you can often make twice the impact using half the words. The longer you speak or the greater detail you go into, the more likely you will be to misspeak, ramble, contradict yourself, or venture into areas you are not prepared to address. Many job candidates fail to be concise with their communication and end up repeating themselves or going on and on when they should have simply stopped talking. Don't be afraid to say less. Economy of language is a sign of a confident candidate. If your interviewer wants more information or additional details, they will ask for it.

Proper greeting

When you meet your interviewer, stand and approach them, and smile. Shake their hand while maintaining eye contact and use their name. While a firm handshake is important for anyone interviewing for a job, it takes on even greater importance for women as confidence is often evaluated based on the quality of their handshake, even more keenly than the handshakes of their male counterparts. Just as we have recommended with other aspects of your communication, adapt your handshake to the person and situation. As the greeting ends, you may want to start by mentioning something positive or complimentary, like the commute, the weather, their office, and so on.

Body language

As we have established earlier, your body language tells us even more about you than your words. If you are relaxed, smiling, and gesturing naturally, your interviewer is also more likely to be relaxed. Don't be frozen or stiff and don't be afraid to be expressive, even when seated. Your posture reveals to the interviewer how you feel about yourself as well as the world around you. According to Dr. Mark Reinecke, Chief Psychologist at Northwestern University, "This is something we have implicitly known for a long, long time . . . when you are feeling energized, courageous, and proud you tend to have a stronger, taller posture."[29] Because of this, be sure to control your body language and facial expressions, even when confronted with an unexpected question. To do this, return to the intention you want to convey for your answer and the reaction you want to elicit from the interviewer. Maintain a connection through eye contact, and nod to show that you are really focusing on what the other person is saying. Stay open with your body language as closed positions such as crossed arms and legs signal resistance or a lack of receptivity.

Smile

Studies show that a strong and genuine smile can play in your favor but only if used effectively. In one study, applicants who smiled at the beginning and end of an interview but smiled less during the middle portion were found to have been hired more frequently.[30] Research shows that candidates are seen as more suitable for a job that requires a serious demeanor (such as a lawyer or pilot) if they smile less during the interview process, and those interviewing for a job where they are less serious (such as customer service representative or salesperson) benefited from smiling more.[31] These examples once again underscore the importance of understanding your audience and modifying your intention cues to suit the role for which you are interviewing.

Vocal quality

Make sure you speak clearly and articulately so that your interviewer can understand you. Slow down your pace to show that you are relaxed. Also, remember that downward inflection exhibits confidence and command while upward inflection shows doubt and uncertainty. When asked a question, pause before speaking and carefully consider what you are about to say. Remember: once the words come out, you can't put them back in. You will be accountable for your answer, so give yourself a second or two to formulate a response. Slow your pace as you answer to give yourself more time to answer thoughtfully. This will also help you eliminate verbal viruses and any fillers that will make you seem nervous or unprepared. How common are verbal viruses in our daily speech? One study calculated that the average speaker will use a verbal virus or other speech disruption every 4.4 seconds.[32]

One example of verbal viruses dashing the hopes of a job candidate took place in 2008 when Caroline Kennedy, the daughter of President John F. Kennedy and the former U.S. Ambassador to Japan, was considering a run for the U.S. Senate. While exploring a bid for office, Kennedy gave an interview with the *New York Times* where she used the verbal virus "you know" a whopping 142 times. Asked about President Bush's tax cuts, Kennedy answered:

> Well, you know, that's something, obviously, that, you know, in principle and in the campaign, you know, I think that, um, the tax cuts, you know, were expiring and needed to be repealed.[33]

Try reading that last response out loud and see how credible you sound doing it. In the end, Kennedy's candidacy fizzled out and she abandoned an actual Senate run.

Be engaged
Make sure you are present at every moment during your interview and actively listening to what the interviewer is asking. Remember what has already been discussed in the interview and, if helpful, refer back to it. Make sure you are truly listening and not simply waiting for them to stop speaking so you can interject. Listen with your eyes as well as your ears and observe the nonverbal feedback coming from your interviewer. Research shows there is benefit in mirroring back to your interviewer any body language or vocal cues that you are observing in their communication, such as speech patterns, vocabulary, volume, posture, and so on.[34]

Once the interview is over, it is important to focus on a strong closing. Stand, shake hands, smile, make eye contact, and use your interviewer's name, just as you did in your greeting. Your last impression now supersedes your first impression. Thank your interviewer for their time and tell them you look forward to hearing from them.

With the actual interview complete, the final step in the process is to follow up with the hiring manager. It is always a good idea to send a thank-you letter or e-mail to the person who interviewed you. It reinforces your interest in the position and shows your potential employer that you are thoughtful, courteous, and professional. If possible, mention any notable topic or tidbit that you discussed during the meeting. This will help solidify you in their memory. It will also show that you were listening and present during the interview. You can also include any details you may have forgotten to mention. If your interviewer requests any additional information or materials, send these items to them as soon as possible. Many employers look to fill positions quickly and not providing the requested material right away could result in someone else getting the job.

Blueprint to Bullseye—Chapter 3

Preparation Guide for Interviewing

1. Information you should know about the company:
   a. Interviewer's role

   b. Interviewer's history with the company

   c. CEO's name, education, and history with the company

   d. Company's origin story (where/when founded, founders, etc.)

   e. Any current news stories regarding the company

   f. Main competitors in the industry

2. Information you should know about the position:
   a. Main responsibilities

   b. New role or a replacement position?

   c. Day-to-day schedule for the role (is travel required, does position have people reporting to them, etc.)

   d. Biggest challenges with this role

3. Rapport-building questions to ask if the opportunity arises:
   a. What is the biggest current challenge for you in your role?

   b. Where do you see the company going in the next three to five years?

   c. What are the three most important skills or qualities you are looking for in someone filling this position?

   d. What are the biggest challenges facing the company at the present moment?

   e. What do you think sets this company apart from its competitors?

4. What information can you share or questions can you ask that will utilize the following intentions and generate the corresponding emotions with your interviewer:
   a. Impress

   b. Intrigue

   c. Excite

CHAPTER 4

Communicate Like a Leader
Influencing Emotion through Style and Delivery

Our potential is one thing. What we do with it is quite another.
—ANGELA DUCKWORTH

When it comes to leaders, few names in history are more synonymous with the concept of leadership than the name Roosevelt. Franklin Delano Roosevelt served as President of the United States from 1933–1945 and was the leader responsible for seeing the American people through the depths of the Great Depression and helping them regain their faith and optimism. He was also the first president to communicate directly to the American people through his "fireside chats"—the radio addresses where he would speak about issues of the day and concerns on the minds of the public at large. His wife, Eleanor Roosevelt, was a trailblazer in her own right, a pioneering civil rights activist, named one of *Time* magazine's most important people of the twentieth century. In a time when female leaders were rare or nonexistent, Eleanor forged a path of her own. Her ability to speak to the masses and motivate them to action became one of her trademark skills. Though she was once terrified of speaking in front of others, she was encouraged by her husband to receive coaching to help sharpen her skills. Eleanor practiced diligently, even acting in homemade movies filmed on the Roosevelt estate, and eventually blossomed into a polished orator and someone historian Doris Kearns Goodwin named one of the most influential communicators of the twentieth century. "She gave a voice to people who did not have access to power," said Goodwin. "She was the first woman to speak in front of a national convention . . . to earn money as a lecturer, to be a radio commentator and to hold regular press conferences."[1]

In 1901, with the assassination of William McKinley, Theodore Roosevelt, cousin to Franklin Delano Roosevelt, became the youngest president in America's history. Only 42 years old, Teddy Roosevelt brought energy and excitement to the office. As a young man he had read Shakespeare, drove cattle, and hunted big game—even capturing an outlaw at one point. During the Spanish American War, he was a lieutenant colonel of the famed Rough Rider Regiment. As a speaker, he excited audiences with his high-pitched voice, pounding fists, and a delivery style described as "an electric battery of inexhaustible energy."[2]

After leaving the Presidency in 1909 and going on an African safari, Roosevelt returned to politics in 1912 running on a Progressive ticket. While campaigning in Milwaukee one day, Roosevelt sat in his open-air automobile outside of the Gilpatrick Hotel. He had written a long speech that he had rolled up and placed in the breast pocket of his jacket, along with his glasses case. As he waved to a cheering crowd, an unemployed saloonkeeper named John Flammang Schrank stepped forward, raised a Colt revolver, and shot Roosevelt in the chest before being quickly tackled and subdued. Fortuitously, the bullet had passed through his speech and glasses case, which slowed its trajectory before it entered his body. With the bullet still lodged in his chest, Roosevelt took the stage as the crowd cheered and said, "Friends, I shall ask you to be as quiet as possible. I don't know whether you fully understand that I have just been shot." The horrified audience gasped as the former president opened his vest, revealing his blood-stained shirt. Roosevelt reached into his coat pocket and pulled out his bullet-riddled, 50-page speech. "The bullet is in me now," remarked Roosevelt, "so that I cannot make a very long speech, but I will try my best."[3]

He then went on to deliver the entire 90-minute speech. Only after finishing his prepared remarks did Roosevelt finally agree to be taken to the hospital to receive medical attention.

Strength has been defined as "a person's capacity to make things happen with abilities and force of will."[4] In a business setting, productivity and accomplishment are powerful motivators, and while strength garners respect, warmth reaps support. When someone simultaneously projects both qualities, we look to them for leadership while investing our trust that they have our best interests at heart. Strong and steady leadership is essential for an organization to succeed and thrive. A good leader is someone who influences and inspires others, driving them toward a new vision or desired outcome. Sue Ashford, a professor at the University of Michigan's Ross School of Business, has studied leadership for decades and her findings have shown the world is not divided into leaders and followers. Instead, she believes that the quality of leadership is something anyone can emulate, whether they are a boss or not. "People grant a leader identity by their willingness to follow [them]," says Ashford. "We come to see ourselves a certain way based on our own thoughts but also based on the messages the world gives us."[5]

Leadership is essential for a team or organization to move forward, but the word itself has many definitions. A leader could be a CEO or a new hire. Anyone who leads others toward mutual success is a leader. In this chapter, we will help readers understand what is required for strong leadership and identify what leadership qualities they personally display and which leadership style is right for them. Thinking like a leader and acting like a leader are not the same thing. Leadership takes focus and a unique set of problem-solving skills.

> *If you want your life to be simple, you shouldn't be a leader.*
>
> —JACK MA

As a leader, every decision you make sends a message to the people around you, as does every decision you choose not to make. Every choice becomes a signal that will be interpreted by those with whom you work and interact. Are your decisions consistent? Are your decisions fair? A good leader takes the responsibility of leadership seriously, understanding that humility is required to guide and support every member of the organization. Jeff Immelt, the former CEO of General Electric, discussed the humbling aspects of leadership in his 16 years running GE, describing how he went to bed every night feeling like a failure but woke up every morning feeling on top of the world. Leadership, for him, was what happened in the space between those two extremes.[6] Being a leader is a journey into yourself where you will be forced to navigate various challenges and opportunities on a daily basis. The ways in which a leader communicates information to their team or workforce can have a significant impact on the level of inspiration and engagement they experience while carrying out their role. An interesting example of this involved former Secretary of Defense Donald Rumsfeld and the unique way he communicated with the members of his department as Pentagon Chief.[7]

Donald Rumsfeld twice served as U.S. Secretary of Defense, from 1975 to 1977, and again from 2001 to 2006, where he demonstrated a very unique way of relaying information to his teams. A hallmark of his communication style was something that came to be known as "snowflakes." Snowflakes were memos that Rumsfeld would draft himself and record into a machine or dictate through a secretary before distributing to his associates and subordinates in note form. The memos were known as snowflakes because they were white and seemed to descend like a blizzard from Rumsfeld's third-floor office. These snowflake memos generally covered a range of topics, from concerns Rumsfeld had about the progress being made in the war, to extended instructions to his subordinates, to a simple request for a haircut. These snowflake memos turned out to be very unpopular with the men and women who reported to Rumsfeld—these four-star generals and other government officials did not appreciate such an impersonal method of communication. During the five years that Rumsfeld served as secretary of defense, over 20,000 of these snowflake memos were dropped onto desks, slid under doors, and handed off in hallways. When Rumsfeld resigned from his role as Secretary of Defense in 2006, his replacement, Robert Gates, immediately discontinued the practice of communicating via snowflake and engaged instead in more in-person, face-to-face communication. When you think about the ways in which you communicate information to your team members or peers, are there individuals who could benefit from more in-person interactions with you? If you manage remote clients and tend to communicate only through e-mail, consider scheduling more frequent video calls or face-to-face meetings to allow you to stay more connected with them.

Effective leadership serves many purposes such as motivating a team, facilitating change, defining a culture, or overcoming adversity. Psychologist Angela Duckworth has studied leaders and other high achievers for years, trying to understand what makes them successful. What she discovered surprised her. In the end, it wasn't test scores or IQ or a degree from a top business school that was the predictor of success. Instead, said Duckworth, "It was this combination of passion and perseverance that made high achievers special. In a word, they had *grit*." Duckworth found that for the highly successful, the journey and the lessons they learned along the way were just as important as reaching their final destination. "Even if some of the things they had to do were boring, or frustrating, or even painful, they wouldn't dream of giving up. Their passion was enduring."[8]

No two leaders are exactly the same, nor do they possess and exhibit the same sets of skills or competencies. We've all experienced a boss or leader who has lacked the ability to motivate and inspire others by acting indecisively, shirking responsibility, scapegoating others, micromanaging team members, or refusing to apologize for mistakes they have made. True leadership drives an organization toward a specific vision, providing inspiration for every member of the company's hierarchy. There is no definitive list of traits required to be a perfect leader, but effective leaders will be seen by others as inspirational, decisive, visionary, honest, credible, self-aware, proficient, and self-directed. They manage change and handle adversity by relying on a specific set of principles—truths, values, and beliefs—that serve as their guide. These principles dictate how leaders behave and make decisions and serve as the foundational bedrock that grounds them.

Some principles of highly effective leaders include:

Treating team members as individuals

Every team member approaches their work with a unique set of expectations, concerns, and experiences. They bring their own perspectives to the way they perform tasks and interact with those around them. As a boss, it is important to understand the various backgrounds of your team members and stay connected with them at all times by asking questions and soliciting feedback.

Being technically proficient

You don't become great at swimming without getting in the water. If your company sells computer equipment and you are the CEO, you will need to possess a deep and detailed understanding of how your products are used, how they are installed, and who comprises your client base. You will need to know how your company differs from the competition and you will need to understand where your industry is headed so you can innovate and prepare for changes down the road. Leaders take the time to thoroughly train and become skilled at their given profession. They continue to learn and practice so they are able to execute their job duties and gain the credibility they need to lead those around them.

Developing the potential of others

As Jack Welch, the former CEO of GE, reminds us: "When you were made a leader you weren't given a crown, you were given the responsibility to bring out the best in others."[9] As a boss, it is important to recognize the unique talents and abilities of every member of your team and work to empower them so they can grow and excel within the organization. In most cases, people would rather work *with* a boss than *for* a boss. As such, give your team members a clear task and then support them with the resources they need to successfully complete it.

Making sound and timely decisions

Good leaders make decisions based on facts rather than emotions or assumptions. They set goals and honor timelines to make sure they are adhering to a plan. We work in a world that moves fast. Deadlines, budgets, schedules, bosses—all contribute to the stress we encounter as part of our roles. Being able to manage time while delivering results is not an easy feat but remains an important principle of effective leadership. As deadlines approach, tension and stress can often rise. Good leaders are aware of this and manage people and projects accordingly, understanding that as the end draws near, people generally become more focused and productive.

Developing a coherent team and strategy

To engage employees or team members, leaders must create a coherent strategic plan for the organization or individual project. And they must clearly set expectations that reaffirm or adhere to the company's vision and values. This helps to keep everyone aligned so as to avoid errors that can cost time and money. A great leader serves as the guide to get their team and the project itself across the finish line on time and on budget.

> *To achieve great things, two things are needed: a plan and not quite enough time.*
>
> —LEONARD BERNSTEIN

Motivating others to follow or take action

Leadership is about drive. It is about convincing others to do more or reach higher than they thought was possible. At times, it is about recognizing the achievement of superior workers and demanding improvement of those who do not meet set standards or benchmarks. Work to gain the trust and respect of your team by being an honest and open leader with your behavior and actions.

Clearly communicating information and vision

A team cannot align behind a vision or follow a specific process if it has not been clearly defined. An effective leader is responsible for setting goals and laying out how a process will work, who will handle each task, and also when those tasks are expected to be completed. By setting clear goals and defining benchmarks and expectations, you will avoid confusion that could result in frustration or low morale among team members.

Leading effectively by example

McDonald's founder Ray Kroc said, "The quality of a leader is reflected in the standards they set for themselves."[10] If you are in a leadership position, you have a responsibility to serve as a model for your team members to emulate. A large part of the perception you create as a boss involves leading others with your own actions. Workers look to those at the top for how to behave and what priorities are important to an organization. This includes the way you speak about clients, how you run meetings, and even how you emulate your company's values. By presenting yourself as a passionate, motivated leader who believes strongly in the mission of the organization, you become someone others will want to follow.

Seeking and accepting responsibility

Leaders manifest responsible behavior from others by demonstrating a willingness to take charge and make difficult (or unpopular) decisions. It also means staying on top of problems or challenges within an organization and figuring out solutions. An effective leader also accepts criticism for mistakes they have made. By acknowledging and owning up to errors, you will set a tone for others to emulate. If you are accountable, others will be inclined to be so.

Knowing personal strengths and limitations

As a leader, self-awareness is key to understanding how you are perceived by others within your organization, as well as what specific strengths and weaknesses you possess. A leader needs to understand how they make decisions, what triggers their anger, what bores or interests them, as well as what makes them happy.

Polls during the 2016 presidential campaign showed that the trait "has the right temperament to be president" was Donald Trump's biggest weakness in the opinion of the voting public. Yet when he was asked about this fact during one televised debate, Trump confidently declared, "I think my strongest asset, maybe by far, is my temperament. I have a winning temperament."[11] The audience in the hall roared with laughter as the comment demonstrated the candidate's obvious lack of self-awareness.

HOW MEN AND WOMEN LEAD DIFFERENTLY

According to recent studies, there are some slight differences in the ways men and women lead in the workplace and these differences can play a significant role in how individuals advance in their careers.[12] Alice Eagly, a leader in research on gender differences, found through multiple studies that the differences between men and women are small, but these minor differences often end up having a large effect on the way men and women communicate, and are perceived.[13] Leaders often possess unconscious biases with regard to race, gender, and education level, among others, so it is vital that we check in on occasion to make sure our decisions are fair and sound ones. Says Barry L. Reece of Virginia Polytechnic Institute and State University, "When people are influenced by one or more of these filters, their perception of the message may be totally different from what the sender was attempting to communicate."[14] These biases are real and can have a serious impact on the ways in which people lead or collaborate. One example of such bias took place in 2017, when a Polish nationalist member of the European Parliament named Janusz Korwin-Mikke, said that women "must earn less than men because they are weaker, smaller and less intelligent." The statement caused outrage and resulted in Korwin-Mikke being suspended for 10 days.[15]

In an experiment conducted in 2003, Columbia Business School had students read a case study about a successful venture capitalist.[16] For half of the group, the entrepreneur's name was Howard and for the other half the name of Heidi. When they asked participants in the study what their impressions were of the entrepreneur, "Howard" was described as likeable and appealing while "Heidi" was seen as selfish and not "the type of person you would want to

One of the best ways to influence people is to make them feel important.

—ROY T. BENNETT

hire or work for." This is an example of inherent bias, as the data for both case studies was exactly the same—the only difference was the gender of the venture capitalist. An interesting

update to the Howard/Heidi study: In 2013, Anderson Cooper repeated the experiment with New York University's business school during a segment on his CNN show. This time around, 10 years later, students rated the female entrepreneur as more likable and desirable as a boss than the male.

When it comes to the overall effectiveness of leaders, new research has revealed some interesting distinctions between male and female bosses. For example, women tend to be rated higher in areas such as achieving results, completing tasks, being transparent, and building rapport with others, while men scored higher in aspects that dealt with strategic planning, persuasion, and tasks where the ability to delegate was required. Past studies have suggested that women are better at using and decoding the nonverbal intention cues of others, such as facial expressions, and are generally stronger with the use of gestures than their male counterparts.[17] And while research suggests that female leaders are more skilled overall at sending and receiving nonverbal messages, studies on gender communication in the medical field alone have demonstrated some significant differences between the way male and female doctors treat patients.

In a new study published in *JAMA Internal Medicine*, researchers from Harvard wanted to find out whether patient outcomes were affected by the gender of their doctors.[18] A few studies had already shown that the gender of a patient's physician did influence the quality of the care they received, but up until then, there were no statistics detailing whether or not it affected actual mortality rates. What they discovered when they delved deeper into this research was remarkable.

The Harvard team found that patients being treated by a female doctor actually had a 4 percent lower risk of dying prematurely than those being treated by a male doctor. "Your chances of dying are lower if your doctor is a woman," said Harvard's Ashish Jha, one of the coauthors of the study and director of the Harvard Global Health Institute. "There are about a dozen studies out there that suggest women seem to practice differently." And precisely *how* do female doctors practice differently? "They communicate more effectively with patients."[19] According to Dr. Anna Parks of the University of California, "Previous work has shown that female physicians have a more patient-centered communication style, are more encouraging and reassuring, and have longer visits than male physicians." Would there be benefits if male doctors started operating and communicating more like their female counterparts? According to JAMA, the results would be significant and could save lives. "We estimate that approximately 32,000 fewer patients would die if male physicians could achieve the same outcomes as female physicians every year," they wrote.[20]

For years, traditional gender roles have dictated that traits such as assertiveness or aggressiveness are considered more masculine while silence and submissiveness were seen as more feminine. For decades, women in leadership roles were forced to play by rules established by men about how to behave in the workplace—how to act, speak, disagree, manage conflict, and handle emotions. In the past, while men have been more comfortable "taking space" during a meeting or discussion—speaking up and asserting themselves—women were more likely to "give space"—remaining quiet or ceding the floor to others. If a woman in the modern business environment asserts herself or speaks up—taking on what is seen as a more traditionally "male" role—it violates gender norms and can be met with disapproval. This creates a challenge for female executives when it comes to assertiveness and advocating for their ideas. In their book, *The Confidence Code*, authors Katty Kay and Claire Shipman say there is a definite confidence gap between the genders, "a chasm, stretching across professions, income levels, and generations."[21] Which begs the question: Does a woman in the corporate arena need to behave more like her male counterparts to be a successful executive? "The quick answer is no—except when it comes to confidence," says Tacy M. Byham, a global human resource consultant. "Women need to do a better job of declaring themselves and becoming their own advocates—speaking and acting confidently and mentally promoting themselves to a future-focused role. With this mindset, our own behaviors change. And a woman's impact is strengthened and improves her ability to get that seat at the table."[22]

Women in the workplace have gradually become more comfortable taking on more behavioral characteristics that are typically seen in men, amid the challenges of a traditional system that has previously limited their choices and even punished them for self-advocacy. According to recent polls by Gallup, female bosses give more frequent praise than male bosses.[23] Another difference involves access to opportunity. Studies show that female executives are more likely to create a pipeline that results in the hiring of more women and minorities than their male counterparts.[24] Currently, the percentage of women in the workforce stands at 47 percent of the labor force, up from 29 percent in 1950, according to the Bureau of Labor Statistics.[25]

And which gender do employees prefer working for—a male boss or female? According to Gallup, both genders report a preference for a male boss—with 33 percent of Americans saying they would prefer a male boss and just 20 percent preferring a female boss (with the rest saying it makes no difference).[26] While women were more likely than men to say they preferred a female boss, they were still more likely to prefer a male manager over a female manager when given the choice. For female leaders such as Sheryl Sandberg, Chief Operating Officer of Facebook, and Marissa Mayer, the former CEO of Yahoo!, promoting female leaders to executive positions is important because it sets a precedent. Simply seeing women in leadership roles can inspire other rising females to be leaders, a sentiment echoed by Tony-Award winning Broadway producer Kristin Caskey, who said, "For girls, you have to see it to be it."[27]

According to Sandberg, when it comes to numbers of female executives versus male, there is still work to be done—of the 197 heads of state, only 22 are women and of the top 500 companies by revenue, only 21 are run by females.[28] Why the lagging numbers for women in positions of power? For Sandberg, the problem is a result of the way we talk to children about leadership. "We start telling little girls not to lead at very young ages," says Sandberg, "and we start telling little boys to lead at very young ages, and that's a mistake. I believe everyone has inside them the ability to lead, and we should let people choose that, not based on gender, but on who they are and who they want to be."[29]

One example of this type of gender bias mindset occurred in 2016 when Jameis Winston, the quarterback for the Tampa Bay Buccaneers, spoke to a group of elementary school students in St. Petersburg, Florida. Attempting to preach self-confidence to a classroom of students, Winston's pep talk went like this: "All my young boys, stand up. The ladies, sit down. But all my boys, stand up. We strong, right? We strong! Now a lot of boys aren't supposed to be soft-spoken. But the ladies, they're supposed to be silent, polite, gentle. My men, my men [are] supposed to be strong."[30] No one doubts Winston's sincerity or the good intentions behind his pep talk, but what was the message for the children listening to him speak in that classroom? Men, stand up and be strong. Women, sit down and be quiet. This type of historical bias positioning men as leaders and women as followers is ingrained in society and female leaders encounter it in direct or indirect ways in the workplace every day.

In 2016, Hillary Clinton famously became the first female politician ever to run for the office of president as a candidate representing one of the two major parties. Although she received 3 million more votes, she lost electoral college votes and the presidency to Donald Trump. Throughout the campaign Clinton struggled to define what it means to communicate as a female leader. She knew there were challenges she would need to navigate. Raise your voice as a female leader and you could be seen as shrill or strident. Show vulnerability or shed a tear and you are weak or overly emotional—challenges that don't apply in the same way for male candidates. "It's hard work to present yourself in the best possible way," said Clinton. "You have to communicate in a way that people say: 'Okay, I get her.' And that can be more difficult for a woman. Because who are your models? If you want to run for the Senate, or run for the presidency, most of your role models are going to be men.

And what works for them won't work for you. Women are seen through a different lens."[31]

According to recent study from Clear Company, 86 percent of employees and executives cited a "lack of collaboration" or "ineffective communication" as the source of most workplace failures.[32] This statistic is alarming for anyone who manages others because it is the job of a boss to lead a team to success. If an organization fails to grow its profits or satisfy its shareholders, everyone will look to leadership for answers or to shoulder the blame. To manage and lead effectively, you need to be mindful of the team's overall objective, the team itself and each of the individuals involved.

EFFECTIVE LEADERSHIP COMMUNICATION

Great leaders must be great communicators. They have to be able to create a vision that others will want to follow. Their words must be supported by strong and active intentions and their objectives must be clearly defined, appealing to the aspirations and emotions of their team members. Without clarity, a leader's ideas will not be understood and without passion their proposals will not be championed. There are some very specific tools in a communicator's arsenal that a leader can use to shape the delivery of their message and influence the emotions of their audience, including the following:

Embrace silence

Actors and leaders understand the use of silence can have a powerful effect on the attention and emotions of another person, allowing a listener to ponder a question, consider a thought, or weigh a new option. As inventor and artist Leonardo da Vinci reminds us, "Nothing strengthens authority so much as silence."[33] Great speakers are never afraid to let an important thought hang in the air so their audience has time to consider its importance and impact. Stanislavski spoke of the three types of pauses that actors use to influence their audience and they are the same ones a leader can employ to impact a listener: *logical pauses* (moments where you stop so an audience can read information or look at a new visual aid), *psychological pauses* (where you pause for dramatic effect), and *physiological pauses* (when you simply need to take a drink of water or catch your breath).[34]

Vary the pace

Leaders can use a varied speaking rate to captivate an audience and draw them in. As excitement builds, speed up your pace to signal urgency to your listeners. By slowing your pace, you signal what you have to say is important by giving them a chance to process and consider the information you are providing. If you are delivering a message that is complex or technical in nature, it is even more important to slow down and also check in frequently with an audience to ensure comprehension. Listeners need time. Most likely, your audience is hearing information for the first time. When you introduce yourself to a new client or team member, say your name slowly. Too many times people rush through the introduction of their name and forget that most people have never heard it before.

Avoid hedging language

When projecting confidence and being assertive with communication, words matter, so try to avoid passive words and phrases, such as "I think," "kind of," and "I mean." These are examples of *hedging language*, words that are vague or tentative, meant to soften the impact of one's message. They often weaken an argument or make a speaker appear less than committed to a particular point or assertion. They also make it easier for others to offer differing opinions or challenge someone's ideas. Linguistically, a hedge is a marker of uncertainty for a speaker, and according to one cognitive scientist, "When you use a hedge, it marks the information as unreliable."[35]

Beware of generalizations

Generalizations are broad statements, covering whole groups of people or things. Generalizations can be problematic because they infer to an audience that there are very few exceptions to a statement and often occur when leaders rush to a conclusion before gathering all the facts or base their opinion on insufficient information or bias. In 2012, presidential candidate Mitt Romney ran into trouble when he was secretly recorded saying, "There are 47 percent [of the American electorate] who are dependent upon government, who believe that they are victims, who believe the government has a responsibility to care for them, who believe that they are entitled to health care, to food, to housing."[36] Hillary Clinton stumbled in a similar way during her campaign when she described half of Trump voters—nearly 31 million people—as "a basket of deplorables."[37] Trump himself angered many when he proposed banning all Muslims from entering the United States and referred to large groups of Mexican immigrants as "rapists" and "bad hombres."[38] In a business environment, leaders should be careful when using generalizations that could be perceived as unfair or untrue, such as: "That client always pays invoices late," "That department is so disorganized," or "He never shows up on time."

Limit jargon and acronyms

Many companies or industries use terms that serve as shorthand ways of naming things, much like a tribal language of sorts. And if you are not part of the "tribe," you may not understand what each one means. While some acronyms or industry jargon can be a shorthand way of claiming membership or creating a brand, excessive jargon or acronyms should only be used if you are confident that every audience member knows what they mean. Analyze your audience before you speak and make sure your language is inclusive and relatable to everyone present. You want your language to show you are thoughtful and well-versed but not make you appear snobby or pretentious. Too many buzzwords can alienate an audience and make it harder for you to get your message across.

Strive for simplicity

It is much easier to complicate something that is simple than simplify something that is complicated. Keeping your message simple is the key to making it clear.[39] Keep this in mind as you prepare for any form of communication, no matter the topic, no matter the setting. Steve Jobs frequently peppered his presentations with words like "amazing," "unbelievable," and "beautiful." He used them because they were simple and because each one created an emotional reaction in his audience that supported his objective of getting them excited to learn about the new product.

> *Knowledge is a process of piling up facts; wisdom lies in their simplification.*
>
> —MARTIN H. FISCHER

Whether designing a visual aid, creating a meeting agenda, or putting together a client proposal, make simplicity a priority. The easier your message is to communicate, the easier it will be to understand. John Maeda, a professor from MIT, puts it like this: "Simplicity is about subtracting the obvious and adding the meaningful."[40]

LEADERSHIP AND POWER

Power is about influence and authority and leaders require it to get things done for their organization. Winston Churchill spoke of the essential link between power and effective communication at the age of 23 when he said, "Of all the talents bestowed upon men, none is so precious as the gift of oratory. He who enjoys it wields a power more durable than that of a great king."[41] In essence, when we use power, we're utilizing our authority to get something we want or need from others. And while a leader may hold power, the way he or she wields that power depends on factors such as leadership style, the specific audience, and even their situation or surroundings. Power comes in different forms and understanding the types of power you possess as a leader is essential to understanding how you can effectively use that power to lead those in your organization and drive results. The types of power a leader may possess include the following categories.

Positional power comes from the position a person holds within an organization, such as their title or job responsibilities. It is based upon a person's ability to bestow rewards or punishments, in the form of job assignments, schedules, and pay or benefits to others. The higher the position of power, the more authority they will have to direct and influence the actions of others.

Network power is based upon who knows whom, or whom a person can have influence over, such as other powerful people within a given company. If you have trusted allies in positions of influence, you are more likely to be able to walk into their office and make a request or suggest an idea that will be given serious consideration than someone who does not have those same connections and relationships.

Expert power comes from a person's expertise, education, knowledge, or experience on a given topic or in a given field. If you are a thought leader or possess a unique set of skills or experiences that are essential for an organization to thrive, it is only natural that you will begin to gather expert power if these particular abilities or information become important or required for a company to be able to achieve a desired outcome.

Informational power can derive from someone who possesses or has access to valuable or important information that others may not know. This can be information that is secret, classified, or has only been shared exclusively with select people within the organization. If you are friends with your company's CEO and they tell you over drinks that the company is being acquired by a competitor and everyone is being given severance packages, you are able to make decisions and plan accordingly because you have information that equates to power.

STYLES OF LEADERSHIP

The way someone in the corporate environment provides feedback and direction, implements plans, and manages others demonstrates their leadership style. There are many different leadership styles for bosses to exhibit and it can be useful for a leader to employ different leadership styles depending on their audience and the situation in which they are involved. According to the American Psychological Association, men generally exhibit a more command-and-control style as leaders while women usually employ a more collaborative style. Men are more direct and task-oriented, while women are more cooperative.[42] Both styles can be effective but it is also important to modify your style at any given moment to suit the needs of your audience.

Five common leadership styles that executives use most frequently are:

Autocratic leadership
With this style of leadership, the person knows exactly what they want done, who is to do it, and when it should be completed. They often make decisions without consulting with team members and generally solicit little input. This can be effective when decisions need to be made quickly but can be detrimental to morale in the long run as it does not create a feeling of trust and sense of ownership for workers. Because of this, it can often lead to high levels of absenteeism and turnover within an organization. In Chapter 2, we told the story of "Tiger Mike" Davis, the Texas oilman who despised making small talk with his employees. He is one example of an autocratic leader, as are Genghis Khan and Napoleon Bonaparte.

Democratic leadership
This type of leader will often make the final decision, but leading up to it will encourage and include employees and other stakeholders in the decision-making process. They value the input and opinions of others. The democratic style can be a positive and motivational experience because team members feel they are

contributing by being allowed to share ideas and offer suggestions. Because everyone is included in making decisions with a democratic leader, the process can often require more time to get things done; therefore, if time is a consideration or the situation that presents itself is an emergency, this style of leadership can be less effective. Dwight D. Eisenhower, Abraham Lincoln, and John F. Kennedy are examples of democratic leaders.

Delegative leadership

A leader who gravitates toward this style generally adopts a more "hands-off" approach to leadership and gives employees freedom as to how they do their work and how they meet their deadlines. This autonomy often results in high job satisfaction, but can be ineffective or even detrimental if team members do not manage time well or lack the skills or self-motivation required to handle their responsibilities effectively. Ronald Reagan was a delegative leader and explained his approach like this: "I don't believe a chief executive should supervise every detail of what goes on in his organization . . . I think that's the cornerstone of good management: set clear goals and appoint good people to help you achieve them."[43] Besides Reagan, other delegative leaders include Warren Buffett and Herbert Hoover.

Transactional leadership

This type of leader operates via a style based primarily on a system of rewards and punishments for job performance. Often leading "by the book," this type of leader is more concerned with following existing rules than with making changes to the organization or its processes. First described in 1947 by Max Weber, this style of leadership is centered on a management process that involves controlling, organizing, and short-term planning.[44] Studies show that men exhibit more of a transactional style of leadership than women, defining responsibilities for their workers and then rewarding them for meeting objectives or disciplining them when they do not.[45] This style can be helpful to make sure routine work is getting done on time but does not generally inspire creative thinking or initiative from team members. Many military leaders, CEOs, and NFL coaches are known as transactional leaders, including Vince Lombardi, Norman Schwarzkopf, and George H.W. Bush.

Transformational leadership

This type of leader is often brought in when it is necessary to completely change the culture or direction of an organization. It is currently one of the most popular styles of leadership and can be applied across various industries. A transformational leader is usually charismatic and challenges or inspires team members by creating a sense of excitement while charting a clear vision and path forward. Studies have noted that women often gravitate toward this style of leadership, which allows them to more easily gain the trust and confidence of their workers.[46] Transformational leadership allows a leader to make necessary changes to an organization's current business model and perhaps even reinvent it, if needed. Examples of transformational leaders include Oprah Winfrey, Marissa Mayer, Nelson Mandela, Steve Jobs, and Franklin Delano Roosevelt.

Effective bosses lead based on strength and vision, not titles or threats. They empower others and modify their leadership style for each audience with whom they interact. In a landmark study by psychologist Daniel Goleman published in the *Harvard Business Review,* his research revealed that a manager's leadership style is responsible for 30 percent of a company's bottom-line profitability.[47] That is a huge number and should provide a wake-up call for any organization where members of the leadership team don't know how to lead effectively. Think about your own organization and your personal leadership style, as well as the communication of those with whom you interact on a weekly basis. By making slight adjustments to your communication and leadership style, you can strengthen your ability to influence others and create passionate, inspired teams willing to collaborate and push forward toward a common objective and mutual vision.

Blueprint to Bullseye—Chapter 4

Leadership Assessment Guide

1. I articulate my company's vision and purpose to others.   Agree   Disagree

2. I inspire others to excel and strive to improve.   Agree   Disagree

3. I show empathy when providing feedback to others.   Agree   Disagree

4. I actively involve others in all change processes.   Agree   Disagree

5. I encourage collaboration among my team members.   Agree   Disagree

6. I listen actively and am open to the ideas of others.   Agree   Disagree

7. I solicit input from diverse team members.   Agree   Disagree

8. I provide feedback to others in a timely manner.   Agree   Disagree

9. I identify and seek to tap people's potential.   Agree   Disagree

10. I model the behavior I expect in others.   Agree   Disagree

Complete these sentences:

I see my dominant leadership style(s) as _____
    because _____.

My strongest trait as a leader is _____.

The leadership trait I need to develop is _____.

CHAPTER 5

Inspire and Motivate Others
Engaging Workers and Leading a Team through Change

If you let a person talk long enough you'll hear their true intentions.
—Tupac Shakur

"Your voice makes a difference," Barack Obama said, recounting an incident that took place during one of the lowest moments of his 2008 campaign for president. As a communicator, Obama's ability to inspire others and connect with a crowd has always been widely regarded as one of his strongest assets. But the story Obama was referencing in this instance was not an example of him providing inspiration, but instead of someone who inspired him and provided the future president with an experience that would define him as a political candidate and leader.[1]

It was 2007, in the middle of his first presidential campaign, and things were not going well for Barack Obama. He had flown to Greenwood, South Carolina, for a campaign rally. His alarm had just gone off and he had wakened feeling sick and exhausted from the relentless pace of the campaign schedule. Opening the curtains to his hotel room, he looked out to see the weather was miserable and pouring down rain. He retrieved the newspaper from outside his hotel room and on the front page of the

New York Times was a particularly negative story about him. After getting dressed, he walked outside and his umbrella blew open. He was soaking wet. Quite a start to the day.

After a 90-minute drive to the rally site, Obama and his aides arrived to discover an audience of fewer than 20 people who were not particularly enthusiastic to see him. As he did his best to mix and mingle—introducing himself, learning people's names—Obama heard a voice from the back of the room shout, "Fired up!" To his surprise, everyone in the crowd suddenly yelled, "Fired up!" And then the voice said, "Ready to go!" and everyone yelled back, "Ready to go!" Obama looked around, not sure what to make of this sudden, unrehearsed call-and-response session. Where was this voice coming from and what was happening? Obama scanned the back of the room and spotted a small, middle-aged woman. She had one gold tooth and was dressed colorfully, wearing a big church hat. The woman's name was Edith Childs and she was a member of the local NAACP branch, as well as a local private detective. As it turned out, Childs was known to do this chant at the different meetings that she frequently attended in her community. It was her trademark phrase and was intended to pump energy into a room and get people excited to be there.

As the chants went on, growing louder and more intense, Obama noticed something happening. After a while, he was starting to get fired up himself. His mood changed and his outlook and attitude felt different, better. "I started to feel like I'm ready to go," recalled Obama. "And all those negative thoughts . . . started drifting away."[2] Obama eventually adopted the phrase, "Fired up! Ready to go!" on the campaign trail and used it to energize his crowds and supporters. The phrase worked and carried him all the way to the White House. Edith Childs showed Obama that if you want others to be excited by your message, you need to project excitement yourself through intentional delivery. For a leader, passion can be contagious. And Childs provided Obama with another, even greater lesson when it comes to motivating and inspiring others. Said Obama, "It just goes to show you how one voice can change a room. And if it can change a room, it can change a city. And if it can change a city, it can change a state. And if it can change a state, it can change a nation. And if it can change a nation, it can change the world."

As the previous story demonstrates, passion and purpose are powerful tools for a leader. In the workplace, passion can spread across teams, and studies have shown that people who attack their work with passion experience *flow*, a euphoric, effortless state of mind we will discuss in an upcoming chapter that is five times more productive than the norm.[3] "Fired up! Ready to go!" served as a rallying cry for Obama and helped him mobilize a movement that eventually delivered him the presidency. Leaders in the corporate arena face challenges not unlike what Obama went through on the campaign trail, as every day brings new challenges and setbacks that must be managed and overcome.

Globalization and technology have changed the way corporations do business as well as how leaders communicate. Because of an increasingly flatter and more far-flung international workforce, it is important for bosses to understand and consider the different cultural differences and expectations that employees bring to the work environment and how to best motivate them. While organizations have been forced to evolve over the past decade, the workforce itself is starting to change as well. Currently, there are up to four different generations working together in the corporate arena—the Silent Generation, baby boomers, Generation X, and millennials (sometimes called Generation Y). Millennials have now overtaken baby boomers as America's largest living generation, with 53 million workers and growing. In fact, more than one in three workers now are millennials.[4] And according to recent findings published by Deloitte, 66 percent of millennials are expected to leave their current jobs in the next three years and only 5 percent think they will still be in their current job in 10 years.[5] This is a much different mindset from that of workers of past generations who often stayed in the same job or with the same company for decades. While all learners grow through similar means and methods, employees of different generations bring with them different values, different expectations, and different styles of working. Studies have shown that workers communicate and lead based on their generational backgrounds, therefore effective leaders must consider the attitudes and habits of each individual worker to inspire or motivate them. Failing to do so can inevitably lead to resentment, high turnover, and low morale.[6]

Millennials (those born from the early 1980s to the early 2000s) want flexible work schedules and a more casual work environment. They want their work to have purpose and serve their community or society in a positive way. Rebecca Ray and Evan Sinar have studied current research on younger workers and found "For millennial leaders, the prototypical leader is an inspiring coach, a compelling communicator and one whose choices and actions are informed by an intercultural perspective."[7] Millennials are used to technology and social media being an integral part of their lives and are comfortable with it being part of their work as well. They also hunger for feedback from bosses. One study found that 80 percent of millennials said they want regular feedback from their managers and 75 percent want mentors who will provide them with advice and guidance that can serve them in their lives and careers.[8] Younger workers prefer a "flatter" organizational structure where titles and hierarchy are less important and most want to work in an environment where they feel a sense of belonging, where they are heard and their opinions matter. One study found that 76 percent of millennials think their bosses could actually learn something from them if they took the time to listen (compared to only 50 percent of baby boomers who felt the same).[9] For bosses trying to motivate a younger team and create a positive and supportive work environment, adjusting their communication and leadership styles to accommodate these needs is essential.

UNDERSTANDING EMPLOYEE ENGAGEMENT

The concept of employee engagement first appeared as a business concept in the 1990s, when William Kahn, a professor of organizational behavior at Boston University's School of Management, provided the first formal definition, calling it "the harnessing of organization members' selves to their work roles."[10] According to Kahn, employee engagement is how people "employ and express themselves physically, cognitively, and emotionally during role performances."[11] Employee engagement does not mean employee happiness or even employee satisfaction. It means the level of emotional commitment and investment a worker has to the goals of an organization. Wellins and Concelman (2004) talked about employee engagement as "the illusive force that motivates employees to higher levels of performance" through the employee's "commitment, loyalty, productivity and ownership."[12] Much of Kahn's work originated from the observations of Erving Goffman, the psychologist we discussed in previous chapters who viewed people as "social actors." Goffman used the concept of "embracement" to describe the investment of self

You aren't a leader if you aren't creating new leaders.

—JA'MAL GREEN

and energy a worker puts into their "role" and to what extent they "presented" or "absented" their selves during the "performance" at work.[13] The less committed or attentive a worker was to the role they were meant to embrace, the less engaged they were as an employee.

Organizations have started paying attention to employee engagement in an effort to understand what motivates their workers so they can better influence them to drive performance. According to research, one way to improve employee engagement within an organization is to improve their manager's communication skills. According to 83 percent of respondents in a 2016 Association for Talent Management study, communication is the most important skill area required for managerial success.[14] And this makes sense, as managers are tasked with putting strategic plans into action, securing employee buy-in, ensuring day-to-day operations run smoothly, and communicating progress up and down the organization. The ability for managers to effectively communicate in each of these instances is critical and research has shown that effective communication between workers and bosses has a direct influence on the level of productivity and job satisfaction seen within an organization.[15]

As a boss or leader, do your employees carry out your vision and follow your direction because they *want* to or because they *have* to? Do you lead them by inspiring them or by intimidating them? Every good relationship—including that of a boss and worker—should be perceived as equally beneficial to all parties. Think about it. If you are the boss or manager, you derive benefit from an employee who is punctual, skilled, collaborative, and delivers what they say they will deliver when it needs to be delivered. Conversely, if you are an employee, you find benefit as well if a boss or senior leader recognizes your hard work, appreciates your time and talent, and allows you to develop within the organization. Studies have shown that engaged employees are not only conscientious about their work and enthusiastic about what they do, they are also committed to maintaining a high level of performance within an organization.[16] Good attitude equals good work. If you want to achieve the highest levels of motivation for a worker, research has shown that you must involve not only physical and cognitive effort, but also an emotional investment from workers as well.[17] According to Kahn's findings, employee engagement rose when people were emotionally connected to their work and that work was aligned with the overall vision of the company.[18] Think about how much easier it is to motivate a team member who is passionate about a task versus one who is detached, resistant, or apathetic.

And, as it turns out, engaged employees are also very good for business. The energy and passion that a committed worker brings to their efforts can boost productivity and help grow an organization. An engaged employee will consistently outperform their disengaged peers and achieve new standards of excellence that can then serve as inspiration for other members of their team. If workers believe in the vision of an organization and are engaged in their work, studies show they will willingly take on additional responsibilities that are above and beyond their specific job description, thus creating a more collaborative and supportive work environment.[19] According to Tamara Erickson, professor of organizational development at London Business School, "The younger generation tends to put a higher premium on the quality, experiences, and self-growth associated with work rather than money."[20] A good manager needs to take this into account and do everything they can to create a culture that will be attractive to younger workers. When a team develops they will bring passion and purpose to their work and will go above and beyond to accomplish their goals. But that trust doesn't happen without attention being paid to the way individual stakeholders interact and communicate with each other. According to the National Wellness Institute, there are six dimensions that contribute to a person's individual wellness: *spiritual, emotional, occupational, physical, social,* and *intellectual.*[21] As a manager, you can engage your workforce more effectively by a keen awareness of all six categories and by helping your workers integrate their lives across all six dimensions. This will not only allow the members of your team to stay motivated by facilitating a healthy work/life balance, it will also help them to avoid common work pitfalls such as burnout or boredom.

Numerous studies show that the best way to bolster emotional commitment is to increase communication. According to the *Harvard Business Review*, highly engaged organizations enjoy double the rate of success versus lower-engaged organizations.[22] Think of what this could mean to the bottom line or a company's prospects for future growth. Studies have also found that an open and honest relationship between a supervisor and their subordinates affects their engagement level. Employees who get twice the number of one-on-one meetings with their manager relative to their peers are 67 percent less likely to be disengaged.[23] Conversely, in situations where managers don't meet with their workers on a frequent basis (or fail to provide on-the-job training), employees were four times more likely to be disengaged.[24] They were also twice as likely to view leadership unfavorably than those who met regularly with their managers.[25] The message here is a simple and powerful one: To better engage your employees, you have to start by listening to them.

Research has shown that more than half of workers who leave their job do so because of a poor relationship with their boss.[26] Often this dissatisfaction is a result of poor communication on the part of the manager—either overworking them or not recognizing their efforts. Research has shown that 78 percent of workers said that being recognized for their efforts motivates them and 69 percent said they would work harder if they were better recognized for their efforts.[27] Over-working an employee can be especially problematic when managing star employees. When a manager knows how skilled and disciplined their A players are, it is tempting to direct more and more work that person's way, knowing that they will always deliver a stellar performance or result. The problem with doing this is that it can be seen as a punishment by the star employee and can lead to burnout, resentment, or a feeling they are being taken advantage of because of their skills or work ethic. When managing a valuable employee such as this, it is vital to keep the channels of communication open at all times. Check in frequently to gauge their level of satisfaction at each stage of a project or task.

Another danger for managers is employee burnout. "Like employee engagement, burnout is personal," says researcher Mollie Lombardi. "The threshold for fatigue and dissatisfaction can be very different from individual to individual, and often high performers who expect a lot of themselves may be even more prone to its impact. Managers need to stay on top of this and help their employees be aware of potential burnout before it's too late."[28] New research out of Stanford has shown that productivity for workers declines sharply when their workweek exceeds 50 hours. And when their workweek exceeds 55 hours, productivity drops off so much you don't get anything out of employees working longer hours.[29]

Another reason bosses fail their workers is they don't engage them creatively or challenge them intellectually. No two workers are exactly alike, so it is important to understand what drives them. What are their passions? What are their goals? What areas do they want to develop? By taking time as a manager to understand what excites each of your workers, you will have a better idea of how to engage them and keep them motivated. Most workers enjoy being challenged in their work, so a good manager will help them set goals that are lofty or perhaps even out of their comfort zone. By pushing their workers to achieve something even they didn't think was possible, a boss demonstrates they care about developing their workers' skills and talents. One of the greatest gifts a boss can provide to their workers is opportunity and the chance to learn, develop, and grow.

LEADING A TEAM THROUGH CHANGE

As discussed in previous chapters, technology and globalization are sweeping us forward like the rapids of a rushing river. Great leaders are often called upon to provide clarity and to exhibit decisiveness amidst chaos. In his book *The Actor and the Target*, Declan Donnellan speaks of change like this: "Every living creature at every moment of its life has to deal with a situation which will either get better or worse. This better or worse might be infinitesimally small, but there will always be some degree of better or worse. All we can be sure of is change."[30] This is not only true for every character in every play, it also is just as relevant for everyone who kicks off a meeting, sits down for a job interview, or presents their ideas to a boss or client. At the end of their communication, they will likely be better or worse off than before they began.

> *You don't drown by falling in the water; you drown by staying there.*
>
> —EDWIN LOUIS COLE

Change can be an emotional process for team members, and if not managed and communicated properly, it can damage trust. Aristotle spoke about change way back in 350 BC, pointing out that if communication is meant to influence another person's behavior, it must be grounded in the desires and interests of the receiver. This idea hearkens back to the first step in our Pinnacle methodology: *analyzing your audience*. Poor change management can result in resentment, absenteeism, cynicism, distrust, confusion, conflict, and anger. According to Angela Kenyatta, CEO of Strategic Change Solutions, "A robust communication strategy must consider the communication needs of all key stakeholders, to keep them informed and engaged." As human beings, we are naturally resistant to change because change shakes our foundation, making the future seem uncertain. It also creates the possibility to fail, which can create anxiety among the members of a team. Says Kenyatta, "Resistance is a natural and normal response to change and can be quite useful when understood as valuable feedback from those impacted by the change. This is why competencies such as active listening, inviting feedback, and leaning into ambiguity are of immeasurable value during periods of transformation when the stakes—and often tensions—are especially high."[31] Change also creates the opportunity for growth and development, and a good leader will remind others of this fact when difficulties arise. To be sure, organizational change is a process with many moving parts. It can be complicated or messy and doesn't occur overnight. But the process of creating a strategic plan to implement change is key to the long-term success of an organization. It is important to remember that not all organizations are the same and not all people deal with change in the same way. Additionally, different kinds of change require different strategies to gain employee acceptance and engagement. Because change often involves disruption, leaders communicating during organizational change should expect resistance from team members. This makes open and transparent communication a necessary tool for a team to embrace change and move forward together. When managing change, it is important to assess any situation and understand what you can change and what you cannot. Interestingly, 46 percent of change management efforts fail during execution, according to a Robert Half Management Resources survey.[32] The reason? Lack of communication. According to Tim Hird, executive director for the company, 65 percent of respondents said that "communicating clearly and frequently" is the most important action to take when going through organizational change.[33] Common mistakes people make when managing change include:

- Not involving people at all levels in the change process
- A lack of vision and foresight from leadership
- Not appreciating that people have different reactions to change
- A lack of transparency with team members during the change process
- Improper system or framework to sustain the changes
- Not incorporating new strategies into a company's culture

The process of implementing organizational change is not always a smooth or easy one. One clear example of change that was not handled effectively, according to Angela Kenyatta, was the initial launch of the healthcare.gov website under Barack Obama. From the start, the web portal for the health insurance marketplace, commonly referred to as Obamacare, was plagued by problems. A series of technical snafus resulted in an absolutely abysmal experience for consumers who attempted to enroll during the first week the site was up. In addition to the poor end-user experience, the flawed launch generated bad press for an initiative that had already attracted numerous detractors. When the post-mortem of the launch was conducted to figure out exactly what had gone wrong, numerous instances of inadequate project scoping, process omissions, and lack of oversight were noted. To the credit of the Obama administration, the feedback from the initial launch was leveraged to make significant improvements which resulted in a more solid registration portal and a greatly improved user experience. By acknowledging and acting swiftly to correct early gaps, the site's bumpy start was overcome and the implementation ultimately became a stellar example of what's possible when the agility and resilience that wide-scale transformational efforts require is effectively applied.

For any type of change to be implemented effectively, three aspects of the change initiative are needed from the company and its leadership. First, there needs to be a high level of support for the initiative itself from leadership. Second, the support needs to be effectively communicated throughout the entire organization. Third, workers at all levels must be given the tools and authority needed to implement the change initiative. Think about the changes that have taken place within your organization recently. How have they affected the morale or engagement levels of your workers? Were the changes communicated clearly and did all levels have the support they needed from management to implement them effectively? As we have discussed previously, there are different types of change that can happen in an organization and understanding the differences of each can help a leader manage more effectively.

The three main types of changes that occur in an organization include:

Developmental change

This takes place when a process that currently exists is slowly and continually improved over time without any drastic or dramatic difference in the way an organization operates. For leaders, this is the easiest type of change to manage as it is the least disruptive to your workers. Examples of developmental change might include upgrading computer systems, utilizing new and improved software, changing vendors, etc. This type of change usually causes little stress to employees if communication has been clear throughout the process.

Transitional change

This is a little more intrusive than developmental change and involves eliminating an existing process and replacing it with one that is completely new. As a leader managing transitional change, it is important to clearly define what changes are occurring and, perhaps more importantly, why they are needed. Managing expectations and listening to the concerns of your team members is vital in this type of change. Examples of transitional change might include a corporate reorganization, merger, or the addition of a new product line. The success of transitional change often rests on how smoothly and efficiently the transitional phase is communicated by a company's leadership. Without constant and clear communication, employees can feel anxious or uncertain about their jobs and even the future of the company itself.

Transformational change

This is the most dramatic and sweeping type of change that can happen within a company and has a large emotional impact on a workforce. With transformational change, a company decides to change its basic underlying strategy and processes by which they have previously operated—often based on a change in supply and demand, lack of revenue, growing competition, or the emergence of new technologies in the field. In order to stay competitive in the marketplace, they choose to make radical changes to the way they have previously done business. Transformational change is usually enacted over time and can involve both developmental and transitional change. As a leader managing this type of operational change, being transparent with your intentions and involving all stakeholders from the start is essential for a successful transition.

Pat Wadors, the former Chief Human Resources Officer at LinkedIn, advises, "If the lines of communication are open from the beginning, you will earn [workers'] respect and trust much faster and your working relationship will benefit . . . let them know you are about listening and understanding, that your goal is to be as informed as possible about everything that is important in order to best help them overcome their challenges and achieve their goals."[34] Studies have shown that "without effective employee communication, change is impossible and change management fails" and, conversely, if you involve your team members in the change process by soliciting their input, they will more readily engage with all aspects of the initiative as they happen.[35] Change is an unavoidable aspect of business. By embracing it and clearly communicating all aspects of it throughout your organization, you not only help employees cope and manage, you also build a pool of nimble, informed workers who can help drive growth and move an organization forward.

ENGAGING YOUR TEAM MEMBERS

As we have discussed previously, a good leader must define a vision and chart a path forward for the members of their team. George Lucas, the creator of *Star Wars*, employs a favorite analogy when it comes to the collaborative process of a team or organization. He sees collaboration like a wagon train headed west—a group of like-minded pioneers, filled with purpose, on a long journey toward a common destination.[36] And as with any type of journey, detours and setbacks are likely to occur. But an effective, visionary leader manages these situational challenges and keeps everyone on board and headed in the same direction. A good boss will lead in a manner that allows team members to make their way without shoving them along or holding their hand at every turn. A good leader will create an environment that brings out the best in their people. Few workers enjoy a boss who breathes down their neck or micromanages every aspect of their work. Micromanaging your employees will almost surely result in your employees disengaging from you and the company. Workers want to feel trusted to make independent decisions. Empowering your team members by allowing them a certain level of creative freedom encourages them to contribute to the overall mission and allows them to grow and develop along the way.

Managers are responsible for putting strategic plans into action, ensuring day-to-day operations run smoothly, and communicating progress up and down the organization. Lack of communication between managers and direct reports can dramatically decrease employee engagement. In fact, according to Gallup, as much as 70 percent of the variance in a team's engagement levels can be traced to the manager's influence.[37] As author Daniel Goleman explains, "Quite simply, in any human group, the leader has maximal power to sway everyone's emotions . . . how well leaders manage their moods affects everyone else's moods, which becomes not just a private matter, but a factor in how well a business will do."[38] A recent Society for Human Resource Management study revealed that 58 percent of employees say it's very important to have a good relationship with their manager,[39] yet only half of employees reported feeling respected by their boss.[40] The more trust you have with a team member, the more they feel empowered, the better your working relationship with them will be. The more time spent between a boss and employee, the deeper the connection and the more engaged they will be. According to *Forbes* contributor Mark Murphy, "Most people spend only half the time they should be spending interacting with their boss. People who do spend an optimal number of hours interacting with their direct leader (six hours per week) are 29 percent more inspired, 30 percent more engaged, 16 percent more innovative, and 15 percent more intrinsically motivated than those who spend only one hour per week."[41]

When you talk, you are repeating what you already know. But if you listen, you may learn something new.

—DALAI LAMA

And just as a leader can learn important lessons from an effective boss, they can also learn a great deal from ineffective bosses. It's a safe bet that most people, over the course of their career, can probably name someone they have worked for who was not up to the task. They lacked the ability to lead, to communicate a vision, or to motivate others. Working with poor leaders and observing their mistakes firsthand can provide valuable lessons on how you choose to lead. Billionaire and *Shark Tank* star Mark Cuban shared an experience he had with a bad boss early in his career that affected how he ran his businesses years later.[42]

Cuban was living in Dallas, working as a bartender, when he landed his first sales job at a software company. "About nine months in," said Cuban, "I got an opportunity to make a $15,000 sale . . . I called my boss, the CEO, and told him I was going to pick up the check. I thought he'd be thrilled. He wasn't. He told me not to do it. I thought: 'Are you kidding me?' I decided to do it anyway. I thought when I showed up with a $15,000 check, he'd be cool with it. Instead, when I came back to the office, he fired me on the spot. I had disobeyed him. He was one of those CEOs who is all pomp and circumstance, one of those guys who seems to scream: 'Don't you know who I am?' He tried hard to look and act the part of the CEO. He wore the right suits. But he had a huge flaw: He never did the work. He never demonstrated the initiative to go out to sell. I had realized by that time that 'sales cures all.' That's a phrase I still use to this day. He was my mentor, but not in the way you'd expect. Even now I think back to things he did, and I do the opposite." The lesson here for rising leaders is to use every opportunity you encounter, the good and the bad, to learn from those around you—emulate the best qualities you observe and avoid the bad ones.

Here are four ways to maximize employee engagement within your organization.

Listen to feedback

One thing a leader can do to instantly improve communication and engage their workers is to talk less and listen more. Employees who feel listened to will reciprocate by listening to others. By doing so, you make your workers feel appreciated and understood, which increases their sense of loyalty to an organization. "Active listening is a powerful tool," says Hollywood producer Peter Guber, "Because it emotionally connects you to your audience and makes them feel valued."[43]

When Barack Obama first took office in 2009, about two-thirds of his staff were men and female staffers often felt it difficult to get a seat at the table or have their voices heard. According to National Security Advisor Susan Rice, "It's not pleasant to have to appeal to a man to say, 'Include me in that meeting.' "[44] To address the problem of not feeling heard, a group of female staffers met privately and developed a simple strategy, which they called *amplification*—to make sure their voices were being heard. Here's how it worked: During a meeting or policy discussion, if a female staffer made a key point or important observation, other women in the room would repeat it and give credit to the staffer who made the point. Something like, "I think Jennifer's point here is a very important one . . ." or "Jennifer's observation is spot on and we should take it into consideration . . ." By doing this, female staffers were supporting each other by "amplifying" points that were being made—holding a microphone to them, so to speak—so male staffers in the room were forced to recognize the point that was just made as well as the person responsible for making it. Amplification can also help prevent male staffers from taking credit for a female staffer's idea at a later date or claiming it as their own. The technique worked and President Obama took notice, gradually including more female staffers in meetings. By the end of his second term, there was an equal split of men and women among his top aides, and half of all White House departments were headed by women. Think about how discussions during the meetings are conducted at your organization. Are there certain louder voices that are always being heard? Are there less assertive voices that sometimes get crowded out? If there are team members who struggle to advocate for their ideas or get drowned out by louder, more assertive voices, use this amplification process to help them be heard.

Set expectations

Employee engagement begins with alignment and making sure employees understand an organization's strategic goals and vision.

What are the company's short-term and long-term priorities and how will they be accomplished? Employees need to be clear about how they can contribute their efforts to have the greatest impact. Most workers generally feel empowered by transparency, so give them clear and actionable guidance and feedback. Your team members are not mind readers—if you are unhappy with something they are doing you've got to let them know. Provide this type of information in a timely manner so they can make changes before it's too late. Keep the communication channels open and be clear about what you expect from them. According to a Gallup poll, employees were three times more likely to be engaged if their managers held regular meetings with them.[45] To create a strong company culture within your organization, adopt a leadership style in which every employee feels like they have a voice. Commit to transparency, and create an atmosphere of trust so that team members understand you are open to their ideas and input. Studies have shown that when bosses set clear expectations for their workers it can actually stimulate employee commitment levels to the organization itself by increasing the quality of task-related communications. This means the information should be timely— the right information getting to the right place at the right time.

Show appreciation
Recognizing the efforts and accomplishments of those around you goes a long way to employee engagement. As mentioned previously, a Gallup study found that 69 percent of people said they would work harder if they were recognized for their efforts.[46] If your team members do not feel appreciated, it's going to be hard for them to be engaged and motivated. Conversely, if employees feel valued and acknowledged for the work they have done, it has a direct effect on their brains and the emotions they feel. According to Alex Korb, a neuroscientist who has studied the brain extensively, "The benefits of gratitude start with the dopamine system, because feeling grateful activates the brain stem region that produces dopamine. Additionally, gratitude toward others increases activity in social dopamine circuits, which makes

social interactions more enjoyable."[47] This means that workers who feel acknowledged will feel more positively about the work they are doing and the collaboration with their coworkers. And a positive attitude can be contagious, as can a negative one. Resentment or apathy can serve as a poison within a team or company if people do not feel appreciated by their boss or an organization's leadership. A recent study from Oracle found a 60 percent increase in engagement simply by recognizing employees—acknowledging their great work or their accomplishments.[48] This statistic proves there is a definite benefit to recognizing employee achievement. As a boss, this can be done in many ways: an e-mail, a phone call, a gift card, a cash bonus, or a well-deserved promotion. Employees want to be seen as partners and they want their efforts to matter. Recognizing their work makes them feel valued. It also helps unify a team around a common goal and encourages others to succeed while reminding everyone they work for a winning and supportive organization.

When it comes to providing incentives as a reward for achievement, bigger is not always better. The size of the award or incentive may not always create the feeling of gratitude you seek. While common sense would suggest that the bigger the incentive, the more the engaged the person would be, that is not necessarily the case. Often a smaller incentive that is more easily attained can be even more effective than a larger one. Why? Because a larger incentive can end up creating increased anxiety in workers. In fact, one study that measured creativity, memory, and motor skills, found that a participant's performances sharply decreased when the incentive was large because it caused them to "choke under pressure."[49] Also, it is critical to understand the objective you hope to accomplish by giving the award to make sure the incentive supports the overall mission of your company. Says Susan David, a psychologist at Harvard Medical School, "If your goal is to motivate, you need to assess what the risks are to your game plan if you give a bonus to recognize outstanding work performance to only one person on the team versus everyone who participated."[50] The danger you run into by recognizing only one person is that the rest of the team who contributed to the project's success may feel resentful or demoralized, and this may undermine your goals in awarding the incentive in the first place.

Empower others

Employees want a strong sense of purpose. They want a specific objective to accomplish and a clear vision to help guide them. They want support and also to be challenged. But they also want freedom. Everyone thrives on creativity, so give your team members the space to spread their wings. As we've stressed previously, they will be much happier working *with* you, than *for* you. One study of millennials found that 86 percent of these younger workers were more inclined to stay at a job longer if leadership provided them with an opportunity for personal development.[51] This is a frequent requirement for today's workers and something a leader must account for if they hope to be effective.[52] Recently, while working with William "Andy" Freels, President of Hyundai America Technical Center, Inc., he mentioned how it was often a challenge in his industry to retain young talent, especially skilled engineers. We asked him what these young engineers were looking for in the job—did they want more money? Better benefits? A lighter workload? As it turned out, it was none of those things. Instead, Freels pointed to the parking lot outside of his office window and said, "They want to be able to walk out there, open the door to one of those cars, and point to a knob or a button and say, 'I designed that.' It's important for them to have a strong connection between the work they spend their life doing and a result that has some effect in the world. Their designs become a part of other people's lives and that makes a difference."[53]

> *Statistics rarely drive me. Feelings, intuition, and gut instinct do.*
>
> —JASON FRIED

These feelings of having a purpose and doing work that makes a difference are not unique to any one generation or any one time in history. Most of us want to do work that matters—that contributes not only to the success of our company but also, in some way, to the betterment of society as a whole. Benjamin Franklin used to wake up every morning at 5 a.m. and ask himself the same question: "What good shall I do this day?" He then went about his work: reading, writing, inventing, building relationships. At night, before retiring to bed, Franklin concluded each day by asking himself, "What good have I done today?"[54] Connecting these two questions and then acting intentionally throughout his day, Franklin was able to accomplish amazing things such as inventing the lightning rod and bifocal glasses as well as exploring the phenomena of electricity. Research done by The Wharton School found that when people are able to connect their jobs to something meaningful, their productivity increases by as much as five times.[55]

THE FORMULA FOR THE PERFECT PEP TALK

We have all seen leaders who deliver inspiring messages that create urgency in the minds of their listeners that move them to action. Obvious examples include Steve Jobs's "How to Live Before You Die" speech at Stanford that gave us the famous phrase "Stay hungry. Stay foolish"; J.K. Rowling's "The "Fringe Benefits of Failure, and The Importance of Imagination" speech at Harvard, and John F. Kennedy's 1961 inaugural address, in which he delivered the famous call to action: "Ask not what your country can do for you, but ask what you can do for your country." Speeches that inspire us do so by influencing our emotions. As a result, we see things differently and choose to act or think in new or more decisive ways as a result of hearing it. Think of classic movies such as *Rudy* or *Any Given Sunday* or *The Wolf of Wall Street* and you will see examples of speeches meant to motivate and inspire behavior change. While most people in the corporate arena don't have the same responsibilities as a world leader or professional football coach, we have the same objective: to motivate action in others. Whether you are a college basketball coach pumping up your team at halftime, a manager motivating your sales force to reach their monthly target, or a high school teacher helping a class rehearse a graduation ceremony, the ability to inspire change in others through the delivery of your message is a necessary tenet of effective leadership. But how does someone deliver an inspiring message—is there a scientific formula that can be utilized to craft a compelling message? As it turns out, there is.

Jacqueline and Milton Mayfield, a husband-and-wife team at Texas A&M International University have studied what is called *motivating language theory* (MLT) and how it can be applied in the business world for nearly three decades.[56] Throughout the process, they have consulted sports psychologists and military historians to better understand what makes a pep talk effective. What they found, based on scientific findings, was that most winning formulas include three key elements:

- Direction giving
- Expressions of empathy
- Meaning making

The evidence uncovered in their research convinced both researchers that once a leader understands these three elements, and the purposes they serve, they can employ them as a framework to craft more compelling messages. The "direction giving" section of a motivational speech is meant to provide information and instruction about how to accomplish a task and how the efforts or performance will be evaluated. If you are a basketball coach at halftime, you detail what adjustments your players need to make to win the game. If you are a sales manager, you suggest what tactics your team needs to focus on in order to hit their target sales number. If you are a teacher, you set benchmarks and deadlines to make sure the graduation ceremony is rehearsed and ready in time. The purpose of the direction giving section is to provide clarity, what the Mayfields described as "uncertainty-reducing language."

The "expressions of empathy" section helps to connect a leader with their audience or listener by offering praise, encouragement, or gratitude. It could also be accomplished by acknowledging the difficulty of the task or the level of effort expended to date with phrases like, "No team has more heart than this one," "This sales quota is something I know you can achieve," or "The hard work you have done so far preparing for this ceremony is breathtaking."

The final portion of the formula is "meaning-making"—employing language that drives home the importance of the task and seeing it through to a successful conclusion. This is where a leader can tie the objective of the work to the mission of the organization itself or the personal goals of the listener. If the basketball team wins the game, they will be remembered as a championship team. If the sales team hits their goal, then everyone receives a commission bonus. If the class pulls off the graduation ceremony, their parents will be proud of their accomplishment. In the meaning-making section of the speech a leader can even detail how accomplishing their objective will not only benefit themselves and their team, but will also make a difference in their community or even in their society at large.

Research shows that employing these types of simple, motivational speeches has a positive impact on the individuals receiving them.[57] Tiffanye Vargas, a sports psychology professor at California State University at Long Beach, has published extensive studies detailing which types of speeches are best at motivating athletes in different situations, and how these principles are also applicable in the business sector. Her research suggests that a coach's pregame remarks really do affect the performance and outlook of the athletes, with 90 percent of players saying they enjoy listening to pep talks and 65 percent saying the speeches have a direct effect on the way they play.[58] By understanding each element of the motivating language theory and structuring inspirational messages around the three steps of direction giving, expressions of empathy, and meaning making, a leader will better influence the emotions of others and be more likely to drive results and facilitate behavior change in a team or individual.

Blueprint to Bullseye—Chapter 5

Assessment Guide for Managing Others

1. How often do you check in with your team members to solicit feedback and hear their concerns? Are there specific team members who could use more attention?

2. How effective are you at setting clear expectations for your team members about their work? Are there team members who could use more clarity or direction?

3. How frequently do you acknowledge and reward high-quality work? Are there team members who need recognition that may be overdue?

4. How accessible and responsive are you to the ideas and concerns of your team members? Are there any team members who feel they are not supported by you?

5. Do you clearly and consistently communicate the overall vision of your organization and expectations for each team member and how they contribute to it? How can you better communicate to team members?

6. Are you adequately transparent with your team members about the direction your organization is headed and the specific challenges that can be expected? How can you do this more effectively?

7. How well do you communicate information during times of change? What types of change can your team members expect in the near future and how can you best communicate this to them?

8. How effectively do you track and reward achievement within your team? How can you improve the ways in which you privately or publicly recognize the efforts of your workers?

9. Do you provide adequate opportunity for coaching and mentoring for members of your team? Are there team members who could use more attention?

10. How effectively do you empower your team members and allow them the freedom to complete their work? Are there instances when you could step back and allow them to make more decisions or show individual initiative?

CHAPTER 6

Build Relationships
Making Connections, Establishing Trust, and Earning Respect

If you want to go quickly, go alone. If you want to go far, go together.
—African proverb

Teddy Roosevelt once said, "The most important single ingredient in the formula of success is the knack of getting along with people."[1] We all present ourselves on a daily basis by interacting with those around us—during meetings, while attending a church service, or even while waiting for yoga class to begin. Each of these meetings or interactions are important because they provide an opportunity to build a new relationship or strengthen an old one. Some of this communication is personal, some is professional, and some is a mixture of both. But no matter what your role or industry, being able to develop trust, listen actively, and show genuine concern for others will serve you well in your career and life. In the end, people need to feel safe and supported to do their best work. This means being respected, valued, and heard by management and anyone else with whom they interact on a daily basis.

Business relationships, like all other relationships, need to be established, developed, and maintained. They need to be based on trust and consistency and both parties should feel their interactions will provide mutual benefit to all involved. The information age in which we live provides many exciting opportunities for connection but also some distinct challenges. Being hyper-connected through our smart phones makes us easily accessible, but can also create distractions that hinder the development of authentic relationships. Making a conscious effort to maintain and protect your relationships will allow you to build a network that can offer support and guidance throughout your career. Without a willingness to work together to maintain a strong connection, relationships erode over time. Leadership is not a solitary endeavor, and all successful leaders can point to the mentors or partners they have worked alongside who have contributed to the success of their organization. As General Douglas MacArthur once said, "A true leader has the confidence to stand alone, the courage to make tough decisions, and the compassion to listen to the needs of others. He does not set out to be a leader, but becomes one by the equality of his actions and the integrity of his intent."[2] The most successful leaders and CEOs understand that to accomplish great things they need to surround themselves with like-minded people with whom they can collaborate.

In 1919, a Chicago paper called Henry Ford, the father of the modern automobile, an "ignorant pacifist." An angry Ford brought a libel suit against the paper and, in a move that surprised many, actually took the witness stand to testify in the case. As the attorneys for the newspaper peppered Ford with a range of questions such as "How many soldiers did the British send over to America to put down the Rebellion of 1776?" it became clear that Ford did not know the answers. As the questions became more obscure and outrageous, Ford pointed his finger at the lawyer asking the questions and made a statement that ended the hearing and instantly won him the case: "If I should really want to answer the foolish question you have just asked, or any of the other questions you have been asking me," said Ford, "let me remind you that I have a row of electric push-buttons on my desk, and, by pushing the right button, I can summon to my aid men who can answer any question I desire to ask. . . . Why should I clutter up my mind with general knowledge . . . when I have men around me who can supply any

knowledge I require?"[3] The lesson Ford provides here is to resist
the urge to know or do everything yourself. No leader has all
the answers. A lone decision-
maker can never match the col-

A relationship, I think, is like a shark. . . . it has to constantly move forward or it dies.

—WOODY ALLEN

lective brainpower of an entire organization, so embrace the process of collaboration. Welcome new ideas or alternative viewpoints. Leverage the expertise of others. Smart managers are aware of their strengths and they hire for their weaknesses.

One of the best ways to create connections and develop contacts is to network. This means getting out to attend industry events, meeting others within your given field, and not being afraid to introduce yourself (and your company) to others. Being able to meet new people and expand your network provides potential benefits such as generating referrals, uncovering opportunities, getting advice, and building friendships. But effective networking takes work and there are a few important guidelines you will want to follow to make sure you are building these connections in a positive and constructive way.

While Ronald Reagan is certainly known for his talent as an influential speaker, he possessed another important trait that served him well throughout his career: the ability to forge networks and create powerful and lasting relationships. Dick Wirthlin, one of Reagan's pollsters, put it this way: "To [Reagan], getting to know someone *was* his business."[4] Reagan's ability to collaborate with others was a result of his experiences as an actor working in Hollywood movies and collaborating with teams of people focused on the pursuit of a common goal. As a leader, Reagan was comfortable delegating and trusting others to do their best. During his time in the White House, when asked if he missed being an actor, Reagan responded, "Why should I? I have the biggest stage in the world, right here!"[5]

Reagan's ability to forge bonds and nurture relationships started back in his early radio days in Des Moines, Iowa, when he worked as an announcer for WHO Radio. Reagan would often be assigned the task of interviewing Hollywood celebrities and he frequently used these opportunities to build relationships and make contacts that would serve him well as his career progressed. In 1937, Reagan made a trip to California for the radio station to cover spring training for baseball and it was on this visit that his desire to be a movie star was suddenly stirred. Using the Hollywood contacts and connections he had made during his years on the radio, Reagan was able to arrange a meeting with a Hollywood agent and secure an audition for Warner Brothers Studios. These meetings eventually led to Reagan winning a lucrative seven-year studio contract and leaving Des Moines for the bright lights of Hollywood.

As a contract player at a major studio, Reagan enjoyed an elite position as a performer and he put in the hard work needed to capitalize on the opportunity. Using his renowned abilities as a charismatic and engaging personality, Reagan began accepting invitations to speak to community groups such as the American Legion, various women's groups, and other fundraisers. "Step by step, speech by speech, he polished his abilities and fine-tuned his skills," wrote Margot Morrell in *Reagan's Journey*.[6] Reagan soon discovered that giving speeches was a reliable way to get his name in the newspapers and keep his profile high. By continuing to increase his visibility by speaking to these different organizations, Reagan began to establish valuable relationships that, over time, would serve as the wind in his career sails. He was constantly working the phones to stay in touch with his network of contacts—many of whom were willing to offer guidance and introductions. In 1947, he was elected president of the Screen Actors Guild. Reagan continued to learn as much as he could about leadership and managing others during his tenure as SAG president. Said Morrell, "[That's] where he got this skill—he referred to it as round-tabling things. He would sit in these meetings and not say a word and let everyone talk, and then he would synthesize a response . . . He let other people do what they did best. He didn't micro-manage . . . [he] always listened to people and appreciated their input, took it into account."[7] And, as we all know now, Reagan's rise was only beginning. The former radio host would go on to serve two terms as governor of California and two terms as president of the United States. In 1984, Regan won re-election by a landslide—capturing 49 out of 50 states. It was was one of the largest electoral victories in American history and much of it was a result of Reagan's ability to connect and collaborate with those around him. Fittingly, during his time as president, Reagan kept a small plaque on his desk in the Oval Office, which read: "There is no limit to what a man can do or where he can go if he does not mind who gets the credit."[8]

Dr. John Gottman, a professor emeritus of psychology at the University of Washington, has done extensive research on the nature of building and maintaining relationships. Though much of his work has been primarily focused on romantic relationships, his findings can just as easily be applied to relationships in the workplace. According to Gottman, when people connect with one another they do it through what he calls "bids for connection."[9] A bid is any effort made by a person to get someone's attention and indicate a desire for connection. For example, asking a coworker how she enjoyed her vacation is a bid. Asking a client out for coffee is a bid. Swiping right or left on a dating app is a bid, as is the decision to accept or reject a friend request on Facebook. In his research, Gottman suggests that someone's ability to recognize and respond appropriately to bids actually impacts the success rate they have connecting with those around them.[10] Because bids for connection are not usually as explicit as someone saying "Hey, I'd like to connect with you," it is important to be open to bids that come your way and respond appropriately. Like a professional actor, this means being present in the moment and staying attuned to any intention cues or shifts in mood or tone that you observe. As Daniel Goleman points out in *Emotional Intelligence*, "Actors, of course, are artists of the emotional displays; their expressiveness is what evokes response in their audience."[11] This ability to pick up on the emotions and intentions of others with whom we interact is called *social awareness*.

Of course, not all bids are the same. Choosing to ignore a bid from a Nigerian prince asking for your bank account information is different from ignoring an e-mail from a potential client who wants to place an order. Bids can be verbal, such as someone saying, "You won't believe what I just saw downstairs," but can also be nonverbal, such as someone smiling at you, sharing a link that you may find interesting, or baking cookies for a team member's birthday. When someone makes a bid, they are looking for a response that they can use to gauge the other person's level of interest in connecting. The bigger the bid (such as asking someone out on a date), the bigger the risk. And the bigger the risk, the bigger the reward. Because people are busy and their workdays are filled with distractions, they often miss bids that are being made. If you are in a leadership position, this can be problematic because failing to respond to a bid sends a message of its own: that you are not interested in connecting with the other person. Gottman found in his studies that when someone makes a bid, there are three ways the other person will generally respond: by turning toward the bid and responding favorably, by turning away and ignoring it, or by turning against it and responding in a hostile or angry way.[12]

Awareness is an essential ingredient when you are networking or building connections with others. Look for the intention cues being communicated. Once you understand how to spot subtle shifts in the vocal delivery or body language of others, you can better interpret the various bids for connection and respond to them accordingly. A good place to see bids in action is during a meeting in your workplace. Next time you attend a meeting, focus on the various bids taking place. Look at people's posture as well as who they are facing. Notice who makes eye contact as well as who gets the audience's full attention and who doesn't.

Bids for connection in the workplace can happen virtually as well. Coworkers send bids to one another constantly as relationships develop and alliances begin to form. If a colleague sends an e-mail request to you, the manner and efficiency by which you respond signals to that person how important their bid is to you. If you return the e-mail within an hour, you are signaling the desire to connect is strong. Conversely, if you take a week to get back to them or don't respond to their e-mail, you are signaling the opposite: that they are not a priority to you. When we don't respond to bids, we make the other party feel unimportant, which can lead to resentment or frustration in the workplace. The more open and responsive you are to bids you encounter, the more valued the bidders will feel. Another important finding in Gottman's research: If a bid is made and not met by the other party, the probability of the person rebidding again after such a rejection is almost zero.[13] This is why it is important as a leader to be present with those around you and take time to carefully consider your responses to the bids coming your way. Because how and when (or even if) you

The meeting of two personalities is like the contact of two chemical substances: if there is any reaction, both are transformed.

—CARL JUNG

choose to respond to a bid will determine the quality of the relationships you will develop with the people in your immediate sphere of influence.

Being able to consider the thoughts and feelings of others whose circumstances are different from their own is something every actor masters as they develop their craft. Empathy—the ability to show genuine concern and feeling for another person—is an essential trait for any person who leads a team or runs an organization. This means being able to feel for those with whom you work to consider their specific challenges, concerns, and emotions and take them into account when making decisions. Sadly, a recent report in the *Harvard Business Review* found that empathy is most lacking among senior executives and middle managers.[14] This is especially problematic as it is these types of workers in leadership roles whose decisions have the biggest impact on a workforce. When speaking to his actors, Stanislavski often discussed the idea of empathy and seeing situations through the experiences of others. "You draw . . . principally upon your own impressions, feelings and experiences," said Stanislavski, "From life around you . . . from communication with other human beings."[15] This, in a nutshell, is how a person develops empathy and how they are able to consider the thoughts, feelings, and motivations of their peers, clients, and friends. In their book, *Emotional Intelligence 2.0,* authors Travis Bradberry and Jean Greaves, stated that, "Actors do this all the time—they walk in a character's shoes for a living. Actors channel the same emotions and feelings, embodying the minds and motivations of the characters. . . . Walking in the shoes of another is social awareness at its best—and it's not just for actors. It's for all of us who want to gain perspective and a deeper understanding of others [and] improve our communication."[16]

Demonstrating to another person through your communication—both verbal and nonverbal—that you hear them and understand them can be a powerful tool for a leader. It can help align a team, engage an employee, and make your workers feel valued. For a leader to show empathy, they have to be genuine and nonjudgmental when considering different or opposing points of view or opinions. When one is empathetic to others, they momentarily project themselves into the other person's circumstances and sense what that person is feeling, much like a professional actor tackling a new role. Empathy comes into play when you listen to another person and make a sincere effort to understand how they feel and what they need in any given moment. Demonstrating empathy can be used to build trust and forge new bonds. When running for senator of New York in 2000, Hillary Clinton understood the importance of building trust and developing relationships with her constituents. To be able to do this effectively she embarked on what she called "listening tours" in which she would travel up and down the state speaking to as many voters as possible to better understand their questions and concerns.[17] At each stop she and her staff would write down what she had learned on slips of paper and then stuff them into a suitcase. Once back at their campaign headquarters, Clinton and her staff would dump out the crumpled papers and separate them by topic so they could organize policy ideas or brainstorm solutions to problems based on what she had gleaned from the conversations. These listening tours proved successful and Clinton won the election.

When you think about your peers and the team members within your organization, how well do you listen to them and show them empathy? Do you feel like you have a clear understanding of the challenges they face each day? Are you aware of any impending deadlines that are stressing them out or specific budget concerns that may be weighing on their mind? If you can't name the specific challenges or stresses they are experiencing, this probably means you need to be more connected to these employees.

As it turns out, there is a psychological basis for human beings to have empathy. Robert Levenson, a psychologist at the University of California at Berkeley, has studied empathy and how it relates to the communication of married couples and their ability to guess what the other person is feeling.[18] Here's how it works: Levenson would film couples during heated arguments as they discussed a topic of conflict in their relationship—how to discipline the kids, spending habits, and the like—and then he measured their physiological responses. Each of the partners then reviewed the tape and described what he or she was feeling from moment to moment. Next, each partner reviewed the tape a second time, now trying to see how accurately they could read the *other's* feelings. What Levenson discovered was that the most accurate measure of empathy occurred in those partners whose own physiology mirrored that of the spouse they were watching—in other words, when their bodies mimicked the subtle, physical reactions of their spouse. If the viewer's physiological patterns simply mirrored their own during the original interaction, they were very poor at interpreting what their partners were feeling. Only when their bodies mirrored the behavior of the other spouse was there empathy. There is a big takeaway here for anyone who has to communicate a message that carries an emotional charge, namely, that when we are angry or upset and the emotional brain is driving the body, there can be little empathy. True empathy requires a calm and receptive presence, open enough to receive the subtle signals of feeling from the other person so that they can be subsequently received and mimicked by one's own emotional brain. The same can be said for showing genuine excitement and interest in others. In a recent article in *Time*, neurologist Michael Trimble described how the same areas of the brain become activated when we see someone who is emotionally aroused as when we are emotionally aroused ourselves. When we encounter another person, especially if it is the first time we are meeting them, we are likely to have an emotional reaction of some sort, either positive or negative, as a result.[19]

> *I sometimes worry about my short attention span, but not for long.*
>
> —HERB CAEN

The ability to listen actively is essential for anyone hoping to build rapport and develop relationships with others. But technology is filling the world with distractions and this affects how we communicate and connect with one another. Studies show that our attention spans are shrinking and this can be problematic for anyone hoping to create a bond with other people. Giving someone your complete and undivided attention is essential if you want to truly connect with them. Think about how your intention cues during an average meeting—facial expressions, body language, eye contact—are interpreted by others. If you are constantly checking your phone or answering e-mails while people are talking, it sends a message that what they are saying is not as important to you as what is happening on your phone. The same idea applies to social communication. Picture yourself out to dinner with friends who sit down across from you and immediately pull out their phones and place them on the table. They are sending a message that they are only partially present and that something more interesting could take place and they don't want to miss it. Research from Elon University found that pulling your phone out during a conversation lowers both the *quality* as well as the *quantity* of face-to-face inter-actions.[20] Conversely, putting your phone away during a meeting or dinner sends the message to the other parties that you are present, they are important, and you are not going to make them compete with outside distractions for your attention. Effective communicators keep the channels of communication open at all times so others feel heard and valued. Whenever possible, when communicating with others, close your laptop, put your phone away, and give the other party the gift of your complete, undivided attention. Additionally, resist the urge to dominate the conversation. Find the flow of give-and-take with each of you contributing to the conversation. Here's something important to remember: if you are more interested in what you are saying than the people listening to you, something is wrong. Be aware of how your engagement levels are being interpreted by the people with whom you are speaking. Michael Strahan, the charismatic football-player-turned-actor-turned-television-host, puts it this way:

> The way you are with people and the energy that you give off . . . Are you somebody who's divisive or inclusive? Are you somebody who genuinely sees people? Or are you somebody who only sees the people that you need to see? A lot of people only see people that they need to see. When I grew up, I was cutting grass. I was washing dishes for years when I was in

college. I was moving furniture in my parents' moving business. I was the guy people didn't see, so I'm very conscious of everybody, because I want to see everybody and make them feel valued.[21]

When asked during an interview with the *New York Times* about the best leadership lesson he learned during his time as a business student, Charles Schwab CEO Walter Bettinger recalled an experience toward the end of his college career that had a huge impact on the ways in which he came to interact with members of his organization. It involved an incident that took place in a business strategy course his senior year. Bettinger said,

> I had maintained a 4.0 average all the way through, and I wanted to graduate with a perfect average. It came down to the final exam, and I had spent many hours studying and memorizing formulas to do calculations for the case studies. The teacher handed out the final exam, and it was on one piece of paper, which really surprised me because I figured it would be longer than that. Once everyone had their paper, he said, "Go ahead and turn it over." Both sides were blank. And the professor said, "I've taught you everything I can teach you about business in the last 10 weeks, but the most important message, the most important question, is this: What's the name of the lady who cleans this building?" And that had a powerful impact. It was the only test I ever failed, and I got the B I deserved. Her name was Dottie, and I didn't know Dottie. I'd seen her, but I'd never taken the time to ask her name. I've tried to know every Dottie I've worked with ever since. It was just a great reminder of what really matters in life, and that you should never lose sight of people who do the real work.[22]

While leaders of successful organizations are often the ones who get the credit and glory, it is the people who work for them that do the work to make them shine. According to Jim Collins, author of *Good to Great,* effective leaders "channel their ego needs away from themselves and into the larger goal of building a great company. It's not that [they] have no ego or self-interest. Indeed, they are incredibly ambitious—but their ambition is first and foremost for the institution, not themselves."[23] Team members want to know they are valued and they want that communicated in their relationships with the boss and senior leaders. An honest and transparent working relationship, where information (meaning the good as well as bad) can be shared openly and honestly is essential. A recent study from the Foster School of Business found that workers rarely take a boss or leader's words at face value. They judge the leader's sincerity by looking for congruence between the leader's words and their actions. "[Team members] are not just mindless automatons," says lead researcher Christina Fong. "They think about the emotions they see and care whether they are sincere or manipulative." According to the study, it is far easier to build strong, trusting relationships if a leader inspires trust through their actions rather than by their words alone.[24] As mentioned in previous chapters, authenticity is important but it is only valuable if that authenticity is demonstrated through action and example. Genuine leaders must walk the walk and talk the talk. Simply going through the motions won't cut it if you want to build strong and highly-motivated teams.

CONNECTING WITH OTHERS TO BUILD A NETWORK

The term "networking" often has negative connotations and conjures images for many people of being stranded alone at a cocktail party where they don't know anyone and have nothing in common with the people in attendance. When we enter into a conversation with a stranger, our first impulse is to put ourselves forward in a way that maximizes the potential for enhancement or advancement with regard to our personal or profes-sional status. People often get nervous meeting new people or attending a party made up of mostly strangers—for good reason. Stefan G. Hofmann, a professor at Boston University, explains, "People are social animals, and we have a strong desire to be part of a group and to be accepted by the group. Social anxiety is a result of the fear of a possibility that we will not be accepted by our peers. It's the fear of negative evaluation by others, and that is [part of] a very fundamental, biological need to be liked."[25] Instead of dreading or avoiding networking situations, it can be helpful to reframe your attitude about attending such events and turn it into something more positive—an interaction that can provide an exciting benefit to you and the people you will meet. By doing this, you start to remove the negative stigma attached to networking and the anxiety that becomes associated with it. Those who are good at networking make it a personal challenge to establish new connections and spread awareness about themselves at every event they attend and with each new person they meet.

Younger workers, brought up on screens and more comfortable communicating via text or instant messaging, have shown some distinct challenges when it comes to their comfort level communicating with people face-to-face. And this can be a problem when they collaborate with workers from older generations. One recent study found that young people who spent low amounts of time in real-life social interactions but high amounts of time on screens or social media were more likely to be depressed, less happy, and less prepared for adulthood than past generations.[26] Julie Lythcott-Haims, the former dean of Stanford, says that being able to talk to strangers such as teachers, landlords, coworkers, and other professionals in the real world is the number-one skill a young person should master and it needs more focus and priority for kids growing up. "We teach kids not to talk to strangers instead of teaching the more nuanced skill of how to discern the few bad strangers from the mostly good ones. Thus, kids end up not knowing how to approach strangers—respectfully and with eye contact—for the help, guidance, and direction they will need out in the world."[27]

Human beings have evolved over time by responding to the intention cues—eye contact, facial expressions, and shared laughter—of others with whom we interact. When we encounter a new person, we want them to walk away with a positive feeling about us and a sense that we are someone who can be trusted. Harvard psychologist Amy Cuddy has spoken about the two questions people will quickly answer when they first meet you:

1. Can I trust this person?
2. Can I respect this person?[28]

By analyzing your audience and adjusting your behavior you will ensure these two questions are answered in the affirmative. When Hillary Clinton became Secretary of State under Barack Obama, she knew she would need to win the trust of the career staff at the State

Department as well as gain the respect of any people who didn't know her. Clinton knew that without trust and respect, it would be much more difficult for her to do her job. To accomplish this, she took steps to establish these essential relationships and create a positive impression even before she had met many of the staffers in person. She did it by doing her homework and learning all she could about them. According to Ezra Klein of *Vox*, "One thing [Clinton] would do is invite these diplomats and researchers to big meetings, and then she would reference something they had written deep in an obscure memo years ago. They were thrilled that a Secretary of State was actually digging into their work. It helped her win over a lot of support . . . they felt respected."[29] Taking a lesson from this example, next time you meet with a new client or a newly promoted leader within your organization, you can create a positive impression by simply doing a bit of research ahead of time to learn what you can about their background, experiences, and communication styles.

Another important example of relationship-building happened in 1939, just prior to World War II, when President Franklin Delano Roosevelt took notice of a rising star in Britain named Winston Churchill. At the time, Churchill was simply a cabinet minister but Roosevelt saw great potential, so he forged an early relationship with Churchill, writing frequently, saying, "If you have anything you would like me to know, please send it and I will answer."[30] The relationship between the two men grew and deepened so that during the following year, when German troops invaded the Netherlands, Luxembourg, Belgium, and France, and Churchill became prime minister of Great Britain, a genuine trust and respect had been established. Roosevelt and Churchill understood each other, and this bond came in handy when they needed to work together and forge a plan to defeat Hitler and his Third Reich. Said Eleanor Roosevelt of the relationship between the two men, "The friendship and affection between my husband and Mr. Churchill grew with every visit, and was something quite apart from the official intercourse."[31]

Trust is built with consistency.

—LINCOLN CHAFEE

Familiarity and proximity can also have an influence on the rapport you are able to build with another person. For example, if you see the same crossing guard every day while walking your daughter to school, chances are that you will grow to like this person or feel connected to them because of their proximity to you, especially if the experience is pleasant. The daily exposure creates a familiarity. These repeated exposures, even the briefest encounter, exert a tremendous influence on the way you perceive other people. Repeated exposures not only influence our perception of another person but they can influence our actual behavior as well. If you look forward to your morning greeting with this particular crossing guard, it will make you more likely to take that same route to school each day because it is an experience you find pleasant. Conversely, if the crossing guard is grumpy, with a constant scowl and a negative demeanor, you may try to avoid the daily encounter altogether and choose to take a different route. Think about the clients or coworkers with whom you enjoy interacting versus the ones you dread having to meet or work alongside.

Ritualistic greetings among strangers such as "How are you doing" or "Good morning" or "Nice day today" are simple ways to connect that are quick and nonthreatening. They are also helpful phrases if you don't know someone well but don't want to appear rude. These phrases are what linguists call *phatic communication*.[32] When we use these types of phrases with strangers in a public setting, the actual content is less important than the fact that you are taking the time to affirm the other person is there and worthy of connection or comment. We need other people in our lives, both socially as well as in a work environment. We need the FedEx driver to deliver the package to us. We need the client to give us a timeline for the project we are proposing. We need a team member to provide us with the data we requested. We need our neighbor to water our lawn when we are out of town. We rely on others to thrive in our lives and jobs. Therefore, the way we communicate and interact with them has a huge impact on the success we will achieve day-to-day. It is these sustained connections that contribute to our well-being, our health, and our happiness.

Whenever we encounter someone unexpectedly or something surprising happens, is takes our focus off whatever we were thinking or doing in the moment and calls us to full attention. It forces us to be present in the moment. Conversations with strangers can lead to something all human beings desire: a feeling of genuine connection. The connection we feel when meeting someone for the first time gives us a momentary bit of intimacy and can lead to exciting places if we are willing to follow it and let it blossom. Of course, the intimacy we have with our spouse or best friend will be different from what we experience with a person we just met in line at the airport. This type of fleeting connection is called *street intimacy* and usually happens in a public setting such as a cocktail party, sporting event, or in a theater before a play or movie begins.

Cities provide ample opportunities to interact with strangers, since more than 50 percent of the global population now lives in urban centers. Because cities generally contain more people and a more diverse population, it is more likely that city dwellers will have greater opportunities to encounter strangers and connect with others on a more frequent basis. But living in an urban environment offers challenges as well. The hustle and bustle of the city—the noise, the crowds—all create an atmosphere where it is easy to put on our protective shells and retreat by shutting out the people around us. When interpreting the intention cues of others, you also need to be mindful of how people operate in a public space. The baseline for this will depend on cultural factors as well as social norms. Again, as we have discussed since the beginning of this book, you have to know your audience, understand how you want them to feel, and then modify your delivery appropriately. For example, how you behave and interact with those at a rock concert in Chicago will be different from how you connect with the people attending a religious ceremony in Abu Dhabi.

The way we interact with others during a busy workweek will most likely be influenced by the setting and circumstances in which we find ourselves. Next time you are in an airport, look around and notice the various behaviors people are communicating with their body language and intention cues. The woman who is late for her flight, running frantically to her gate, probably won't notice you (unless you are standing directly in her path). The man looking for a place to sit who approaches you, perhaps offering a friendly smile, and asks if the empty seat next to you is taken. The objectives of the woman and man in these examples (to get to the gate without missing her flight and to find a place to sit down) are clear, so the intentions they use to accomplish them need to be clear as well. Depending on our objective at any given moment, we may want to be seen or we may want to disappear. We open ourselves to certain encounters and close ourselves to others. If we have just finished work and are heading home on the subway we may simply want to be left alone. In this case, our intention cues will need to communicate that—by avoiding eye contact with those around us, listening to music on headphones, or choosing a seat in the back of the train, away from the other riders. All of these tactics are intention cues that signal to others that we are not interested in connection at this moment. If the opposite is true and our objective is to connect or make new relationships, our body language will need to support that objective as well, meaning lots of eye contact, smiling, and approaching those who signal openness in return.

BUILDING YOUR NETWORK

So where should you look to begin building your professional network? The answer: all around you. Look to your friends and family, your coworkers, any business owners you may know, former employees and employers, club members, school or college acquaintances, vendors, or even your neighbors. Social media sites like Facebook or LinkedIn can also be a good place to start. Everyone has a network, and tapping into the networks of others can serve you well as you grow and advance within your organization and in your career. Even chance encounters can lead to important connections somewhere down the road. When meeting someone for the first time at a cocktail party or networking event, take your time to get to know the person and build rapport. If you immediately begin the conversation by selling your product, pushing your business card, or pitching your

Small opportunities are often the beginning of great enterprises.

—DEMOSTHENES

services, you will likely put the person off and ruin any chance of future partnerships or collaboration.

For those who get nervous about having to meet new people or mingle with strangers at a cocktail party, there is good news: the more you do it, the easier it gets. The more familiar you are with the experience of talking to someone you just met or engaging in conversation with a stranger, the more likely it will be that you not just tolerate it, but actually start to enjoy it and look forward to the opportunity. This is what social psychologists call *exposure effect*.[33] A good conversation between two people will have a natural flow from one person to the next and appear effortless. Each person should take turns as the conversation flips back and forth between partners. Studies show that on average each turn during a conversation lasts for around two seconds, and the typical gap between each turn is just 200 milliseconds—hardly enough time to utter a word.[34] Let's take some time now to discuss specific actions you can take to build rapport when networking or meeting someone for the first time.

Learn to be comfortable with breaking the ice

Initiating a conversation with someone you don't know is an essential tool for building relationships and expanding your network. Using an icebreaker—a quick question or comment—to initiate a conversation with someone you don't know is an easy way to get things going. It could be as simple as offering a compliment ("That's a beautiful bracelet"), asking for help ("Do you know what time the band is set to start?"), or commenting on the environment ("This is such a unique venue"). Another approach might be to ask the other person a question such as, "What brought you to the event?" or "How do know the host?" One benefit of being able to ask questions in a social setting is that the mere act of doing it actually increases our level of likability in the eyes of others. According to one study, people who ask more questions are found to be more likeable by the people they just met. In a series of experiments at Harvard Business School, researchers assigned people to either ask a lot of questions (at least nine) or only a few questions (at least four). Afterward, they chatted with the study participants to find out how much they liked their conversational partner. The result? Participants tended to like those who asked a lot of questions more than those who asked only a few. As the researchers looked deeper into their findings, they found that it was not only the quantity of the questions that played a factor in the questioner's likeability but also the types of questions they asked.[35] They found that the best questions to ask were follow-up questions. Why? Because these questions showed genuine interest by providing proof the other person was actually listening to what they were saying. The lesson here for anyone trying to build rapport with someone they have just met is to ask the person questions, listen actively to their responses, and then follow up with questions based on what they just said. And remembering the information they provide is important as well. The information you glean can be used in subsequent meetings with the person to show you were truly listening to them during your initial meeting. If your memory if not always reliable, you can discreetly write down bits of information you learn about a person immediately after meeting them and file your notes away for future use.

Remember names

Many people have trouble remembering names when they are first introduced to someone. This can be awkward and embarrassing and is generally a result of nerves in the moment. But learning someone's name is an important way to make a positive impression. Remembering names is not a complicated process but it must begin with the objective of actually wanting to learn their name. When you shake hands with the other person, try to avoid distractions. Give them your total focus in the moment, including a smile and direct eye contact. Repeat their name back to them. If it is helpful, make an association that will allow the name to stick. In most instances, people generally like to hear their name spoken, so using someone's name occasionally during your conversation will help draw them in. Also, by repeating their name, it will help you remember it. Be careful not to overuse the person's name as this can backfire and come off as corny or insincere.

Be present and pleasant

Striking a balance between warmth and confidence helps you not only seem credible but also makes you more relatable as a human being. Often, people seen as more likable by others use conversations as an opportunity to learn more information about another person. Dr. Joe Dispenza, a neuroscience expert, points out that, "Every time we have a thought we make a chemical. If we have good, elevated thoughts or happy thoughts we make chemicals that make us feel good or happy. And if we have negative thoughts or bad thoughts or insecure thoughts we make chemicals that make us feel exactly the way we are thinking."[36] By giving people the space to speak, you allow them to feel important and heard. This creates a feeling of likeability. Conversely, there are things you can do to make people immediately dislike you, such as dominating a conversation, boasting, demonstrating prejudice or bigotry, and being overly negative or opinionated.

Use mirroring

When you "mirror" back to your conversation partner the body language, vocal dynamics, or speech pattern they are demonstrating, you are using *isopraxism*, the involuntary phenomenon that involves the mirror neurons that fire in our brains. John Cacioppo, a social psychologist at Ohio State University, has studied the way people communicate. "Just seeing someone express an emotion can evoke that mood," says Cacioppo, "Whether you realize you mimic the facial expression or not. This happens to us all the time—there's a dance, a synchrony, a transmission of emotions. The mood synchrony determines whether you feel an interaction went well or not."[37] This is why being aware of the intention cues coming from someone you just met and then mirroring them back can help you create a positive impression. Recent studies in the field of neuroscience found that when two people are in each other's company, their brain waves will begin to look nearly identical. "The more we study engagement, we see time and again that just being next to certain people actually aligns your brain with them," said Moran Cerf, a neuroscientist at Northwestern University. "This means the people you hang out with actually have an impact on your engagement with reality beyond what you can explain. And one of the effects is you become alike."[38] This is why, when soliciting feedback from an employee or listening to a client explain why they are unhappy with the quality of your services, it is helpful to mirror back to them the same intention cues to show them that what they are saying is being heard and considered with genuine concern. This could be done verbally by paraphrasing what they have expressed or repeating certain words or phrases verbatim, and also nonverbally by simply mirroring back body language that shows you understand their feelings and concerns.

Do your homework

If you are attending a work function, take some time to learn any information you can about the people attending. Ask others what they know about them and what information or insights they are willing to share. Prepare a few talking points or questions that may demonstrate you have an understanding of their background, area of expertise, or some of the current challenges they may be experiencing at the moment. Let these points emerge organically during the conversation to avoid your interaction seeming scripted or disingenuous. Guy Kawasaki, the famed Silicon Valley executive and best-selling author, has said the key to great networking is to "Ask good questions, then shut up." If you are able to get others to talk instead, "Ironically, you'll be remembered as an interesting person."[39]

Discover where you can add value

One of the most basic rules of networking is you should give more than you get. Many people see networking only as an opportunity for getting something for themselves. This is a mistake. Networking should be an opportunity for mutual benefit for all parties involved. It is a chance for you to demonstrate what you can do for people, so it is unwise to start by asking what they can do for you. Showing how you can add value can take place by asking a question such as, "How can I help?" This simple yet powerful phrase allows you to quickly build trust and rapport by showing your willingness to assist. As you meet people, try to pinpoint how you can add mutual value to their company or mission. If you offer a service they require, let them know how you can assist. If you know someone who can assist them in their work, offer to make an introduction. Whenever possible, connect like-minded people; this will only serve to grow your network. When he was first starting out in business, billionaire Mark Cuban understood the value of building relationships and learning from others. While working at Mellon Bank in Pittsburgh, Cuban started something called the "Rookie Club" in which he would invite senior executives to a happy hour so they could talk to the younger bankers and share stories or insights that would allow them to develop and grow.[40]

One benefit of cultivating a solid network of contacts involves something called the *norm of reciprocity*. Reciprocity is the social glue that helps us build and maintain relationships. The norm of reciprocity is the expectation that people will respond favorably to one another by returning benefits for benefits, and responding with either indifference or hostility to slights or harms. For example, if you are a server at a high-end steakhouse and you need a specific weekend off to attend your sister's wedding, it is more likely that a fellow server will cover your shift if you have performed a similar favor for them in the past. Benjamin Franklin often used reciprocity as a strategy when dealing with an adversary—something that became known as the "Ben Franklin Effect." At some point in their relationship, Franklin would make a point to ask the other party if he could borrow a certain book from them. This favor flattered the person and gave them a positive feeling because now they knew that Franklin was indebted to them and would owe them a favor at some point in the future.[41] Reciprocity creates an inner sense of obligation and is our attempt to avoid any uncomfortable feelings that may result from the social rejection that occurs when someone does not reciprocate.

Show humility

Stanislavski often warned against arrogance, writing, "Self-admiration and exhibitionism impair and destroy the power of charm."[42] Humility is a very undervalued leadership trait in the corporate arena but an important one that can nurture collaboration, motivate others, and drive results. We often do our most productive networking when we offer to teach or instruct others or, conversely, when we ask others to teach us. By sharing knowledge or expertise, we benefit from the norm of reciprocity, in that the person we are teaching will feel an appreciation and feel obligated to somehow return the favor at a later date. If you meet a stranger and they listen to your thoughts and feelings, they are more likely to open up and offer feelings of their own. A mutual trust can develop and a level of vulnerability can be achieved. By sharing facts, opinions, and experiences, a bond can be made.

Be curious

Another important aspect of building relationships is the ability to demonstrate genuine curiosity about others. The best way to get to know someone is by learning more about them. That means asking questions and listening to their answers, while providing them with your full attention and supportive nonverbal cues to show you are not only being attentive but also interested in the information being provided. Though it sounds simple, this is an area where people often fall short. "Most people spend the majority of their conversations sharing their own views rather than focusing on the other person," according to a paper published in the *Journal of Personality and Social Psychology*.[43] Recent studies found that, on average, people spend 60 percent of their conversations talking about themselves (and the number jumps to 80 percent when communicating on social media platforms such as Twitter or Facebook).[44] When meeting someone new, assume that person has passions, interests, or hobbies—most likely even some that you share. Try to uncover those commonalities by asking questions and sharing similar information about yourself. Recent studies support the idea that when two strangers communicate with each other, "disclosure begets disclosure."[45] When you meet someone new and you dominate the conversation or boast about your accomplishments, it signals a lack of interest in the other person and contributes to a negative first impression. Why do people enjoy talking about themselves so much? As it turns out, there is a biological reason for it. Studies suggest that self-disclosure—revealing personal information about yourself to others—fires up the neural regions of the brain associated with motivation and reward. Simply put, talking about yourself is intrinsically rewarding.

Exit like a champ

When making your exit after an encounter with someone you've just met, the generally accepted practice is to let the person with the higher status end the interaction or step away first. When it comes time to exit, do it in a way that leaves a positive lasting impression. This will set you up for success next time you encounter this person because you will have established positive feelings about the previous encounter. Use your body language to signal you are leaving, perhaps beginning in small increments. Gradually breaking eye contact, starting to step away by putting distance between you and the other person, changing the position of your torso—these are all good intention cues to show you are about to move on. If the person with whom you are interacting is being observant and interpreting these cues the way you intend, it should make for a smooth transition.

Blueprint to Bullseye—Chapter 6

Preparation Guide for Building Business Relationships

1. What are your networking goals for the next six months? One year? Three years?

2. Identify five people in your personal network who can help you advance your career.

3. What does each of these people have to offer you and how can you best access it?

4. Name someone at your current company who could serve as a mentor or adviser to you.

5. List two people at your current company who could benefit from your personal advice, guidance, or experience.

6. What stories or experiences can you share with others to inspire them?

7. Identify five organizations that you could benefit from joining or supporting.

8. How will each organization help to build or strengthen your network?

9. What seminars, conferences, or events can you attend to grow your network?

10. How can you best stay in contact with your current network connections?

CHAPTER 7

Create a Memorable Narrative

Leveraging the Power of Storytelling in Business

Great stories happen to people that can tell them.
—IRA GLASS

Storytelling is an art form that traces its origins back to the time of earliest man. For thousands of years now, communicating information through story has been an effective way for human beings to pass along messages, teach lessons, and define cultures. Anyone working in today's business environment can benefit from the use of storytelling as a communication tool. When delivered effectively, a story resonates emotionally with a listener and impacts the way they think or feel about a subject or topic. Different stories often contain different lessons and the same story can be interpreted in many different ways, depending on the storyteller's point of view and the perspective from which the story is told. Hollywood producer Robert Evans once said, "There are always three sides to every story: your side, my side, and the truth. And no one is lying. Memories shared serve each differently."[1] A story, even in the form of a simple illustration or anecdote, can also serve to connect a listener to what they already feel is important to them—what they want or need. As author and expert storyteller Jonah Sachs points out, "One of the main reasons we listen to stories is to create a deeper belief in ourselves."[2] All great leaders are great storytellers, and all great communicators understand the power of narrative. The ability to tell a good story is a crucial tool for anyone who wants to impact an audience and influence others.

When we think of the Olympic Games, we think of the world's greatest athletes performing feats of physical excellence most people can only imagine. Sports stories are powerful because they tap into our deepest dreams and desires and provide lessons with regard to success and failure, commitment and preparation, and overcoming incredible odds on the road to victory. For centuries, story has served as an essential element of this elite sporting competition. Think of Jesse Owens facing down Adolph Hitler during the 1939 games in Berlin, the U.S. men's ice hockey team beating the defending gold-medalist Russian team in the "Miracle on Ice," and swimmer Michael Phelps, dazzling crowds by winning a record 28 Olympic medals. But for every famous Olympian like Greg Louganis, Mary Lou Retton, or Sugar Ray Leonard, there are countless other athletes with stories to tell. And these stories, while not as well known to the general public, are often just as remarkable for the lessons they contain. One such story involves a soft-spoken city worker in Chicago named Albert Robinson and something that had remained locked away for nearly 30 years.

Albert Robinson grew up in Chicago and discovered his passion for track and field early on, excelling as an athlete at Hales Franciscan High School, where he won two state championships. Robinson knew the only way he would be able to attend college would be by winning a scholarship, so he set his mind to making it happen—eventually receiving a full-ride from Indiana University. Through commitment and a solid work ethic, Robinson stood out, eventually winning seven Big Ten titles, twice being named Male Athlete of the Big Ten Championships, and running the fastest 200-meter race in the world at the time in 1984. In 1987, Robinson set his sights on his most ambitious dream to date, something he had dreamed about since he was a young boy: earning a coveted spot on the 1988 Olympic team in the 400-meter relay. As with other goals Robinson had set for himself, he accomplished this one as well, joining the elite group of sprinters who would be representing the United States in the Olympic Games in Seoul, South Korea, in the 400-meter relay.

To say that the United States dominated this event would be an understatement. In the previous 15 Olympic Games, going all the way back to 1920, the United States had won the gold medal 13 times. Carl Lewis, the legendary sprinter and Robinson's childhood idol, had anchored the 1984 400-meter relay and was back again as part of the 1988 team, along with Dennis Mitchell, Lee McNeill, and Calvin Smith, a former world record-holder at 100 meters and, at the time, the world champion at 200 meters.

Robinson and his team arrived in Seoul and settled into their dorms in the Olympic Village. For Robinson, the sights and sounds of Korea and the hustle and bustle of the international athletes arriving to compete felt like a dream. He had worked his entire career, put in countless hours of sweat and toil on the track and in the weight room for this opportunity, and it was finally here. He was an Olympian and the gold medal he had dreamed about since childhood was within his grasp.

Winners focus on winning.
Losers focus on winners.

—UNKNOWN

As race day arrived, Robinson changed into his uniform and sweats, grabbed his duffle bag and headed to the stadium. Waiting on the warm-up track with his teammates and the other relay teams, Robinson felt his heart beating in his chest. He breathed deeply and took in the sights and sounds of the stadium and crowd. He had been chosen to run the second leg of the preliminary qualifying round of the relay, getting the baton from Mitchell, and then handing it off to Calvin Smith. Lee McNeill would be anchoring this race for the team as Carl Lewis was sitting out and resting up for other races.

Finally it was time, and the teams took their positions on the track. The gun went off and Mitchell blasted out of the blocks. Robinson took the baton and ran his leg of the relay, passing to Smith who finally passed to McNeill, handing him the baton with a 10-meter lead. Robinson watched from his place across the track as McNeill crossed the finish line and raised his arms in victory. The U.S. team easily won the heat and moved one step closer to their gold medal.

But then something unexpected happened.

Thirty minutes after the race results had been posted, the Soviet Union, France, and Nigeria filed protests with the International Amateur Athletic Federation, the organization overseeing the games. Their complaint involved the baton pass between Smith and McNeill, specifically, that the runners had passed the baton outside of the required zone, which was a violation of the rules. After watching the tape of the baton pass, the IAAF judged the pass to indeed have occurred outside of the 20-meter zone. The U.S. relay team was immediately disqualified. For Robinson and the rest of the team, the news was like a sucker punch to the gut. They were stunned, speechless. "There was nothing to say," said Robinson. "It was over and done with. The race is gone. You're out." Robinson headed back to his dorm room and packed his suitcase. The next day he flew home, his Olympic dreams finished. In the years that followed, Robinson replayed the race over and over in his mind, picturing every practice and every baton pass. "You work so hard to get there and it all falls apart because of something you didn't have any control over. That's hard to swallow."[3]

Albert Robinson retired from track and field a year after the Seoul Olympics and left his athletic pursuits behind him. He eventually moved back to Chicago, got married, and took a job as a city employee, working on cases of fair housing and discrimination. For Robinson, his Olympic experience was something that was not easy to process. "I really just kept it to myself." The possibility of what could have been but never would be hung over him like a cloud that wouldn't lift. To cope, Robinson chose to pack his Olympic experience away in a box, a difficult memory, but one he refused to let define him. "To me, this was just one part of who Albert was. But Albert likes house music, Albert likes dancing, Albert likes other things than just track and field." He rarely talked about what happened in Seoul, something he now refers to as a "dream deferred." Even his coworkers had no idea that Robinson was an elite athlete and former Olympian. The Seoul experience would remain locked away in that box for nearly 30 years, until circumstances changed for Robinson and it became necessary to open the box and revisit his athletic past.

In 2004, Robinson and his wife, Aileen, had twin daughters, Rachel and Sydney, and as luck would have it, when they reached their teens, they began to show great promise and passion for one sport in particular: track and field. Recognizing the natural talent that each of his daughters possessed, Robinson decided that he would be their coach. He approached their training with the same fire he had approached his own training all those years ago. As he watched his daughters gradually begin to improve and excel, his passion for track and field suddenly was rekindled. For Robinson, with life experience and the passage of time, his collection of stories and experiences suddenly became a treasure chest of useful lessons he could now use to motivate his daughters, both on the track and in the classroom. "I've learned from my shortfalls and my successes," says Robinson. "I've learned to channel these stories and break each lesson down, step by step, for their benefit. Bottom line: You have to do the hard, bitter work if you want to achieve your dreams, because that work will lay the foundation for what you do for the rest of your life." Like Robinson, we all possess the power of story and anyone can benefit from using their individual experiences to influence or inspire those around them. As Stanislavski once wrote, and Albert Robinson's story demonstrates, "Time is a splendid filter for our remembered feelings . . . it not only purifies, it also transmutes even painfully realistic memories into poetry."[4]

In a business context, stories can serve as springboards to communicate new strategies, structures, policies, identities, and goals. A quick anecdote that establishes common ground between you and a colleague can forge a bond that might have taken weeks to accomplish otherwise. A good story can help you personalize the information you are trying to convey and can be used to build rapport, establish trust, overcome objections, communicate value, and demonstrate results. In his best-seller, *Thinking, Fast and Slow*, Daniel Kahneman breaks it down even simpler: "Good stories provide a simple and coherent account of people's actions and intentions."[5]

A recent article in the *MIT Sloan Management Review* discussed new research that showed how storytelling, when used in executive development, actually outperformed many other initiatives with regard to leadership skills. When leaders become comfortable using storytelling in the workplace, it "builds strategic competence and strengthens organizational character."[6] A good story not only makes a message more memorable, it can also help

Sometimes reality is too complex. Stories give it form.

—JEAN-LUC GODARD

you clarify meaning and illustrate a concept or idea. And as it turns out, anyone can be a good storyteller by following a few simple rules and utilizing a structure than has been successfully used by playwrights and screenwriters for hundreds of years.

Telling a story effectively starts by considering the journey your listeners will be taking as a result of hearing it. Each story you tell should suggest an adventure that your audience will enjoy embarking upon. Good stories should take a listener on a journey, beginning in one place and then dropping them off somewhere entirely different at its conclusion. In the process, the listener should have learned something new, felt something genuine, or experienced something memorable as a result of hearing it. Richard Branson, the billionaire founder of Virgin, has said,

> The best way to get somebody to take in something you want to share—a lesson, a business pitch, anything—is to do it in the form of a story. When we hear stories, we can be simultaneously involved in the tale being told. We can empathize, relate and understand far more that way. The ability to tell a story with passion, humor and heart will help build trust. When I am listening to business pitches, if I can understand the vision of the entrepreneur through their storytelling, I am far more likely to get interested. The purpose and products of the business still need to be right, but storytelling can help to bring these to life.[7]

Of course, as with any communication, you must start by analyzing your audience. This will help you decide whether or not the use of storytelling will resonate with them. For example, if you are presenting numbers to a CFO or data to a scientist, it may be wise to forgo a story and let the data you are presenting create the narrative instead.

A recent Stanford University study found that the average person will retain 5 to 10 percent of what they hear in a business presentation consisting of statistics alone, but 65 to 70 percent if that information is coupled with a memorable story or anecdote.[8] The reason for this is simple: emotion. "Psychological studies show that we don't get infected by a story unless we are emotionally transported—unless we lose ourselves in the story," says author Jonathan Gottschall. "Great epic poems to office scuttlebutt—are almost uniformly about humans facing problems and trying to overcome them. Stories have a problem-solution structure. Stories are always about trouble."[9] Good stories have the ability to cross cultures and engage us in an emotional way—this is actually what gives them their power. Stories are a way for our brains to organize information and help prepare us to make decisions. They reveal character and they build trust. According to research, presentations that scored high for storytelling were more likely to influence an audience to change its beliefs or actions.[10] Steve Jobs once said, "The most powerful person in the world is the storyteller. The storyteller sets the vision, values, and agenda of an entire generation that is to come."[11] Ed Catmull, the president of Pixar and Walt Disney Animation Studios, worked closely with Jobs during his time at Pixar, saying, "[Steve] knew how important it was to construct a story that connected with people. This was a skill he used in his presentations at Apple. When he got up in front of an audience to introduce a new product, he understood that he would communicate more effectively if you put forward a narrative."[12]

One recent study found that when managers used storytelling to resolve conflicts and address issues with their teams, they were more successful in reaching the specific outcomes (and objectives) they desired.[13] When situations are complex, stories can simplify information and make it easily understood and accessible. A good story or anecdote can make a point quickly and cover ground that otherwise may have taken hours to explain. An illustration can help overcome a client objection or get buy-in from a senior leader. Human beings are wired for stories, which is why being a good storyteller should be a part of any leader's personal brand. Think about how stories are used in television commercials. Many companies are increasingly using storytelling to strengthen their brand in an effort to attract top talent. As contributor Lars Schmidt wrote in *Forbes*, "These narratives are revealing a more human side of the business. They often go beyond 'This is *what* I do here,' instead illuminating 'This is *why* I do what I do—*here*.' "[14] Stories can be used to illustrate a concept or idea, show value, establish credibility, demonstrate collaboration, and foster better relationships. Stories can also be used for persuasion or to overcome a sudden objection in a business setting. Studies have shown that when you use a narrative story to make a point or paint a picture, the viewer or listener will naturally empathize with the characters in the story by feeling what they are feeling. People are more likely to buy into a proposal or purchase a product if they see themselves in the story and find it relatable. This is especially true for people tasked with presenting complicated or technical information. This can be a challenge for someone who believes that the data is what matters and the numbers should speak for themselves. "Often technical people are not accustomed to telling stories," says Jay Bonansinga, author of the bestselling *Walking Dead* novels. "They are more accustomed to filling people's ears and brains with numbers and data. But it also makes narrative more important because an audience will sit up and lean in when they hear a story. Subject matter experts often fail to realize that it's not the quantity of the information they are imparting to an audience—if they're showing three pie charts, it won't make it twice as good to show six. The key that will unlock success is telling a story that generates emotion."[15]

I believe in the power of storytelling. Stories open our hearts to a new place, which opens our minds, which often leads to action.

—MELINDA GATES

While overt selling or persuading are *push* strategies, stories involve more of a *pull* strategy for a communicator. A story happens more slowly, gradually drawing a listener in and forcing them to follow the characters—feel what they feel, experience what they experience—and make an emotional investment in their eventual outcome. Because of this, leaders can leverage storytelling to energize a team, shatter complacency, and galvanize a vision. As discussed in previous chapters, active intentions such as energize, shatter, and galvanize will fuel the delivery of a message and provide energy to the telling of the story itself. Leadership, driven by passion, can move an audience emotionally and enhance a leader's ability to influence. Team members in a meeting or presentation want to feel something as a result of a speaker's message and recent studies show that good stories are a scientifically proven way to do just that. According to Paul Zak, a pioneer in the field of neuro-economics, the reason for this is that stories actually trigger the release of oxytocin, a chemical that encourages empathy in the receiver of the story.[16]

Another positive benefit of being a good storyteller is that it can make you more attractive to others—at least if you are a man. According to research from the University of North Carolina at Chapel Hill and SUNY Buffalo, when a man is perceived to be a good storyteller, he is seen to be more attractive as a long-term partner. Interestingly though, women who were seen as good storytellers were not seen as more attractive. While it is hard to pinpoint the cause of this gender disparity, the authors suggest that for women it has to do with the fact that "storytelling ability reflects a man's ability to gain resources [and] positions of authority in society."[17]

Every experience you've had and every hardship you've endured has contributed to you becoming the person you are today. We can all think of famous hardships or challenges that shaped the lives of leaders, past and present. There's Steve Jobs getting fired from Apple, Franklin Delano Roosevelt being stricken with polio, and Barack Obama being forced to produce his birth certificate, just to name a few examples. Every moment of your life—every triumph and every mistake—follows you to the present and contributes to the ways in which you are seen in the workplace. As comedian Louis C.K. rightly points out, "If you went back and fixed all the mistakes you've made, you'd erase yourself."[18]

Storytelling can serve as a vital tool for defining your brand. A simple essence story can let people know how you think, how you make decisions, and how they can expect you to interact with those around you. Many successful business leaders have stories that trace their personal journeys to the top. Examples include Oprah Winfrey using her skills as a communicator to create a broadcasting empire, Donald Trump receiving a million-dollar loan from his father to start his real estate business, or Steve Jobs and Steve Wozniak inventing the personal computer in their garage. These stories resonate with people. They not only become an integral part of the person's brand but also an important part of the company's culture and, subsequently, the public's consciousness. In this way, stories can help to define the culture or the organization itself. Every organization has an origin story about how it came into being that gets passed down from person-to-person until it becomes part of a company's lore. Think of famous brands such as Nike and Facebook. With Facebook, there's the story of Mark Zuckerberg and his Harvard classmates coming up with the idea of a social network that eventually became Facebook, today used by over 2 billion people around the world. For Nike, we have the story of Phil Knight and how he used a waffle iron in his kitchen to create the distinctive shoe soles that defined the Nike brand, a company valued at more than $32 billion.

Marketing is no longer about the stuff that you make, but about the stories you tell.

—SETH GODIN

Jerome Bruner, the great Harvard psychologist who pioneered the modern study of creativity, has observed that stories always rise out of the unexpected. And because surprise rewards our brains with the release of dopamine, good stories provide pleasure and make us feel good. Writes Bruner: "Narrative deals with the vicissitudes of human intentions. And since there are myriad intentions and endless ways for them to run into trouble—or so it would seem—there should be endless kinds of stories. But, surprisingly, this seems not to be the case."[19] We all possess hundreds of stories from our lives and experiences that can be drawn upon in business to influence others. To break it down into simple categories of business stories, we have detailed the five types of stories every leader should have at the ready in their communicator's toolbox, including:

The Origin Story

This is a story that provides a window into how your company does business, articulating its values and priorities. For example, the origin story that details how and why the company was formed is always insightful for someone unfamiliar with your organization. Also, the story about how you became part of the organization or how you first became interested in your given field is a good tale to have ready to share with a prospective client or interviewer.

The Value Story

This is a story whose purpose is to generate excitement and develop trust by clearly establishing the value your company has delivered for clients or customers in the past, and how the work you do benefits your customers, the community, or society at large. Identify the benefit you or your company can provide to a listener and drive that point home through the telling of your story.

The Challenge Story

This is a story that demonstrates a difficult or demanding situation your company has encountered and how your organization was able to adapt and overcome it. A story such as this shows flexibility, resiliency, and tenacity—all traits that will be admired by a customer or prospective client.

The Implementation Story

This is a story that shows how your company devised a plan and successfully put it into action. It provides a client or customer with a clear idea of how your team collaborates, operates, or shifts priorities when necessary to achieve success.

The Solution Story

This is a story that demonstrates how your organization identified a problem or customer need and addressed it through the use of your products, services, or expertise. This type of story can be used to persuade a potential customer to sign a deal or consider a proposal by showing a clear example of how you provided value for a previous client or customer.

Stories can be used to draw people in and guide them toward the point of view that aligns with the objective you seek to achieve. To do this, as we have mentioned previously, you need engagement. Just as audiences enjoy twists and turns in the plots of movies and plays, including these same types of revelations and surprises in a story can help build excitement and generate interest with an audience. As a storyteller, you build suspense by withholding key facts or details as long as you can, revealing information only when absolutely necessary. Think of great movies like *The Sixth Sense, Chinatown,* or *The Crying Game,* and how effectively they use the element of surprise. A skilled storyteller will hold back pertinent information during a story to help build the tension, revealing details bit-by-bit, on a need-to-know basis. By gradually ratcheting up the suspense, a storyteller hooks their listener in and engages them fully with the circumstances and stakes of the message. According to anthropologist Dr. Helen Fisher, this teasing of information and the mystery it creates in the mind of a listener actually triggers the flow of dopamine, a chemical in the brain that provides a natural high.[20] The pleasure of following a good story comes from the release of tension as information is finally revealed and the various elements of the story fall into place. For leaders or teachers tasked with motivating or empowering others, surprise during the telling of a story can actually increase a listener's motivation to learn. Steve Jobs often used the element of surprise when launching Apple products, repeatedly using the phrase "one more thing . . ." to build suspense and draw people in.[21]

In their book, *Surprise: Embrace the Unpredictable and Engineer the Unexpected,* authors Tania Luna and LeeAnn Renninger, break down the science of surprise and shed new light on why human beings gravitate toward it. As it turns out, we are all hardwired to enjoy new experiences—we like the shot of dopamine we get when we make a new purchase, get a text mail alert, or meet a new friend. "Surprises point us to dangers, opportunities, and new information," said Renninger. "Research shows that surprise intensifies our emotions by about 400 percent, which explains why we love positive surprises and hate negative surprises."[22] When we are able to surprise an audience with a twist or reveal in our story, we force them to pay attention and be present in the moment. Says Luna, "Surprise hijacks all of our mental processes and pulls our focus into one thing."[23] Other research backs up this idea as well, finding that surprise makes people more aware of their environment and actually assists with concentration and engagement levels.[24] Good stories create a situation where the audience or listener feel emotionally invested in the characters and content. This can be an integral factor in someone's ability to engage with and retain the information you are presenting to them. As experts have discovered, surprise "builds new neural pathways in our brains, leading us to think more flexibly and creatively."[25] Surprise jolts us out of complacency and demands our focus and attention. It challenges our assumptions and makes us question the decisions we make and even how we make them.

Everything you do becomes material that can be drawn upon when telling stories. Educators Joe Winston and Miles Tandy have studied the influence of storytelling in our lives. "We communicate our daily experience to ourselves and to others in story form," they write, "We make sense of the behavior of others by inventing stories to explain why they act as they do."[26] David Green, the former Global Marketing Officer for McDonald's, has always valued the power of story during his time at the fast-food giant. "I came to understand how important campfire stories are in big institutions," said Green. "For instance, at McDonald's, if there was a little man in the parking lot picking up cigarette butts you knew you were in trouble, because that was [McDonald's founder] Ray Kroc. There was a time when Ray went into a restaurant that was filthy, and he jumped on top of a table and yelled out, 'Ladies and gentlemen, you are not getting what McDonald's is best at. This restaurant is now closed. Please come back tomorrow; it will be a lot better.' That kind of story, just like fireweed, spreads throughout an organization. Every great company, whether Walt Disney or Steve Jobs at Apple, has this kind of institutional story that goes around and tells you what the culture is about."[27]

One of our favorite business stories has been around for many years and grown into something of an urban legend. The story involves the upscale retailer Nordstrom and their renowned customer service. As the story goes, a man brought a set of tires back to a Nordstrom location in Alaska to return them and get his money back. There was only one problem: Nordstrom, a retailer of apparel, shoes and other accessories, didn't sell tires. Still, as the story went, Nordstrom allowed the man to return the tires and gave him a full refund. While a story like this seems implausible, it actually happened, according to Nordstrom spokesman Colin Johnson. Turns out the location of this particular Nordstrom had once been occupied by a tire shop where the man bought the tires in question. The man returned to the same spot where he had purchased the tires, not realizing the building had changed ownership. Said Johnson, the Nordstrom manager who allowed the man to return the tires did so to demonstrate the company's superior customer service and also to forge a positive relationship with a potential new customer. Whether or not this story is true is not as important as the fact that it has been told and retold for over fifty years, shining a positive light on both Nordstrom and their superior level of customer service with each new telling.[28]

Stories can often be more powerful for an organization than a company vision statement or motto when it comes to defining a culture or promoting company values. A story, illustration, or anecdote can offer an immediate lesson that is relevant and applicable to an audience or listener. In her book *The Story Factor*, Annette Simmons writes, "'We value integrity,' means nothing. But tell a story about a former employee who hid his mistake and cost the company thousands, or a story about a salesperson who owned up to a mistake and earned so much trust her company doubled his order, and you begin to teach an employee what integrity means."[29] By sharing a story such as this you can demonstrate the values of a team or organization and show how these examples have tangible effects if they are put into action.

As you begin to comb your past experiences for stories that

People are going to tell stories about you whether you want them to or not. Choose which ones they tell.

—BOB MCDONALD

can be used in your work, consider the following tips that need to be addressed when delivering an effective business story:

Identify the takeaway first

There is a reason you have chosen this story to tell. As with any communication, figure out the objective you are pursuing as a result of telling the listener your story. Always keep your audience in mind and make sure the content and lesson of the story address their needs. Stories should be clear and concise so as not to waste people's time. To accomplish this, start your story as close to the end as possible.

Utilize clear intentions

Once the objective and purpose for the story has been identified, choose active intentions for a congruent delivery during the telling of it. If your story is meant to inspire or empower, your word choices and delivery should support that and your verbal, vocal, and visual channels of communication should be aligned.

Don't make yourself the hero

Avoid making the story about you—even if it actually is about you. Focus the telling of the story on the benefit you are providing to the listener. Make them feel something, learn something, or do something as a result of hearing it. You can do this by identifying the value you are providing for them ahead of time and then focusing your story on that.

Appeal to emotion

While facts are important, people are more likely to be driven to make decisions based on emotion. As such, if your story can generate a feeling or emotion within the listener, they are more likely to be engaged and persuaded as a result. One way to do this is by using short sentences and small words to drive the action of your story. Using an active voice will make your story more compelling and will anchor your listeners' attention to the present moment.

Keep it simple

Make your story personal and stick to only the information needed to construct a concise and streamlined story. An effective business story should last no more than three to five minutes so don't get bogged down with extraneous details or unnecessary side stories. Wind a story up tight. Tell your story using the least number of words possible. Use simple language and avoid jargon or acronyms. Every sentence you choose to include should do one of two things: reveal character or advance the action.

Drive your main point home

Once you've built to the climax and payoff of your story, drive home the moral or lesson so it is clear to your listeners why you shared this particular tale. If your intention is to inspire or motivate, this is where your delivery and the congruence of your message needs to make us feel something so we walk away from your story feeling the emotions you want us to feel.

CREATING HEROES AND VILLAINS

Shark Tank is the popular reality television program where unknown inventors pitch their new products or companies to successful billionaire investors in the hopes of securing a partnership or investment of capital. The producer of *Shark Tank* is Mark Burnett, who also carefully shaped the brand and image of Donald Trump on *The Apprentice*. Burnett understands the importance of storytelling, of creating a context and characters and building tension and suspense by creating heroes and villains that viewers can either root for or against. Every episode of *Shark Tank* starts by introducing viewers to the inventors through the telling of their story and the challenges they have faced. By creating empathy in the sharing of each inventor's personal story or struggle, it creates an emotional investment from viewers. If we like the inventor or investor we root for them; if we dislike them we root against them. This is important for any leader presenting information in a business setting, whether pitching a new product or implementing a new process or procedure. A good influencer will set up a problem or pain point during a pitch or presentation that serves as the villain and then presents their product or proposal as the hero who will solve their problem. An HR manager implementing a new procedure within a company must first present the "why" to an audience to explain the reason for the change or shift in policy. Defining the problem or challenge that makes the policy change necessary will help you set context and overcome any objections or resistance. The "why" in this case serves as the villain and the new procedure or policy becomes the hero that will make things better as a result.

Political strategist Mark McKinnon thinks one of the main reasons Donald Trump won the election of 2016 was his experience as a television star on *The Apprentice* and his ability to tell a story with clear heroes and villains: "Voters are attracted to candidates who lay out a storyline. Losing campaigns communicate unconnected streams of information, ideas, speeches. Winning campaigns create a narrative architecture that ties it all together into something meaningful and coherent."[30] The same could be said for anyone delivering a message in the corporate environment. A data dump of information and numbers is not going to motivate an audience as effectively as a well-structured presentation that tells a compelling and coherent story. This is where Trump excelled and Clinton fell short, according to McKinnon.

> How do you tell a story? Identify a threat and/or an opportunity. Establish victims of the threat or denied opportunity. Suggest villains that impose the threat or deny the opportunity. Propose solutions. Reveal the hero. That's what Trump did. The reality TV star understands the power of narrative. He identified a threat: outside forces trying to change the way we live. And an opportunity: make America great again. He established victims: blue-collar workers who have lost jobs or experienced a declining standard of living. He suggested villains: Mexican immigrants, China, establishment elites. He proposed solutions: build a wall, tear up unfair trade deals. And the hero was revealed, Donald Trump.[31]

Trump's ability to frame nearly all of his messages in the form of heroes and villains, winners and losers, is a touchstone of his leadership and communication style. During a sales pitch or presentation at your job, if you are able to set up a problem that needs to be solved and then suggest a solution that involves your company or product, you can use the hero/villain dynamic to your advantage by presenting yourself, your company, or your product as the solution they need to effectively solve their problem.

When it comes to constructing your material or developing your story, you have to build a foundation and structure that serves the overall objective you are attempting to accomplish. Think of an architect designing a building. With the design of a building, every beam, every pipe, every nail, every window, serves a purpose and is necessary for the overall structure of the building. This same concept is applicable when developing your business story. Every detail you include must be specific, carefully chosen, and meticulously placed. Transitions are also important elements to keep a listener engaged. They serve as a connective tissue as you move from point to point. Without smooth transitions, your story's pacing will come across as halting and it will be difficult to follow.

Storytelling is a skill that most people can master, but it helps to understand the elements that create the framework of an effective story. Playwrights, screenwriters, and novelists nearly all use variations on a particular dramatic structure developed by Gustav Freytag, a nine-teenth-century German novelist. Freytag noticed patterns in the plots of classic stories and novels and devised a diagram known as "Freytag's Pyramid."[32] This diagram was used to analyze and provide a structure for storytelling, and we have adapted a version of it into our storytelling work. Take a look at the model below to understand the various elements that comprise an effective story.

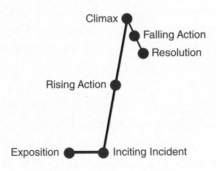

Exposition

This is the who, what, when, and where of a story that sets the stage so your audience can follow the characters and events that will take place.

Inciting incident

The inciting incident is the event in your story that serves as a trigger to initiate the plot and conflict and start the action of the story moving forward.

Rising action

These are the events of the story that drive the plot forward and build the tension from one moment to the next.

Climax

This is the section of the story where opposing forces clash and the conflict reaches its highest point of tension or drama.

Falling action

Once the climax is achieved and the conflict is resolved, these are the few final events that signal we are coming to the end of the story.

Resolution

This is where the story reaches its conclusion and you tie up any loose ends, reveal any remaining secrets, and drive home the moral or lesson of the story one last time.

Think of the diagram for dramatic structure as a story map—a framework on which you can hang the details of your story. It is also quite easy to overlay the elements of a good business story onto this time-tested storytelling formula, as demonstrated below. Use the following model to outline your business story by identifying what details correspond with each of the points on the classic Freytag story map. As you progress from one point to the next, your business story should flow and build in an effective and compelling way. Let's go through each section of the business story map.

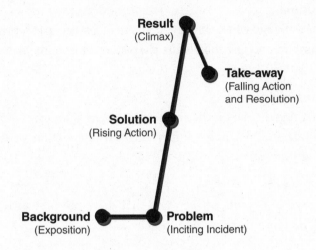

Establish background information (exposition)

You have to start with some background information so your client or team member can follow the journey of your story. Who is the story about and when and where does it take place? As you set up your story, provide the listener with any details they will need to know about the people, setting, and circumstances involved. The more descriptive your details, the better the picture you will paint for your audience to keep them engaged and invested in your story.

Identify the problem (inciting incident)

Now that you've established the basic facts of the story and the specific background information, it is time to develop some conflict. Introduce a pain point or problem that needs to be solved. This gets the action of your story started and will create interest in the mind of your listener to see how the issue will be addressed. Think of your favorite films or books. Can you pick out the inciting incident that gets the story started and grabs your interest? Do the same with your business story. What incident or event gets the ball rolling? What villain can you create and then subsequently vanquish?

Detail the solution (rising action)

As the story takes off, you slowly build and reveal pertinent information that drives the story forward, showing the client or team member what steps were taken to address the problem at hand. At some point, you will want to clearly identify a solution to the problem that was established at the outset. This is the "hero" of the story that will emerge to fix a problem, address a challenge, or create a positive change.

Spotlight the result (climax)

Once you have revealed the solution that will solve the problem at the heart of the conflict, you need to describe specifically how you did it and how a positive outcome was achieved. This is what your listener has been waiting to hear. Focus on the benefit your solution provided and ensure that the climax of the story aligns directly with the objective you have chosen for telling it.

State the takeaway (falling action and resolution)

Now that the problem has been solved and the villain has been defeated, the only remaining element is to wrap up your story with a one- or two-line closing that clearly defines what the listener should have learned from your story. When we use stories as a means to influence, motivate, or teach others, this is the point where the takeaway needs to be delivered so it is clear to your audience what the point was and why the lesson of the story is important to them.

Remember, in most cases, a story is always about the ending—the lesson or moral you want to drive home. Your job as a storyteller is to kick off a story and get to the ending in the fastest, most interesting way possible. Without an exciting climax or a clear takeaway, a story is just a bunch of facts strung together and you run the risk of your audience walking away feeling disappointed or unfulfilled. Winston Churchill was always an enthusiastic proponent of powerful endings in his speeches and stories, saying:

> The climax of oratory is reached by a rapid succession of waves of sound and vivid pictures. The audience is delighted by the changing scenes presented to their imagination. Their ear is tickled by the rhythm of the

language. The enthusiasm rises. A series of facts is brought forward, all pointing in a common direction. The end appears in view before it is reached. The crowd anticipates the conclusion and the last words fall amid a thunder of assent.[33]

Using the story maps detailed in this chapter, choose a personal or professional story from your past experiences and sketch out the framework from which to begin crafting it. Who is the audience that you hope to impact with this story? What background information do you need to set up at the outset? What is the problem your company or client encountered and what solution drives the rising action? What are the result and takeaway? After creating your outline, practice telling the story to someone, perhaps a spouse or coworker who may not be familiar with it. Then solicit their feedback. Did they find it interesting? Which sections dragged on too long or were confusing? Taking their comments into consideration, go back and refine your story and tell it again, this time to someone new. While the facts and information in your story are important, keep reminding yourself that people are driven by emotion. Find stories that have strong emotional anchors. If your story can generate a feeling or emotion in the minds of your listeners, they are more likely to be engaged and persuaded. Choose strong and active intentions (such as excite, frighten, empower, inspire, etc.) to fuel your delivery and elicit the emotional reaction you want from your audience or listener.

We all possess a myriad of stories based on our individual life experiences and each of these stories can be shared to inspire or enlighten others. By using the content discussed in this chapter you can begin mining past experiences for stories and begin to structure each for maximum impact. As you sharpen and refine your abilities as a storyteller, seek out the stories of others, especially those passed down from bosses or coworkers within your organization. These stories can be shared with others who will then pass them along as well. Become a story collector and get comfortable sharing stories and anecdotes. Every story you tell is a gift, as is every story shared with you by others.

Blueprint to Bullseye—Chapter 7

Preparation Guide for Storytelling

1. What is the main theme of your story?

2. What do you want your audience to do as a result of hearing your story (your objective)?

3. What intentions will you use to accomplish your objective?

4. What is the context for your story? (When and where does it take place?)

5. Who is the hero of your story? What does the hero want and what obstacles are in the way of the hero getting what is wanted?

6. Who (or what) is the villain of the story?

7. What temporary setbacks or ups and downs does the hero experience?

8. Where do surprises occur over the course of the story?

9. How does the story end?

10. What lesson do you want the audience to take away as a result of hearing this story?

CHAPTER 8

Handle Difficult Conversations
Providing Feedback, Managing Emotions, and Speaking in the Moment

The words you speak become the house you live in.
—Hafez

In business, people are often tasked with providing feedback to subordinates, delivering difficult news to stakeholders, or presenting information to audiences that can be hostile, distracted or apprehensive. In this chapter, we will discuss techniques to help you effectively communicate difficult news or feedback, handle stress, and be able to speak clearly and confidently in the moment. Handling emotional interactions while clearly and confidently answering questions or clarifying information is an essential trait for a leader to master in order to retain their credibility and influence others. For actors, being present in any given moment and adjusting their communication as circumstances dictate is a necessary part of the job. One such example of an actor having to perform under uniquely stressful and challenging conditions took place in 1953, when Winston Churchill went to the

Old Vic Theatre in London to see Richard Burton perform the title role in *Hamlet*.

"Do be good tonight, dear boy," said the play's director to Burton backstage, "because the old man is in front." Richard Burton had been a huge admirer of Winston Churchill and suddenly grew very anxious upon learning that his childhood idol would be present in the audience that night. In an effort to settle his nerves and focus himself, Burton turned to an old actor's trick: he doused his head in cold water. The pressure to deliver a stellar performance for Churchill filled the legendary actor with anxiety and he tried his best to stay calm. As the house lights dimmed, Burton took a breath and stepped out onto the stage, launching into Hamlet's first speech of the play. As his voice boomed out into the theatre, Burton noticed the sound of another voice, this one murmuring from somewhere around the first few rows of the audience. "It was Churchill speaking the lines with me," Burton recalled, "and I could not shake him off." The actor tried slowing down and speeding up but no matter how he changed the cadence or pacing of the speeches, Churchill continued to parrot the lines from his seat a few rows away. Eventually, in a final exasperated effort to deal with the situation, a frustrated Burton began cutting parts of his speeches short. The tactic worked and the words coming from Churchill's seat near the front of the stage eventually fell silent, replaced instead by an angry growl.[1]

MANAGING EMOTIONAL INTERACTIONS

While most of us will never have to speak in front of someone of Churchill's stature and under such maddening circumstances, there is a high likelihood that we will have to communicate important information to senior leaders or influential audience members at some point. These types of interactions can be fraught with challenges, such as interruptions, technical snafus, or resistance to the message you are attempting to deliver. When the stakes are high or an audience is comprised of powerful decision-makers, our nerves and emotions can often affect the way we communicate. As a speaker or presenter, your ability to stay calm under pressure links directly to your performance and it is your job to keep emotions in check so that they serve the intentions you have chosen to accomplish your objective. As Greg Hicks wrote in his book *LeaderShock*, "When we don't assertively set our intentions, we passively or unconsciously choose something else. Our outcomes are haphazard, and we become hostage to people and events that lead us astray. Intention adds directionality and power to human endeavor."[2]

For anyone tasked with leading others or communicating difficult information in a business environment, stress is an ever-present aspect of the job. While in many ways technology has made our lives and jobs easier, our reliance on technology and this constant connectivity can actually cause stress for many workers. According to Socialist MP Benoit Hamon, "There is far more work-related stress today than there used to be . . . the stress is constant. Employees physically leave the office, but they do not leave their work. They remain attached by a kind of electronic leash, like a dog." Anyone who spends time around children knows how important their phone is to them. They are communicating with others almost constantly through social media or texting. Many feel anxious or upset if they lose their phone or are without it for an extended period of time. Megan Moreno, head of social media and adolescent health research at Seattle Children's Hospital, has noted it is not only teens who are addicted to their cell phones. "Adults are learning to use their phones in the way that teens do," she says, "They're zoning out. They're ignoring people. They're answering calls during dinner rather than saying, 'Okay, we have this technology. Here are the rules about how we use it.' "[3] Author Simon Sinek agrees and warns about how technology is warping social interactions of younger generations of workers who have come of age with the modern convenience of smart phones. Says Sinek, "They've grown up in a world of instant gratification. You want to buy something, you go on Amazon and it arrives the next day... you want to go on a date, you don't even have to learn and practice that skill . . . you just swipe right. Everything you want you can have instantaneously—except job satisfaction and strength of relationships. There ain't no app for that. They are slow, meandering, uncomfortable, messy processes."[4]

During communication with others, individuals often believe their internal states are more apparent to an audience than they actually are. This phenomenon is known as the *illusion of transparency* and derives from the difficulty people have in getting beyond their own experience when attempting to determine how they appear to others.[5] Think about it. You know what you are feeling, what you are thinking, and you tend to believe those thoughts and emotions are clearly visible to others, perceivable to the outside world. In most cases though, research has shown that we overestimate how clearly our message is being communicated because we neglect to factor in how others are filtering our message through their own prism of wants and needs.

When it comes to the illusion of transparency, there is good news and bad news. The good news is research shows individuals are typically better at disguising their internal states than they believe, such as how much of their nervousness or anxiety is being perceived by an audience. The bad news is that people often feel that as long as they are clear about their intentions at any given moment, others will easily understand the tone and tenor of their message as well. This is not always the case. As leaders in the business arena, there are numerous situations that arise where the ability to deliver bad news becomes an important skill to possess, such as having to lay off employees, delivering a performance review for an underperforming team member, reducing a budget or cutting a program, or asking people to do more work without additional pay. Making sure we are delivering these types of messages in a way that ensures they are received in the same way is important for any leader. But it isn't always easy to do.

Nothing travels faster than the speed of light, with the possible exception of bad news.

—DOUGLAS ADAMS

A powerful example of a CEO effectively delivering difficult news took place in 2012 at the tech giant Hewlett-Packard. Meg Whitman, who had become the company's CEO the prior year, had taken the helm during a particularly turbulent time in HP's history.[6] Through mismanagement and a string of poor decisions made by previous leadership, HP was headed for a death spiral if very tough decisions were not made immediately and Whitman knew it. When it came time to make those decisions and communicate them to the workforce at HP, Whitman decided to record a video message for her 350,000 employees that addressed rumors at HP but also detailed a plan forward, including specific actions that she had decided to take:

> At the end of 2009 we reported a workforce of about 304,000. At the end of 2010 we had almost 325,000 employees, and at the end of 2011 that number had ballooned to nearly 350,000. Over that same period, we saw year-over-year revenue growth of 10 percent in 2010, of 1 percent in 2011, and, so far in 2012, revenues have been declining. We're struggling under our own weight. And we've got to restore a healthy balance in order to return HP to its position as a growing, thriving, innovating industry leader. That's what this is all about. And the workforce reduction is only one piece of a comprehensive effort. We see a lot of opportunity to remove complexity, streamline, and reduce costs in a number of areas across HP.

Whitman knew that the news would be difficult to hear for members of the HP organization—the actions she was proposing would reduce the workforce by a stunning 8 percent—28,000 would be losing their jobs. To drive home to employees why the layoffs were necessary to rebuild the organization and position it for the future, Whitman ended the announcement with a message meant to inspire and motivate:

> In times of change, it's easy to lose focus, waiting to see what happens next. We can't let that happen. This is a great organization, full of incredible people who are resilient, committed, and who care about our customers and our company. I'm asking all of you to please keep driving forward. Close every deal. Leave nothing on the table. We need that now more than ever.

By delivering this difficult message in an honest and transparent manner, Whitman demonstrated respect and empathy for her workers and took responsibility for the actions she was taking to save the company. She removed uncertainty for her workers by clearly explaining why she had chosen to take these measures, what changes specifically would take place and where the path forward would lead for the organization.

For an example of a CEO doing a poor job delivering difficult news, look no further than a quarterly earnings telephone call that United Airlines CEO Oscar Munoz conducted in 2017. The airline's stock price had been slipping as of late and investors and analysts were jittery going into this particular earnings call. While answering a question from an analyst during the call, Munoz remarked that he and United had "dug ourselves in a hole" and asked for patience. If his intention was to *reassure* his audience with his response, he did not accomplish it. Because of Munoz's mishandling of the phone call, United's stock price plummeted a whopping 12 percent—losing $2.5 billion of market value in a single day.[7]

> *Communication is health; communication is truth; communication is happiness.*
>
> —VIRGINIA WOOLF

As many of us have witnessed firsthand in a meeting or conversation, once a word or comment is spoken, it can't be taken back. You say it, you own it. Emotions can be difficult to manage when situations get tense or there is conflict or strong feelings from individual stakeholders. In these situations, it is rarely helpful to react in anger when dealing with a client, boss, or team member. It is more advisable to take a breath, step out of the room for a moment, and return when you are calmer and more composed. As a communicator, anger is one of the most difficult emotions to manage because we struggle with our ability to think straight as emotions rise. We get defensive and shift into "fight" mode as our brains gets overloaded. Phap Dung, a senior monk and teacher, offers some helpful insight into dealing with the emotion of anger when interacting with others. "We see the mind like a house, so if your house is on fire, you need to take care of the fire, not to go look for the person that made the fire. Take care of those emotions first; it's the priority. Because anything that comes from a place of fear and anxiety and anger will only make the fire worse. Come back and find a place of calm and peace to cool the flame of emotion down."[8] This is another reason why active listening and mindfulness are important. There is great power in holding your tongue and allowing the other person to speak. It helps you take stock of the moment and be truly present because you are giving the other person the opportunity to be heard. In turn, you will be able to better understand their position and may even learn new information that you did not know before. This is important even when you know you are right in an argument—in fact, *especially* when you are right. By doing this, explains Amy Cuddy, "You're not giving power away; you're allowing [the other person] to feel seen and understood."[9]

Being mindful allows you the ability to take in information and reflect on it before reacting or responding in a way that damages your leverage or the relationship itself. This can only happen if you are engaged fully in the conversation and responding to the intention cues of the other person with whom you are speaking. Here's the advice that Stanislavski gave to his actors on the topic: "Each change of circumstance, setting, place of action, time—brings a corresponding adjustment. All types of communication . . . require adjustments peculiar to each."[10] In other words, be present and aware of the circumstances around you and respond to each in any given moment. This is where intention and objective become essential. If the objective you are pursuing is strong and supported by specific and active intentions, it will create a solid foundation upon which to build your message. Of course, this is easier to accomplish during face-to-face interactions but can grow more complicated when information or ideas are being communicated through e-mail or text. Platforms like Twitter or Facebook are great for making assertions but are not as useful for any type of discussion that requires detailed or careful thought.

Behavioral scientist Justin Kruger has studied e-mail communication and has found that miscommunication is much more likely to occur when messages are relayed through electronic means versus face-to-face. With spoken communication, the messages were interpreted accurately about 75 percent of the time, but when communicated through e-mail the accuracy was only 56 percent.[11] The main reason for this is that in an e-mail or text, there are no vocal dynamics or facial expressions to interpret so context can be easily misconstrued. Kruger found that intention cues such as gestures and vocal inflection act as important indicators of true meaning and by eliminating them we risk leaving too much room for misinterpretation or ambiguity. What made this finding even more surprising for Kruger was how the senders of these misinterpreted or ambiguous messages had virtually no idea their messages were not being received and discerned in the manner they intended. Authors Noah Goldstein, Steve J. Martin, and Robert B. Cialdini describe the problem like this: "Because the senders have full psychological access to their own intentions when they create the messages, they often assume that the message recipient does as well."[12] Returning to the idea of the illusion of transparency, it is the job of the sender of a message to ensure that it is received in the manner intended—even when sending e-mails or texts. As a communicator, what can we do to prevent our written messages from being misinterpreted? One thing is to limit the frequency of sending important or emotional messages in written form. Instead of sending an e-mail or text, try to communicate in person, and face-to-face whenever possible. Pick up the phone, stop by someone's office, or schedule a video call to discuss if the topic is complex and could be misconstrued if handled over e-mail. If you absolutely have no choice but to communicate through e-mail, proceed with caution. Research has also shown that e-mail encourages negativity in what we say—a result of not having to look the person in the eye and see their reactions.[13] Once you've composed the message, take time to read it over before sending it. Ask yourself how you might react if you received a message worded this way. Reflect on your word choices and make changes if you think the words as written do not support your intention or will not help you achieve the reactions you want from the receiver.

During tense or complicated negotiations, communicating via e-mail can present distinct challenges. One study conducted an experiment with MBA students who were made to negotiate with one another through e-mail as well as face-to-face. The results of the study found something interesting: those students who negotiated through e-mail shared much less personal information about themselves than did the students who negotiated face-to-face.[14] This is important to note, as sharing personal information during communication invites the other party to share personal information as well. This helps develop trust and build rapport, crucial tools for building relationships.

HANDLING DIFFICULT QUESTIONS

As the first line of the Greek philosopher Epictetus' manual of ethical advice, the *Enchiridion*, tells us, "Some things are in our control and others not."[15] Although these words were written nearly 2,000 years ago, they still ring true today, especially for anyone presenting material or promoting a new idea in the corporate arena. You can prepare like a champ and still be caught off-guard by a comment or question you failed to anticipate. As Mike Tyson, the heavyweight champion boxer (and Broadway actor), once put it, "Everybody has a plan until they get punched in the mouth."[16] When handling challenging or hostile questions during a meeting or presentation, it is important for you to stay calm and keep emotions in check. Give the benefit of the doubt to the person asking the question and put your focus on the question itself and not the person asking it. When difficult questions arise during a meeting, presentation, or interview, it is important to maintain composure, even in the most unexpected circumstances. When you're asked a question, wait a second or two before responding so you can absorb the tone and spirit of the question and consider your answer carefully. As you begin to answer the question, you might want to take a step toward the person who asked it. Square off your torso and aim your belly button toward them to indicate you are giving them your full attention and interest. Focus on your audience by returning to Pinnacle's three-step process: First, *analyze* the person asking the question and try to figure out what they want or expect to hear from you. Second, *understand* what you need to say and do to elicit the reaction you want. Third, *modify* your delivery to accomplish that objective.

An example of a CEO creating a public relations disaster as a result of answering a question ineffectively happened in 2010 following the Deepwater Horizon oil spill that claimed 11 lives and spewed toxic sludge into the Gulf of Mexico. As people around the world watched more than two hundred million gallons of oil gush from broken pipes, the CEO of British Petroleum, Tony Hayward, became the face of the disaster. But instead of showing remorse or offering an apology for the environmental mess caused by his company, Hayward's handling of his numerous public appearances during the spill and clean-up came across as tone-deaf and arrogant. In interviews, Hayward minimized the extent of the disaster and downplayed the environmental consequences, saying the spill was "relatively tiny" compared with the "very big ocean."[17] In one exchange, things got even worse when Hayward shirked any responsibility at all for the mess and attempted to shift the blame to the owners of the actual rig, saying, "This was not our accident . . . .This was not our drilling rig. . . . This was Transocean's rig. Their systems. Their people. Their equipment."[18] In an interview with reporters during the clean-up process, Hayward created yet another public relations nightmare for BP when he complained about the inconvenience the oil spill was causing him. "There's no one who wants this over more than I do. I would like my life back."[19] His flippant and self-pitying comment showed a lack of concern for the people and wildlife affected by the spill, and Hayward and BP spent weeks undoing the damage that resulted from the negative publicity. While history provides us with hundreds of examples of leaders or politicians flubbing the answers to questions or behaving in a way that damaged their credibility, an appearance by Facebook CEO Mark Zuckerberg at the D8 Summit in 2010 quite clearly shows us why proper preparation and the ability to think on one's feet are essential traits for a leader to possess.

When a man is prey to his emotions, he is not his own master.

—BARUCH SPINOZA

Zuckerberg had been invited to sit down for a live interview at D8 with interviewers Walt Mossberg and Kara Swisher. Dressed in his trademark black hoodie, Zuckerberg looked ill at ease from the start. When Swisher asked a question about privacy controls and the ways in which Facebook protects the privacy of its user's information, things went quickly from bad to worse for Zuckerberg. He was visibly uncomfortable listening to the question and the expression on his face suggested panic. Breaking eye contact with his interviewers, Zuckerberg clearly was not prepared for the question and, instead of answering it, ended up stammering out a long, rambling story about how he started Facebook with his friends all those years ago. Not only did his answer not directly address the question asked, it showed a CEO who was not focusing his response on the needs of his customers. Instead of offering the Facebook origin story that he has probably told a thousand times, Zuckerberg should have chosen to reassure his nearly 600 million Facebook users (at that time) that he was actively protecting their private information so they could continue to use Facebook without worry.

Instead, Zuckerberg's nerves and panic got the best of him. His answer to the question came off as disjointed and overly broad. His physical delivery communicated nervousness and discomfort, with one audience member describing him as "a young man under a lot of pressure, sweating profusely and answering questions . . . with rambling, largely conceptual answers."[20] Another person described Zuckerberg as "literally dissolving in a lake of his own sweat."[21] Since this unfortunate interview, Mark Zuckerberg has begun working on his communication skills with a coach and has made some noticeable improvements, but this incident shows the importance of executive presence, anticipating tough questions, and utilizing intention and objective in your communication to elicit the feelings you want from your audience.

Speak only if it improves upon the silence.

—MAHATMA GANDHI

Answering questions is a form of both reactive communication and impromptu speaking. People ask questions to receive information or get clarification, and in nearly all cases, people value information that they request more than information that is presented to them. Questions that come from superiors, team members, or clients can range from softball questions with simple answers to more difficult questions that require thoughtful consideration. Most communication in a corporate setting happens with little or no time for you to gather your thoughts, much less put together notes or an outline. With impromptu speaking—the delivery mode in which someone is called upon to speak without preparation—you have to speak in the moment and own your words. Despite the fact that we all engage in this type of communication every day, impromptu speaking is the mode that makes people the most anxious. The fear of misspeaking or drawing a blank makes many leaders nervous, but the ability to answer questions in a confident and compelling manner is essential for establishing and maintaining credibility in the eyes of an audience. The way someone responds to an audience's questions is every bit as important as how they delivered the actual presentation itself. To answer questions effectively, follow these simple rules when speaking in the moment:

Project confidence

Your audience creates much of their perception about you as a communicator by what they see, so use a solid home base position and good eye contact to project a confident and relaxed presence. Also, smile before you begin speaking, provided it supports your message and intention. This shows you are relaxed and glad to be there.

Pause before you start

When responding to a question, you have approximately one or two seconds to formulate your answer. Those one to two seconds can make the difference between answering effectively or not, so use them wisely—but above all, use them.

Slow down

When speaking without preparation, a slower and more deliberate pace is your best friend. Slow down the rate of your words so you can control them and shape your message. Because once the words are out, you can't put them back in.

Choose your words carefully

In the one or two seconds before you open your mouth, imagine three mental bullet points that can serve as a roadmap for your speech. This will help you structure your message so it is clear and easy to understand for your audience.

Say less

The moment you begin speaking, you are providing evidence by which a listener will judge you. The longer you speak, the higher the odds become that you will misspeak, go on too long, or lose your audience's attention. Avoid rambling. Less is more when answering a question, so keep your response tight and specific.

ASKING EFFECTIVE QUESTIONS

Effective questioning is fundamental to successful communication. As novelist Thomas Berger once said, "The art and science of asking questions is the source of all knowledge."[22] Asking effective questions, whether in a meeting, during a presentation, or in a one-on-one conversation, is an essential tool—not only to learn new information but also to challenge, stimulate, and engage others. Asking questions helps us grow, solve problems more effectively, and develop better decision-making

A prudent question is one half of wisdom.

—FRANCIS BACON

processes. Think about how much of your day is spent asking questions of others: your spouse, your children, your neighbor, your boss, etc.

While asking thoughtful questions may seem like a simple task, it is perhaps one of the most powerful tools we possess in our communication toolbox. Questioning can assist a group in working with more clarity and purpose toward a common goal. Effective questions should be meaningful and easily understandable for a listener and should aid the questioner in the pursuit of their given objective. When asking questions to which you seek a specific answer, it is helpful to direct the question to a specific person. If you ask your question to a crowd, you run the risk of no one speaking up and you could end up standing there during a long, uncomfortable silence. There are many benefits to asking questions effectively, such as uncovering needs, clarifying information, solving problems, building rapport, and diffusing conflict.

When it comes to asking questions, there are three types of questions that can be used to elicit information from others:

Convergent questions (*closed-ended questions*) can be answered with a simple yes or no or a specific bit of information. Convergent questions generally have only one correct or acceptable answer. They can be used to get a clear response or bit of information very quickly. Convergent questions are often useful when checking comprehension or when confirming alignment. "Where is your office located?" "Can you have this project completed in three weeks?" and "How large is your staff?" are all examples of convergent questions.

Divergent questions (*open-ended questions*) are exploratory questions that can have more than one possible answer and are designed to elicit expanded thinking or reveal information or insight from the person answering. Examples of divergent questions would include, "How do you think we can finish this project by the deadline?" "What do you see as our biggest challenges for the upcoming sales kickoff?" and "Tell me about yourself."

Rhetorical questions are questions that are asked to make a point rather than elicit an answer. No verbal response from the listener is required. Rhetorical questions can be used to spark the interest of a listener by requesting that they find personal relevance in an idea or a statement. Studies have found that people can be more easily persuaded when arguments are presented in a rhetorical manner.[23] Why? Because by asking the questions rhetorically, you force the other party to relate your arguments directly to their lives and circumstances, making it personal. Examples might include, "Who wouldn't prefer working less hours for more money?" "Are you kidding me?" and "Do you want to succeed at this job or not?"

To ask questions effectively during a meeting or presentation, follow these guidelines:

Organize your thoughts before asking the question
Take a moment to be clear about exactly what information you are looking for before putting a question forward.

Keep questions topic-related

Make sure your question raises the visibility of the concept or information you are discussing.

Make questions as specific as possible

Questions that are vague or too general may not elicit the information you seek. Be direct with what you are asking.

Keep questions concise

The longer or more detailed your question, the harder it will be to follow, so be succinct. Stop after the question mark and resist the urge to ramble on. Focus your attention on the other person and the answer they are about to provide you.

Clearly articulate your question

Be clear, both with articulation as well as your phrasing and word choices when asking questions, to avoid confusion or misinterpretation.

DELIVERING FEEDBACK EFFECTIVELY

Much of our communication during a given workday involves the providing of feedback or opinions to others—be it on a phone call, in a performance review or during a meeting with a client. Feedback is critical to development. Negative (or constructive) feedback allows a person the opportunity to grow, while positive feedback reinforces good habits and results. As discussed in previous chapters, communication is never simply about the exchange of information, it is also about the actions and emotions you want to elicit in your listener as a result of them hearing your message. Being able to deliver feedback to someone in a one-to-one conversation can help clarify meaning, align goals, and deepen trust. According to an article in *Forbes*, 9 out of 10 managers avoid giving constructive feedback to their employees for fear of the employee's reaction. According to the article's author Mark Murphy, "Only 29 percent of employees say they 'always' know whether their performance is where it should be, while 39 percent of employees said if given constructive feedback regularly, they'd take it well, even parsing it to figure out where exactly things went awry."[24] Feedback is useful for both the person receiving it as well as the person sharing it and both contribute to the development of the relationship and growth of the organization as a whole. Remember, providing a genuine compliment or giving credit to a peer or coworker for a job well done doesn't cost you anything. Yet it will make the person receiving it feel better and it will make you feel better for providing it.

Criticism may not be agreeable, but it is necessary. It fulfills the same function as pain in the human body. It calls attention to the development of an unhealthy state of things.

—WINSTON CHURCHILL

Whenever providing feedback or delivering a performance review, it is important that you and the other person have a mutual purpose and an understanding that you are both working toward a common goal. This sharing of feeling is called *mutuality*. Mutuality will create trust and empathy and will help establish a healthy climate for discussion and improvement. Both parties must care about the interests of the other person, not just their own. Communication often fails because people jump to the worst possible conclusion about another person without considering the other person's circumstances or point of view. According to psychologist Judith V. Jordan, the main channel for mutuality is *empathic attunement*, the ability to comprehend the momentary psychological state of another person.[25] "It is a process during which one's self-boundaries undergo momentary alteration," said Jordan, "Which in itself allows the possibility for change in the self. Empathy . . . always contains the opportunity for mutual growth and impact."[26]

Here are some guidelines when delivering feedback:

State feedback clearly and absolutely
Keep your feedback concise to avoid confusion or misinterpretation. Being assertive with your delivery when providing feedback is important so that the person receiving it understands your points are not up for debate. New research out of Brigham Young University found that when it comes to receiving criticism or bad news, most people actually prefer directness, candor, and very little, if any,

small talk or buffer.[27] Focus on clarity and directness and get to the heart of the discussion as quickly as possible.

Ensure the feedback is timely

For feedback to be effective, it should be delivered in a manner that allows the other person adequate time to take in the information and make the necessary adjustments and improvements. Don't wait until it is too late to provide the criticism or feedback.

Monitor intention cues

As you deliver feedback to a worker, maintain eye contact and stay attuned to their body language in the moment. Adjust your approach if you notice the other person displaying discomfort or physically closing themselves off. Intention cues such as crossed arms, avoiding eye contact, or shaking their head signal that the message you are putting forward is not being received or accepted.

Show empathy and concern

Because criticism of our work involves pride and ego, it can be difficult to hear. Think about how you might feel or react to hearing the feedback you will deliver and make sure your delivery communicates mutuality. Make the feedback about the person's performance or abilities and not about their personality or character. Use techniques such as summarizing and paraphrasing to indicate you are listening closely to what they have to say.

Anticipate comments and questions

Once feedback is delivered it is common for the person receiving it to have questions. Be open to them and prepared to clarify information or explain how decisions were made. Allow the other person to share their thoughts or feelings and resist the urge to interrupt them as they speak.

Offer support and guidance

Because feedback is meant to improve performance, it is important to suggest an action plan for the person receiving criticism so that their efforts and improvements can be tracked and assessed. Let them know they can count on you for support and guidance as they embark on a path forward.

RECEIVING FEEDBACK EFFECTIVELY

Sheryl Sandberg recently shared some of the important lessons she learned during her time as an executive at Facebook and Google. During the interview, she was asked: "What's the number one thing you look for in someone who can scale with a company?" Her reply: "Someone who takes feedback well."[28] Just as it is important for someone in the business arena to be able to provide honest feedback, we also need to be comfortable receiving feedback from a boss or coworker. As any effective leader knows, for growth and learning to take place there has to be a willingness on the part of those around you to accept feedback and criticism as necessary tools for improvement. Betsy Sanders, former senior vice president and general manager of Nordstrom, gives this advice, "To learn through listening, practice it naively and actively. Naively means that you listen openly, ready to learn something, as opposed to listening defensively, ready to rebut. Listening actively means you acknowledge what you heard and act accordingly."[29] Hearing criticism is not always easy, as our value and status within an organization become intertwined with our work, therefore any criticism of our performance can be seen as a personal judgment or threat to our ego. Says Joe Navarro, nonverbal communication specialist and former FBI agent. "The minute we begin to sense that something is going to hurt us, someone is going to punish us . . . we begin to tighten down."[30] If you approach feedback or new information from a place of ego or fear, the opportunity for growth diminishes. Learning is a process that never ends. Receiving feedback in an effective manner involves receptivity, openness, and a level of self-awareness on the part of the person receiving it. As Greg Hicks observes in *Leader-Shock*, "When we see feedback as negative, or give all our power to the person giving the feedback, we set ourselves up for a long, hard fall. Our intention should be to see feedback as nothing more than new information; never as an attack."[31]

Perfection is not attainable, but if we chase perfection we can catch excellence.

—VINCE LOMBARDI

Another way to respond to critical feedback is to actively lean in to it. Seek it out. Accept the fact that no one is perfect and we all have areas to develop. According to UCLA neuroscientist Alex Korb, having a constant "perfection only" attitude or mindset can often be counterproductive: "Trying for the best, instead of good enough, brings too much emotional ventromedial prefrontal activity into the decision-making process. In contrast, recognizing that good enough is good enough activates more dorsolateral prefrontal areas, which helps you feel more in control . . . making decisions includes creating intentions and setting goals . . . finding solutions to your problems and calming the limbic system."[32]

When receiving feedback from a boss or superior, follow these guidelines:

Keep an open mind

Start by remembering the benefit of getting feedback: this is for you, to help you grow and develop. The critical information you are about to hear is for your benefit. No one is perfect and everyone has areas where they can continue to refine and improve.

Listen to understand

Try to listen to the information without any preconceived biases or prejudice. While the person provides the feedback, write down any specific points they make so you can capture the information to be able to consider it later.

Don't become defensive

The feedback or criticism you are receiving is not a reflection of who you are as a person. While it is sometimes difficult to hear criticism of your abilities or your performance, don't take it personally. Remind yourself that being open to the process of learning and growing is a desirable characteristic for anyone and will help you develop both personally and professionally.

Check your ego

All of us want to be accepted and appreciated. Think about how this feedback and criticism is going to make you smarter, better, or more productive. Don't dismiss the feedback outright as unfair or unjustified. Don't let your pride or emotions get in the way of progress and growth.

Accept the feedback graciously
This can be challenging but it is a great skill to possess. Respond respectfully as though the feedback comes from a place of gratitude. Be courteous and listen actively. Thank them for their thoughts and their candor and let them know you will consider what they had to say. Ask them if they are available for any follow-up conversations if you require clarification on any specific feedback provided.

Carefully evaluate criticism
As you listen, resist the urge to immediately disagree or interrupt as it will make you seem impatient or defensive. Try to put yourself in the speaker's position and imagine how they feel having to provide this feedback. Hear them out and give them a chance to finish before you speak.

Look for lessons
When receiving constructive criticism or feedback, receptivity is key. Be truly open to what the other person has to say and think about how you can use that information for improvement. Every interaction you have with your peers, clients, or a boss provides an opportunity to learn something about yourself or the other person.

Ask questions to understand feedback
Once the feedback has been given, ask questions of the other person for clarification. Make sure you have a clear and complete understanding of the feedback provided as well as the spirit and manner in which it was intended. This will help to avoid confusion.

Take time to process the information
Once you have received the feedback, it is helpful to take some time to think about it before developing next steps. Share the feedback with a spouse or friend to get their thoughts. Sleep on it for a night. Take time to acknowledge your feelings and internal

dialogue to help you more effectively consider and implement a plan to move forward.

Develop an integration plan

Once you've had a chance to digest and consider the feedback, decide how to implement changes. What steps can you take immediately to develop and grow? What steps might be more long term and how can you set a process in motion for that? Write down an action plan and share it with the person who provided you with the initial feedback or criticism to get their thoughts or suggestions.

Blueprint to Bullseye—Chapter 8

Preparation Guide for Providing Feedback

1. What are the expectations of the person who will be receiving the feedback?

2. What strengths does this person demonstrate with regard to the quality, quantity, and timeliness of their work? (Provide three examples.)

3. What are the areas of development for this person with regard to the quality, quantity, and timeliness of their work? (Provide three examples.)

4. What is your objective at the end of this meeting—what actions or attitudes will you suggest this person could adopt while moving forward?

5. What intentions can help you achieve that objective (reassure, motivate, inspire, persuade, challenge, involve)?

6. What questions might this person ask after receiving your feedback? How will they likely react to what you have to say, and what emotions might they experience?

7. What type of action plan can you suggest that will help this person improve their performance? How can you support them and how do you plan to track and assess progress?

Creating A Master Introduction and Master Closing

Creating a Master Introduction and Master Closing when delivering feedback will help you frame your message by clearly establishing the topic of the meeting, why it's being discussed, and what the path forward looks like for all parties involved. A Master Introduction and Master Closing should each last no longer than 30–60 seconds and should include the following elements.

Master Introduction
1. Greeting
2. Topic of the conversation
3. Purpose or benefit
4. Goal at the end

Master Closing
1. Summarizing of conversation topics
2. Restating of the goal
3. Next steps
4. Thank you

CHAPTER 9

Run Killer Meetings
Facilitating Like a Pro to Get Results

Individually, we are one drop. Together, we are an ocean.
—Ryunosuke Satoro

M eetings are a fact of life and an essential part of doing business and collaborating in the corporate arena. When they are run effectively, meetings can foster relationships, solve problems, and develop stronger teams. Meetings, both good ones and bad, can actually affect the level of an employee's happiness. One study out of the University of North Carolina showed that the feelings a worker had about the meetings they attended at their company had a direct correlation to the general satisfaction or dissatisfaction they felt about their job.[1] Those working in the corporate arena are attending more and more meetings. Research shows that meetings have increased in length and frequency over the past 50 years, with executives now spending an average of nearly 23 hours a week in them, up from less than 10 hours in the 1960s.[2] And because so many of the meetings people attend are poorly run or unnecessary, they often end up undermining effective communication and collaboration instead of improving them.

One survey from Microsoft found that 69 percent of people world-wide (and 71 percent in United States) felt that the meetings at their company were ineffective.[3] Common complaints included: the timing or location of the meeting changing at the last minute, people arriving late or being unprepared, side conversations that distract from the agenda, and action items not being developed. While meetings have a bad rap with people, it is generally the *operation* of the meeting that elicits negative feelings, not the *vehicle* of the meeting. It's not that we object to the meeting itself, it is the frequent disorganization we encounter that makes us feel as if our time is being wasted. In truth, meetings can be very valuable experiences if they are facilitated properly. "Meetings matter because that's where an organization's culture perpetuates itself," says William R. Daniels, a senior consultant who has done extensive research on the subject. "Meetings are how an organization says, 'You are a member,' so if every day we go to boring meetings full of boring people, then we can't help but think that this is a boring company. Bad meetings are a source of negative messages about our company and ourselves."[4] We hate mandatory meetings that go on too long, lack focus, and don't accomplish their objective. An effective facilitator's job is to create value for meeting attendees by guiding them to a successful outcome while utilizing each person's talent and, at the same time, honoring their time.

A meeting is a formal or informal gathering of people for the sole purpose of achieving a common goal through the sharing of infor-mation or debating of issues. Meetings can take place in person, over the phone or via video conferencing. According to a recent study, around 25 million meetings are conducted each day in the United States alone—around 3 billion meetings per year.[5] A 2014 article in the *Harvard Business Review* found that senior executives devote more than two full days every week to meetings involving three or more coworkers and 15 percent of an organization's time is spent in meetings—a percentage that has gradually increased every year since 2008.[6] The bad news is that much of this time spent in meetings is unproductive. Studies have found that more than half of senior leaders surveyed rated the meetings they attended at their company

as "ineffective" or "very ineffective."[7] And the price of these
poorly run meetings is steep,
costing U.S. companies around
$37 billion a year.[8] Ineffective
meetings are not only a waste
of time and resources, they
also contribute to "productivity
drain" for a team or organiza-

Value is not intrinsic, it is not in things. It is within us; it is the way in which a man reacts to the conditions of his environment . . . how they act.

—LUDWIG VON MISES

tion. Humorist Dave Barry once wrote, "If you had to identify, in one word, the reason why the human race has not achieved, and never will achieve its full potential, that word would be 'meetings.' "[9] In this chapter, we will detail ways to plan and execute a meeting that honors people's time and gets results. While cultural norms for meetings vary among industries and countries, having a specific meeting process in place will enable an organization to accomplish its goals in a more positive and collaborative way.

Every leader has different philosophies about how meetings should be run. For example, if you work for Amazon, it is helpful to be comfortable with conflict.[10] CEO Jeff Bezos encourages his meeting attendees to respectfully challenge any decision being made, no matter how difficult or exhausting it may be to do so. Bezos doesn't believe in compromising or agreeing for the sake of social cohesion. But when a decision is eventually made, he expects the entire organization to get behind it and offer their support. Bezos is not a fan of PowerPoint presentations and instead encourages his employees to submit their ideas in the form of four-to-six page memos. In the opening minutes of an Amazon meeting, Bezos and his team conduct what he calls "silent starts"—where everyone in attendance simply reads through the memos in silence. "For new employees, it's a strange initial experience," says Bezos. "They're just not accustomed to sitting silently in a room and doing study hall with a bunch of executives."[11] For Bezos, these silent starts serve a dual purpose: they assure undivided attention and help prepare all meeting attendees for the discussion that will follow. And when it comes to meeting size, Bezos believes that the more people who attend a meeting, the less will get accomplished. Because of this, he has implemented what he calls the "Two Pizza Rule" at Amazon, meaning no meeting should ever take place where two pizzas couldn't feed the entire group.[12]

Steve Jobs, known to prefer simplicity and minimalism in the design of his products, also liked these qualities in his meetings at Apple. He hated when meetings were overattended, believing that too many minds in the room complicated the decision-making process. Once, when Jobs was in a weekly meeting with Apple's ad agency, he saw someone in the room who didn't regularly attend, and politely asked her to leave, saying, "I don't think we need you in this meeting."[13]

Employees of Elon Musk, the visionary founder of Tesla and SpaceX, learned quickly that they needed to have a clear grasp of the topics included on a meeting agenda. Said one SpaceX employee, "When we met with Elon, we were prepared. Because if you weren't, he'd let you know it. If he asked a reasonable follow-up question and you weren't prepared with an answer, well, good luck."[14] During one meeting at SpaceX, Musk noticed a female attendee who had not contributed any ideas or opinions. "You haven't said anything," remarked Musk, confronting her in front of the entire group. "Why are you in here?"[15] Though this exchange may have been seen as rude, it also made Musk's point that meetings are about action and decision-making. And if your presence in the meeting is not assisting in those two aims, your time would most likely be better spent doing other things.

Jeremy Stoppelman, CEO of the online advertising site Yelp, has a different approach to meetings. He likes to meet individually with each of his direct reports on a weekly basis to better understand each worker's current goals and challenges. "Sometimes I feel like the company's psychiatrist," said Stoppelman. "But I do feel like listening to people and hearing about their problems (personal and professional) cleans out the cobwebs and keeps the organization humming."[16]

Whatever protocols you institute for meetings at your company, creating a process to facilitate effective meetings can provide many benefits. But it also requires an understanding of why meetings are important, how different types of meetings have different purposes and how proper preparation, execution, and follow-up will ensure that meetings at your organization are a productive use of people's time. As a general rule, you should facilitate only the type of meeting you would want to attend yourself. According to a recent study, middle managers spend up to 35 percent of their time in meetings and senior level executives spend up to 50 percent.[17] Is all of this time spent in meetings productive? When asked in one study if workers leave meetings with a clear understanding of the next action item, 46 percent of participants answered: "some of the time," "rarely," or "never."[18] Not exactly an encouraging response. Meetings in the workplace should never be about talking; they should be about creating *meeting assets* in the form of decisions, action items or consensus. A meeting should provide a clear benefit to attendees and a clear understanding of their role in the meeting as well as their purpose for being there. We've all been to a meeting that meandered from one topic to the next without a clear point. Experiences such as these are why organizational expert Thomas Kayser once described a meeting as, "An interaction where the unwilling, selected from the uninformed, led by the unsuitable, to discuss the unnecessary, are required to write a report about the unimportant."[19] Too many times meetings are just excuses to gather and talk rather than accomplishing a specific objective that needs to be achieved. Meetings should be about strategies being considered, action items being implemented, and decisions being made. They should be focused and clear, with active participation and accountability expected from all in attendance. Research shows that when employees feel accountable for the work that they do, they are more likely to contribute to solving problems and achieving goals for the benefit of the organization.[20] One reason meetings don't create assets and don't accomplish their objective is the result of a phenomenon called *diffusion of responsibility,* whereby a person is less likely to take responsibility for action or inaction when others are present.

Good meetings should follow an agenda and strive for conclusion. This means turning agenda items into actions for which people will be held accountable. Good meetings should be viewed as an organizational tool that can solve problems and align teams. Done well, meetings can

There is nothing quite so useless, as doing with great efficiency, something that should not be done at all.

—PETER DRUCKER

save time and drive engagement, beginning with an objective that can be clearly stated and that everyone can organize around. If you are a leader and have the authority to convene and facilitate a meeting, you owe it to your team and organization to be prepared for it. Leading a diverse team also means that you will have many different personalities and different people in your meetings. Vanessa Redgrave, a member of the legendary acting dynasty, once said the following about a theatre audience that could just as easily apply to a group of meeting attendees, "We all come . . . with baggage. The baggage of our daily lives, the baggage of our problems, the baggage of our tragedies, the baggage of being tired."[21] This is one more reason to stay attuned to the mood and energy of a room and adjust your delivery as needed. Members of a team also have distinct viewpoints and come to a meeting with individual needs and expectations. As a facilitator, it is your job to make sure the needs of all stakeholders in a meeting are being met and everyone is working toward a common goal.

Research shows that as much as one-third to one-half of the U.S. population identify themselves as introverted.[22] If any of your attendees are introverted, you will need to facilitate your meetings in a different way than you would if the group consisted only of people who are more outgoing or extroverted. An introverted employee may struggle in a meeting that is filled with bigger personalities. If you notice participants who are not being heard, gently encourage them to share their thoughts or views on the subject being discussed. You may also want to wait until the meeting is over to solicit feedback from introverted team members, and then do so in private. Many employees, even those who do not necessarily consider themselves introverted, are hesitant to publicly challenge or disagree with others in a meeting. But good meeting facilitators understand that a certain amount of creative conflict is healthy within a team. Challenging the thoughts and ideas of others in a constructive way not only benefits the person issuing the challenge, it can also create a more collaborative environment for the team as a whole.

Poorly run meetings hurt morale, reduce employee engagement, and waste corporate resources. Andy Grove, the former chief executive at the microchip giant Intel, once wrote: "Just as you would not permit an employee to steal a piece of office furniture, you should not let anyone walk away with the time of his fellow managers."[23] In their book *Rework*, Jason Fried and David Heinemeier Hansson detail the consequences of poorly run meetings, writing: "When you think about it, the true cost of meetings is staggering. Let's say you're going to schedule a meeting that lasts one hour, and you invite 10 people to attend. That's actually a 10-hour meeting, not a 1-hour meeting. You're trading 10 hours of productivity for 1 hour of meeting time. And it's probably more like 15 hours, because there are mental switching costs that come with stopping what you are doing, going somewhere else to meet, and then resuming what you were doing beforehand."[24]

Because the average worker's week is filled with tasks and obligations that need to be met, every hour they spend trapped in an unproductive meeting is one less hour they have to complete their work. Because all meetings have opportunity costs, good leaders keep their meetings short and focused. And just because a meeting is scheduled for an hour doesn't mean you can't end early and let people get back to their other work. There is an adage called *Parkinson's Law* that says work will always expand to fill the time available for its completion.[25] In other words, if you schedule a meeting for an hour, that meeting will most likely fill up that entire hour, whether that amount of time is needed or not. By scheduling that same meeting for only *half* an hour, you create an urgency to keep things moving and get through the agenda in a shorter amount of time. Too often we overestimate the time needed for meetings and end up losing hours of productivity in the process. By shortening your meetings, you will spend your time more efficiently and people will feel more productive as a result.

One study found that 47 percent of people listed "too many meetings" as the number-one time-waster at work.[26] Meetings that are scheduled with no other purpose than to rehash content that was discussed at previous meetings will make people feel like their time is not being well spent. Including too many people in a meeting is also something that should be avoided. The larger the meeting, the less accountable meeting attendees will feel toward making contributions of ideas or effort. Researchers call this *social loafing*. According to Andrew Carton of the University of Pennsylvania's Wharton School, another reason to keep your meeting size small is that victims of meeting bloat are more likely to blame others for their problems versus offering solutions themselves.[27] Other elements that commonly derail a productive meeting include disruptive behaviors, fatigued attendees, lack of involvement, and unclear meeting objectives.

Most people attending meetings in the modern work environment struggle to be fully present and often face numerous distractions. One study found that 92 percent of people admitted to multitasking during work meetings.[28] Actors improvising a scene know that being fully present in the moment is the key to effective collaboration. When one actor is not present and focused on his fellow actor—when he is "soloing"—the forward motion of a scene gets stopped cold. The same principle holds true for a team gathered for a brainstorming or problem-solving meeting. If meeting attendees are not present and engaged with the agenda and their fellow attendees, the group could miss out on an opportunity to discover a workable solution or new idea. Business communication requires being present, listening to those around you and reacting in the moment. While it can be uncomfortable or intimidating to put forward a suggestion in a meeting, a good meeting leader will create an environment where all attendees feel safe to share their opinions and ideas.

Effective leaders are also able to adjust in the moment to circumstances when a change of course is necessary, such as when a new idea emerges or a sudden conflict arises that needs to be addressed. "Yes, and . . ." is a rule-of-thumb response in improvisation that suggests an improviser in a scene should accept what another participant has stated and then expand on that line of thinking. For example, one actor may say, "Boy, it is really cold out today!" and the other person onstage may respond, "Yes, and I forgot my winter coat!" Drawing upon this classic tenet of improvisation and embracing the spirit of "Yes, and . . . ," meeting attendees can let ideas fly without anxiety or the fear of judgment. By creating this open and imaginative

Without data you're just another person with an opinion.

—W. EDWARDS DEMING

space, people will feel free to contribute ideas, confident that their suggestions won't simply be dismissed without consideration. On the stage, as in the boardroom, saying no kills collaboration and shuts down meaningful dialogue. Communicating in the spirit of "Yes, and . . ." allows meeting attendees to listen to each other and suspend judgment by creating a safe space for critical thinking.

One of the challenges of the current work environment is that people attend a lot of meetings, sometimes one right after the other. The danger of scheduling back-to-back meetings means that you can carry the emotions of one meeting into the following meeting without giving yourself a chance to reset and begin the next meeting from a calm and neutral place. Just like a group of actors gathering to rehearse a play, coworkers assembling for a meeting should enter the meeting prepared and ready to offer up their ideas and energy. As Stanislavski advised, "Never come into the theatre with mud on your feet. Leave your dust and dirt outside. Check your little worries, squabbles, petty difficulties . . . outside . . . all the things that . . . draw your attention away."[29] The "mud" that Stanislavski warns us about is anything—stress, personality clashes, or other distractions—that hinders a group's ability to accomplish their objective. Whether you are a meeting leader or a meeting attendee, you should approach every meeting from a focused starting place. Imagine what happens if you have a heated argument with a coworker and then head straight into a meeting with a client to negotiate pricing for an upcoming project. Because your heart is still racing and your mind is still replaying the previous exchange, there is a good chance your emotions may hinder your ability to think clearly and make sound decisions. One way to avoid this happening is to schedule breaks between your back-to-back meetings to give yourself some breathing room to let your emotions settle before proceeding to your next meeting.

Another reason to keep meetings concise and focused is that workers in the modern business environment have limited attention spans. Research by the National Science Foundation suggests that the average person can experience up to 50,000 thoughts every day, so it is no wonder the pressures and stress of our day-to-day responsibilities have affected our ability to listen and focus.[30] One study in the United Kingdom found that the average person's attention span has fallen to just 5 minutes, down from 12 minutes 10 years prior.[31] And modern distractions such as text messages and various other alerts don't help. Research conducted by the University of California at Irvine found that the average worker is interrupted or switches tasks every three minutes and five seconds.[32] And these interruptions, whether they are phone calls, e-mails, or in-person visits, cause the worker to take an average of 25 minutes to get back to their original task.[33] Distractions and interruptions also affect the quality of work that takes place. Researchers at Michigan State found that interruptions of less than 3 seconds doubled the rate of errors on a task.[34]

As previously established, if attendees at your meeting appear bored or disengaged with the topics being discussed, it is up to you to engage them. Start by reading the body language of those in attendance if you want to know how your meeting is going. Are attendees enthusiastically contributing ideas or are they quiet and hesitant? Do they seem engaged or do they look bored or disinterested? Conversely, if your boss or other senior leader is running the meeting, be conscious of the nonverbal cues you are communicating as an attendee. Slouching, dozing off, or checking your phone sends a negative message about your level of engagement and one your boss is unlikely to appreciate. An extreme example of this occurred in 2016 when a government official named Kim Yong-Jin accidentally dozed off during a meeting being run by North Korean leader Kim Jong-un. Un was reportedly so furious at the display of disrespect that he had the man executed by firing squad for the offense.[35]

Power is a tool, influence is a skill; one is a fist, the other a fingertip.

—NANCY GIBBS

Because of space constraints or audience size, meetings often occur in less formal settings such as boardrooms, conference rooms, or offices. When facilitating while seated at a table, body language is still important. It is easy to let all of your energy drain into your chair instead of focusing it outward toward the person you are addressing. Make sure your voice and body language are supporting your intentions when speaking and avoid slumping in your chair as this may make you appear overly casual or too relaxed. Continue to use expressive gestures to underscore or support the points you are trying to make, but since your audience is closer, gestures can be smaller in size. Keep your eyes up and try not to look down at the table while speaking. Connect with every person at the table, including the people sitting on either side of you. Keep both feet firmly on the floor to help you stay grounded and limit extraneous movement such as shifting and fidgeting. Rest both hands on the table, either folded or near each other when you are not using them and be careful not to play with objects such as rings, pens, or paper clips as this can be distracting.

FIVE DIFFERENT TYPES OF MEETINGS

There are different types of meetings that leaders may be required to facilitate as part of their role within an organization: *social, brainstorming, informational, problem-solving,* and *ceremonial.* While most meetings will clearly fall into one of these five categories, it is possible for a meeting to be a blend of two or more types. And just as with any communication, returning to the concepts of intention and objective will help you better understand what you want your meeting to accomplish and also how to best accomplish it.

Here are the five types of meetings:

Social meetings are generally informal in nature and less structured than other types of meetings. The purpose of a social meeting is simply to help maintain a relationship or build rapport with a client or associate. While more casual in nature, social meetings still serve a very important purpose and many deals have been initiated or solidified over a cup of coffee or glass of wine. Examples might include: taking your team out for a drink to celebrate the completion of a project or meeting with a former client over coffee to attempt to win back their business.

Brainstorming meetings are designed to produce as many ideas or options as possible, generated by the group present, to solve a problem or complete a task. Examples might include: gathering the team to discuss the new company logo, talking to senior leadership about ways to boost profit margins, or meeting with fellow human resource managers to come up with ways to promote and implement an upcoming change in company protocol.

To run a good brainstorming meeting, follow these five steps:

1. Define your overall objective for the meeting
2. Create an informal environment and a "no-criticism" rule
3. Keep number of participants low
4. Choose a leader to run it
5. Capture ideas to consider and record them in full view

Participants in a brainstorming session are encouraged to suggest any ideas that come to their mind, no matter how odd or unrealistic they may seem. Creativity should be encouraged and the group should cast a wide net. People should also feel comfortable building upon the comments of others—suggesting improvements or using previous contributions as springboards for new ideas. Once all possible suggestions have been recorded, evaluate each one and decide which will provide the best solution. An important aspect of a good brainstorming session is to postpone all criticism and judgment until all ideas have been collected.

Informational meetings can involve two people or two thousand or more. The main purpose of an informational meeting is to share information (data, insight, or facts) or provide a status update across a team to make sure there is understanding and alignment. Examples might include: a town hall meeting, a sales presentation, or a training session. Note: when people complain about meetings being a waste of time, it is generally an unnecessary informational meeting that is the culprit. Don't schedule an informational meeting if the same information can just as easily be covered in an e-mail or phone call.

Problem-solving meetings are usually intended to tackle a situation or issue that needs to be addressed quickly or urgently. There may be two or more opposing opinions about how to address the issue and the problem-solving meeting is meant as a forum to discuss both the problem and the merits of the various solutions suggested by meeting attendees. The objective is then to arrive at a consensus and the best plan of action to move forward.

Ceremonial meetings can involve two to twenty thousand people or more. In a ceremonial meeting, the purpose is to recognize or honor a person or group of people for their accomplishments and achievements. Because of this, they are often more formal affairs. Examples might include: an awards banquet, a dinner honoring veterans for their military service, or a televised ceremony like the ESPY awards or Oscars.

PART ONE: PRE-MEETING PREPARATION

Good meetings don't just happen; they require careful planning and forethought. The preparation portion of successful facilitation is the most time consuming but, done properly, will allow your meeting to run like a well-oiled machine. One big mistake people make when planning a meeting is deciding on agenda items before they have clearly defined the objective for the meeting. Your objective should dictate your agenda items, not the other way around.

As you begin planning your next meeting, ask yourself these questions:

- *What objective am I trying to accomplish with this meeting?*
- *Why is it important for this to be achieved?*
- *Who do I need in the meeting for it to be successful?*
- *How much time do I need with these attendees to accomplish this objective?*

Once you have taken the time to answer the questions above, here are the steps to focus on during the remainder of your preparation:

Define your objective

Decide what specific goals and objectives you need to accomplish with this meeting. What will a successful meeting look like? This will also help define whether or not you have achieved your meeting objectives once the meeting is over. Without a clearly defined target you can't be sure that all meeting attendees are pointed in the same direction. Try to create urgency for your meeting by developing emotionally driven content that benefits the team and serves your organization's overall mission or purpose.

Invite carefully

Decide which team members need to attend this particular meeting and what their specific roles will be. Don't invite people who will not directly benefit from attending the meeting. Overattendance is just as bad as underattendance. For people whose attendance is not essential to achieving the meeting's objectives, their time could be better spent back at their office getting other work done. Another consequence of "meeting bloat" is a reduction in motivation and effort that occurs when individuals work collectively compared to when they work individually (diffusion of responsibility, which we mentioned previously). Meetings that are underattended are ineffective because without key stakeholders, decisions cannot be made. Optimizing your attendance will not only make your meeting more productive, it will honor the time of nonessential attendees whose time can be better spent doing other things.

Consider the location

The designated meeting site is a crucial decision that can play directly into the success or failure of your meeting. Ask yourself if the space you have chosen will meet the requirements for the participants involved. A room that is too small may make people feel uncomfortable or cramped. A room that is too big may seem cavernous and make it harder for people to connect or be heard. Is the location easily accessible to people or is it out of the way? Is the equipment provided adequate for the meeting?

Create an agenda

It is helpful to establish a clear agenda before the meeting takes place to help keep things flowing. It can serve as a roadmap to make sure everyone remains on the same page. In his *New York Times* article titled "How to Run a More Effective Meeting," Adam Bryant wrote that a meeting agenda "provides a compass for the conversation"[36] and can help keep a meeting on track (or get it back on track) if things begin to stray off course. A good agenda should have a title that provides a headline for the meeting itself and include such elements as: a list of the meeting attendees, the location and time of the meeting, the meeting duration (start and stop time), as well as a brief statement detailing the meeting's overall objectives.

Adjust room set-up

Try to get into the actual meeting space ahead of the actual meeting. If the room is configured in a way that will not allow for your meeting participants to be comfortable and able to communicate effectively, make adjustments. Arrange the chairs and tables in a way that everyone can clearly see the facilitator and any visual aids that may be shown. Also, it is important to make sure that the seating arrangement distinguishes facilitators from attendees, participants from nonparticipants. If it is a group comprised of people who do not know each other, it can be helpful to distribute name badges.

Maximize turnout

Poor attendance can torpedo a promising meeting at the very last moment. It is not enough to simply invite people and hope they show up. Reminders are essential as you get closer to the actual meeting day and time. Calls, e-mails, written reminders, and public announcements are all good ways to make sure turnout is maximized. Keep track of the percentage of people who actually show up to help calculate future turnout.

Prepare your materials

Make sure you have all the necessary materials for the meeting and are ready to distribute them. The care you take in making your meeting handouts look professional becomes a reflection on the quality of the meeting itself. If helpful, distribute meeting materials in advance so participants have a chance to review them prior to the meeting. Make sure you have a contingency plan in case the required materials don't arrive on time. And when it comes to visual aids or slides, remember, these are merely visual "aids." Don't overwhelm your audience with too many pages of notes or overly complicated slides.

PART TWO: FACILITATING THE ACTUAL MEETING

Now that all of the preparation has been done, it's time to facilitate the actual meeting. Meetings should be informative, forward moving and efficient. And above all, they should be enjoyable. Some tips to facilitate a successful meeting include:

Start the meeting promptly

According to studies from the University of North Carolina at Charlotte, 37 percent of meetings in the corporate arena start late, on average by 15 minutes.[37] People get frustrated when they show up on time and have to wait for those who show up late. As a leader within your organization, you have the ability to establish informal rules about how meetings happen. Employees take their cues from leadership so if the meetings you run always start late or bleed over past the designated ending time, they are sent a signal that this is acceptable. Terry Lundgren, the chairman of Macy's enforces a strict policy of on-time meetings within his organization. "If the meeting is at 8, you're not here at 8:01, you're here at 8, because the meeting's going to start at 8," he said. "Busy people that can't get off the last phone call to get there, [need to] discipline themselves to be there on time."[38]

Kick it off with energy

The start of your meeting sets the tone for what will follow. Introduce yourself, if necessary, and welcome everyone to the meeting. If there are people who are new or unknown to the group, take the opportunity to introduce them. Thank attendees for their presence to show them you appreciate their time. Clearly establish the agenda and the overall objectives for the meeting with passion, focus, and clarity.

Set ground rules

Ground rules are important tools for a facilitator to utilize in order to keep meetings on track and under control. Since many meetings in recent years have become less formal, ground rules can be adjusted to accommodate your specific situation and environment. Ground rules that can be set include limiting the use of cell phones or e-mail to breaks only, requesting that only one person speaks at a time, expecting active participation from all in attendance, keeping all discussions to agenda items only, and starting and ending the meeting on time. Ground rules are simple to set for your peers and direct reports but they get more complicated to enforce with clients or senior leaders. For peers and subordinates, you can set whatever rules you deem necessary. The best way to set ground rules is to clearly state them at the start of your meeting, explain why following the ground rules will benefit the meeting attendees, and then ask for agreement that the rules will be followed. Once an audience has publicly agreed to specific rules or behavior, they will feel a social pressure within the group to follow them.

One of the biggest meeting distractors is when people bring their cell phones into a meeting. Limiting or eliminating the temptation to check cell phones during meetings is a good idea. According to one study from McCombs School of Business at The

University of Texas, Austin, your ability to think and concentrate is significantly reduced when your phone is within reach—even when it is switched off. According to the study's researchers, "It's not that participants were distracted because they were getting notifications on their phones. The mere presence of their smartphone was enough to reduce their cognitive capacity."[39] Finally, if you set ground rules at the start of a meeting and attendees do follow them (say, by staying off their cell phones), convey your appreciation at the conclusion of the meeting by thanking them for their attention and engagement.

Encourage participation
It is important that you create a comfortable and open environment for people in your meeting right from the start. This will encourage everyone to participate and be actively involved in all discussions and decisions being made. Attendees who show up late, lack focus, or fail to contribute ideas during a meeting hinder the ability of a group to move forward in a productive way. Also, studies show that men tend to talk more and offer more suggestions during meetings, while women are interrupted more frequently.[40] Since you cannot tap your attendees' skills and expertise without full participation from everyone in attendance, encourage less assertive personalities to sit front and center and then bring them into the discussion if their voices are being crowded out.

Stay on track
Try to keep the meeting moving forward by sticking to the agenda established at the start of the meeting. Stay focused. As Winston Churchill once said, "You will never reach your destination if you stop and throw rocks at every dog that barks."[41] One study by a group of research psychologists found that when people switch back and forth between topics or tasks, they lose up to 50 percent of their efficiency and accuracy.[42] The more complex the task—such as a meeting strategy discussion—the more processing will potentially be lost by discussing nonagenda items. If you feel the discussion veering off topic during a meeting, gently guide it back

to the original agenda item. By doing this, you will ensure you start and end your meetings on time.

Seek action

Meetings are about action items and decision-making. If possible, bring closure to a particular subject or issue before moving on to a new one as groups will often spend much more time discussing an item than is actually necessary. Create a system of accountability and define specific, measureable, time-based next steps for attendees so they can be held responsible for them. This may mean further research or additional investigation. Delegate tasks and get confirmation that attendees can and will deliver.

Close strong

As you draw the meeting to a close, check your agenda to make sure all items were addressed. Review what has been covered, including what decisions have been made and what commitments are still outstanding. Thank the attendees for their time and contributions. Privately solicit feedback from any stakeholders willing to provide it regarding the overall effectiveness of the meeting itself.

PART THREE: POST MEETING FOLLOW UP

Once a meeting concludes, a summary of the meeting assets should be made available to all stakeholders. Ideally the meeting summary should be sent within 24–48 hours after a meeting has taken place and should contain information such as: topics that were discussed, decisions that were made, attendees who were present, and action items that were developed. These meeting assets are what generate value for your team or organization. Without capturing assets and making those assets available to stakeholders, a meeting risks being nothing more than a social exercise without a clear purpose. Additionally, by distributing meetings assets, a facilitator can communicate pertinent information to nonessential stakeholders, saving them time and productivity by not requiring them to be in attendance.

Blueprint to Bullseye—Chapter 9

Preparation Guide for Meeting Facilitation

1. What is the overall objective(s) for your meeting?

2. Where will the meeting be held and what are your requirements to facilitate it (audio/visual, handouts, seating size, refreshments, etc.)?

3. Which team members should attend this meeting and why is their attendance required?

4. What is the title of the meeting (think of this as the main idea or theme)?

5. What challenges could you face and what difficult questions might arise?

6. What are the agenda items for the meeting?
   a. Start time

   b. List of attendees

   c. Location of meeting

   d. Topics to be discussed

     e. Objective for the meeting itself

     f. End time

7. Who will take on which roles during the meeting (leader, timekeeper, recorder)?

8. What action items do you hope to generate and assign during the meeting?

9. How will you track progress once action items have been assigned?

Master Introduction and Master Closing

Creating a Master Introduction and Master Closing for your meeting will help you frame your message by clearly establishing the reason for the occasion and the objectives you hope to accomplish. A Master Introduction and Master Closing should each last no longer than 30–60 seconds and should include the following elements.

Master Introduction
1. Name/role/credibility
2. Hook or attention grabber
3. Reason for the meeting
4. Benefit to the audience
5. Goal at the end of the meeting

Master Closing

1. Summary of main points

2. Restating of the benefit to the audience

3. Reintroduce the goal or ask for action

4. Closing hook or challenge

5. Thank-you to audience

CHAPTER 10

Make the Sale

Being Assertive, Influencing Others, and Preparing to Engage

If you want something from an audience,
you give blood to their fantasies.
—MARLON BRANDO

The ability to convince or persuade others and advocate for your ideas is an essential aspect of work and life. For most workers, resources like money, space, and time are scarce, and many times we are forced to influence or convince those higher up than us regarding the value or validity of each request. Think about how many times during an average week you attempt to convince other people to adopt your position, accept your approach, or take a specific action. Whether you are negotiating with your spouse about who is going to be picking up the kids from school, your children about what time they will be home from the dance, your boss about the promotion you are currently seeking, or a client about the pricing for a recent proposal—without the ability to influence, little can be accomplished. As the famous showman P.T. Barnum once put it, "Without promotion, something terrible happens . . . nothing!"[1]

An excellent example of a leader influencing others took place on September 5, 1978, when President Jimmy Carter summoned Egyptian President Anwar Sadat and Israeli Prime Minister Menachem Begin to Camp David to attempt to achieve what Carter's predecessors had failed to accomplish: a Mideast peace agreement. Carter saw the Middle East and the settlement of the conflict between the Israelis and Palestinians as one of the top goals of his presidency—the first peace between Egypt and the Jews in 2,600 years. In November 1977, Carter sensed there was a window of opportunity to move the peace process forward. Deciding to seize the moment, he invited Begin and Sadat to meet at Camp David. Carter knew that securing a peace treaty would not be an easy feat. Both foreign leaders brought with them a distrust of the other as well as other psychological baggage that would need to be overcome. As discussions kicked off, Carter told Begin and Sadat that, if the discussions failed, he would make public his final proposal and then let each of them explain to the public why they had accepted or rejected it.

Our doubts are traitors and cause us to miss the good we oft might win, by fearing to attempt.

—WILLIAM SHAKESPEARE

The negotiations were intense and took place in secret, with limited access for a hungry media that wanted minute-by-minute updates about any progress being made. Said Carter, "'What's going to happen is we'll be here about two or three days, and once Sadat and Begin realize their historic opportunity and once we isolate them from their domestic politics and the press and create the atmosphere for them to rise to this historic occasion, they're going to sit down and work out the principles on which peace will be done, and we'll announce it to the world."[2] Carter worked as a go-between for the discussions and his staff did their best to prevent any leaks that could damage the forward motion of the talks. Carter had a lot riding on the success of the meeting as polls at the time showed that the American public had doubts about his effectiveness as Commander-in-Chief.

But things did not start out well.

According to reports, by the end of the second day of meetings, people could hear Sadat and Begin screaming at each other at the top of their lungs. At one point, Carter had to physically separate the men to prevent them from coming to blows. He also had to block them from leaving the room and abandoning the talks altogether. Three days passed with no progress. Sadat and Begin bickered and argued but Carter was determined to push them to find common ground. He met with the two men independently in an effort to push through the roadblocks that had stalled the talks. But after a week of discussions, negotiations broke down; there seemed to be a stalemate with neither side ceding any ground on the matter. But Carter had a secondary plan in the works, one he had not communicated to either Sadat or Begin.

Carter had made copies of a photograph that had been taken of the three men at Camp David and went to meet privately with Begin in his cabin. Begin was in an angry mood and very unhappy with the direction and substance of the talks. As Carter listened to Begin rant, he took out the copies of photographs and presented them to Begin as a gift for his grandchildren. Carter had even signed each photo: "Love, Jimmy Carter." Holding the photographs, Begin was overcome with emotion as he read off the names of each of his nine grandchildren. Carter told the Israeli leader that he had hoped to write an additional message on each photo once the peace agreement had been made: a message signifying that this photo had been taken at the place where their grandfather and he had made peace. Begin, still looking at the photographs, began to weep. Despite the emotional display from Begin, Carter remained pessimistic that any sort of resolution would be possible. Reluctantly, he decided he would go to Sadat to inform him that the agreement was most likely off. But before he was able to do so, the phone in his cabin rang. It was Begin saying that he would sign the peace deal. Carter's shrewd lobbying efforts and his appeal to the emotions of the Israeli leader had worked. The famous image of Anwar Sadat and Menachem Begin shaking hands during a signing ceremony in front of the White House became an iconic historical moment and one of the highlights of Carter's single term as president. As a result of the agreement being signed, Begin and Sadat shared the 1978 Nobel Peace Prize and many years later Jimmy Carter was awarded the Nobel Peace Prize (in 2002) partly as a result of his efforts in the Camp David accords.

Authors Erwin P. Bettinghaus and Michael J. Cody define persuasion as "a conscious attempt by one individual or group to change the attitudes, beliefs, or behavior of another individual or group of individuals through the transmission of some message."[3] As an influencer, you need to identify the benefit to the customer or stakeholder. Every time we get in front of an audience to convince them to take action or change behavior, we are not only selling our messages, we are selling ourselves as messengers. Tali Sharot, a neuroscientist at the University of London has studied human behavior and the way people make decisions. "Each time we share our opinions and knowledge, it is with the intention of impacting others," says Sharot.[4] We all communicate on a daily basis with the hope of influencing those around us. Every single day, 4 million new blogs are written, 80 million new photos are uploaded onto Instagram, and 616 million new tweets are posted to Twitter.[5] When people share information or experiences with others, their brain center receives a burst of pleasure. This drives us to continue communicating with others because it feels good. It is also a useful feature of our brains because it ensures that knowledge and information get shared with others, thus benefiting society as a whole. And the desire to share our thoughts and opinions with others is quite strong, as it turns out. Research from Harvard University found that people were actually willing to forgo money if it meant that their opinions would be broadcast to others.[6] Whether your objective is to get the job, win the contract, make the sale, or entertain your client, the task of persuasion is on you.

Facts do not cease to exist because they are ignored.

—ALDOUS HUXLEY

As we discussed in previous chapters, our three-step process, known as The Pinnacle Method, starts by understanding the needs and desires of the audience you are trying to influence. Unfortunately, this does not happen automatically. While we may think that data and facts are enough to get people to react the way we want, that is not the case. Even good data, coupled with logical thinking, is not always enough to change someone's point of view. Says Sharot, "The problem with an approach that prioritizes information is that it ignores the core of what makes us human; our motives, our fears, our hopes, our desires, our prior beliefs." As communicators, we often make the mistake of approaching our message through the filter of our own wants, needs, and biases instead of through those of our audience. "If we want to affect the behaviors and beliefs of the person in front of us," advises Sharot. "We need to understand what goes on inside their head [and] reframe the information we provide such that it taps into people's basic motives."[7] Jayne Benjulian, the former speechwriter at Apple agrees: "Of course a speech is about your central concept, what it is you're saying, but it's also who's saying it and who you're speaking to."[8] By framing your message in a way that highlights the benefit for the person you are attempting to influence, you are more likely to elicit the emotional reaction you need to help drive the other party toward the objective you hope to accomplish.

When attempting to persuade someone to buy your product or service, it is important to focus on the benefit it provides to them, not simply its features. Here's the difference: A feature is a statement about what your product or service can do for your customer while the benefit shows the end result. Getting good gas mileage for a car is a feature. The amount of money it will save you is a benefit. Having no calories or sugar is a feature of bottled water. Gaining less weight and feeling and looking better is the benefit. A higher cut for better ankle support is a feature of a hiking boot. Reducing the odds of ankle injuries is the benefit. Keep in mind that in most cases, audiences don't care what your product can do, they only care what your product can do for them.

PREPARATION IS KEY

The more specific and credible the business speaker's message is, the more likely it is their audience or client will believe it. But this takes preparation and focus. Just like a painter must prepare their paints and canvas, just as a coach must prepare a team for the big game, someone who wishes to influence others with his or her message must take the necessary time to prepare. Without preparation, it is much less likely that a speaker's message will hit its mark and accomplish its objective—whether the goal is instituting a policy, detailing a program, or describing a process. The more prepared you are for your presentation or interview, the more comfortable you will be and the easier it will be to relax and focus on the objective you have set for yourself. By knowing your material, your transitions from one point to the next will flow more smoothly and allow you to focus on your audience and their reactions to what you are saying rather than on what you are supposed to say next. Without adequate preparation, your delivery will lack smoothness and certainty. One example of embarrassingly inadequate preparation took place in 2013 with one of the most recognizable brands in history, a debacle that ended up costing this particular company more than $14 billion.

Stephen Curry, the star point guard for the Golden State Warriors, is an international sensation. As a younger athlete, Curry had worn Nike shoes growing up and also as a college player at Davidson. When he was drafted by the Warriors, he signed a sponsorship deal with Nike and was wearing their shoes in 2013 during his breakout 54-point game at Madison Square Garden. Coming off a great season, Nike owned the first opportunity to keep Curry on their roster and extend his sponsorship. "I was with them for years," said Curry, before admitting, "It's kind of a weird process being pitched by the company you're already with." According to *Forbes*, Nike accounted for 95.5 percent of the basketball sneaker market in 2014. They were the undisputed heavyweights in the battle for market share—which perhaps played into the lack of preparation given to their meeting with Curry to re-up his deal. Often, when people get complacent or overconfident, they get sloppy and fail to put in the time needed to ensure proper preparation.

The meeting between Team Curry and the Nike representatives took place at the Oakland Marriott, three levels below Golden State's practice facility. To the surprise of Curry and his team, Nike power broker Lynn Merritt didn't show up for the meeting and instead Nico Harrison, a sports marketing director at the time, ran the meeting. The pitch itself did not begin well, with one Nike rep accidentally addressing Stephen as "Steph-ON." Said Curry's father, Dell, "I heard some people pronounce his name wrong before. I wasn't surprised," but added, "I was surprised that I didn't get a correction."

The presentation by Team Nike only got worse as it went along. A slide was shown that featured Kevin Durant's name instead of Curry's— a result of someone repurposing slides from a previous presentation without taking the time to swap in Curry's name. "I stopped paying attention after that," said Dell. Though Dell and the others presented poker faces while they listened to the rest of the pitch, the lack of detail on the part of the Nike executives showed sloppiness and a lack of respect toward Curry and his team. Team Curry never got a strong indication that Curry would ever be seen as a signature athlete for the shoe giant and, as a result, the decision to leave Nike was in the works. Famously, this is where Under Armour swooped in and snagged the Curry endorsement. Stephen Curry went on to become a two-time NBA MVP with two championship titles to his credit. His relationship with Under Armour paid off handsomely for the athletic gear maker as they saw a 57 percent jump in footwear sales—a whopping total of $677.7 million. Curry has become such an integral part of the Under Armour brand that the shoe company recently agreed to a contract extension for Curry through 2024, including an ownership stake in the company.[9]

Like a building that rises from the ground one brick at a time, the material for a presentation must be constructed and prepared in much the same way. By organizing your content with a focus on the benefits it will provide to your audience, you will have strong material from the beginning of the process. Be just as judicious with the information you choose to include as the material that you leave out. Less is more. Research shows that people can only remember around five to nine bits of information at a given time, so it helpful to limit the information you are providing so as not to overwhelm or confuse your audience.[10] It is also helpful to divide your material into "chunks." By breaking your presentation into smaller sections, it will not only be easier to under-stand and follow, it will also be easier for audience members to remember. When preparing, work one chunk at a time. Once you feel confident and comfortable with one, you can begin linking each chunk to the next until you are ready to run the presentation in its entirety. As the old saying reminds us, "When eating an elephant, take one bite at a time."

To be properly prepared, it is helpful to do a dress rehearsal—an informal run-through of your entire presentation—for a spouse or coworker. This gives you a chance to practice it on your feet so you can feel the flow as you move from one section to the next and identify which sections or transitions need attention. Transitions help to create a clear and logical journey for your audience. How well you master the transitions in your presentation can often make or break it. By physically running the presentation in an informal, no-stakes setting, you will become more comfortable with the material and this familiarity will boost your confidence. The more time you can spend practicing out loud, the better prepared you will be during the actual meeting or presentation. Interestingly, a recent survey found that only 2 percent of executives practice their presentations out loud.[11] This is a missed opportunity for the 98 percent who don't. Once you've finished your dress rehearsal, get feedback from those who watched it. Ask them which sections dragged or lacked clarity. Solicit honest feedback about your voice and body language and use these observations to refine and sharpen your performance. Also, anticipate ahead of time what difficult questions your audience might ask and practice your answers so you are ready for them.

The two most important requirements for major success are: first, being in the right place at the right time, and second, doing something about it.

—RAY KROC

According to Megan Bruneau, a mental health therapist: "Anxiety feeds off uncertainty, and confidence feeds off familiarity."[12] All the more reason to prepare so you can make your unknowns known. If you have put in the adequate time to prepare your material and delivery, you will be more confident on the day. Remind yourself that no one knows this material better than you. Audiences look for confidence and a relaxed presence from speakers so do your best to enjoy the experience. Dorothy Sarnoff, a professional actress who coached numerous presidents and world leaders over her career, often advised speakers that every audience should get the feeling from a speaker that communicated: "I'm glad I'm here. I'm glad you're here. I care about you."[13]

A common phenomenon that can plague even the best leader is something called *imposter syndrome* whereby a person feels their achievements are "undeserved" or that they will somehow be exposed as a fraud by an audience, despite possessing accomplishments and achievements to the contrary. According to one study, an estimated 70 percent of people will experience at least one episode of imposter syndrome in their lifetime.[14] While this distracting (or crippling, for some) feeling of inadequacy was originally believed to mostly affect women, research has revealed that leaders from both genders, across a range of backgrounds and industries, suffer from it. Even the most powerful leaders experience insecurities and doubts about their abilities. Being prepared and silencing your critical inner voice through positive thought and creative visualization will go a long way toward managing feelings of insecurity or inadequacy in your abilities or power.

In his book *Outliers,* Malcom Gladwell posited that someone learning a skill or trade needed 10,000 hours of practice before they could truly master something—whether it was playing the cello, writing computer code, or speaking in front of an audience.[15] According to Anders Ericsson, the psychology professor at Florida State from whose work Gladwell drew the 10,000-hour benchmark, it is not natural-born talent that makes someone exceptional but rather the time that the person invests to achieve mastery through preparation and "deliberate practice." For preparation to be effective it has to have specific goals that are well-defined. "You don't get benefits from mechanical repetition," says Ericsson, "but by adjusting your execution over and over to get closer to your goal."[16] And billionaire Mark Cuban agrees that proper preparation is essential when communicating in a business setting. "When you walk into a room, if you don't know more about your industry, your customer, your business than anyone else in the world," he said, "someone like me is going to come in and kick your ass."[17]

By stepping up as a leader and promoting your ideas, you are putting yourself forward for judgment. This can be scary as it opens us up for criticism, negative feedback, and, potentially, rejection. This type of exposure can make us feel judged and vulnerable. Additionally, we all have the inner judgments we contend with every day, that critical inner voice that can trip us up or cause self-doubt in the moment. But speaking up and advocating for our ideas can also be a place of great power for a communicator as all eyes and all ears are on you. One of the reasons people are nervous when speaking in front of others is that they fear the unknown. *What if the audience asks me a question that I can't answer?* We fear looking foolish or appearing uninformed. This is a common reason people have speech anxiety. To help calm your nerves, remind yourself that no one is expecting you to know everything there is to know about a topic. You only have to be the expert with regard to what you

Truly great technique has the generosity to vanish and take no credit.

—DECLAN DONNELLAN

are prepared to present in that particular meeting or presentation. If a question comes up that is outside the scope of your message, simply ask the person if you can research the answer and get back to them with the information they seek.

People get nervous when communicating in front of others because of something called the *spotlight effect*, whereby they feel like they are seen and judged and noticed more harshly by an audience than they generally are. The spotlight effect—a phenomenon first coined by Thomas Gilovich and his colleagues—involves the tendency to over-estimate the extent to which one is noticed by others.[18] For example, someone may feel nervous when pitching a new product to a client but generally overestimates how nervous they actually appear to the client in that moment. The key for someone who struggles with the spotlight effect is to first acknowledge the stress and feelings you are experiencing and then shift your focus away from yourself and direct it outward to your audience and onto the objective you are attempting to achieve. The message you are delivering is not about you, it is for the benefit of your audience. By taking the focus off of you and focusing your message on others, you transfer the glare of the spotlight from you to them.

GET COMFORTABLE SAYING NO

Advocating for your ideas and asserting yourself in the workplace is an important leadership trait. While in previous chapters we have extolled the virtues of avoiding the word no as it relates to collaboration and brainstorming, we now want to offer a slight exception to that advice. Being able to assertively say no to a request from someone is also an important skill for a leader to master. No holds power. No saves time and money. No is a verbal brick wall that stops the forward movement of a request or inquiry in its tracks. It has the power to end a negotiation or conversation in a split second. Sometimes no can be used for convenience while other times it can be used out of necessity. We sometimes struggle with saying no because we worry we will disappoint or upset people. We may be afraid of how our relationship will change with the other person if we deny their request or don't grant the favor. Saying no can be scary and stressful. Research done at the University of California in San Francisco shows that the harder it is for someone to say no, the more likely they are to experience stress, burnout, and depression.[19] Conversely, it can also be liberating and can allow you to better manage your time or work more productively by not taking on extraneous work or committing to something for which you don't have the time or the interest. Saying no is unambiguous with regard to intent. It is clear and direct: "Are you available for a conference call next Tuesday?" "No, I'm not."

Getting comfortable saying no can be a powerful weapon in your communication arsenal. It is definitive and unwavering. Warren Buffett once said, "The difference between successful people and very successful people is that very successful people say 'no' to almost everything."[20] According to research, women generally have more trouble saying no than men.[21] Author Jessica Turner has done extensive research about the challenges women face in the workplace and discovered a common theme: "For women," said Turner, "this 'disease to please' can wreak havoc on every area of our lives. We are nurturers by nature. We want to help and love others. But sometimes our actions are not an outpouring of love but a result of wanting to please someone else. This phenomenon is closely related to the disease of perfectionism."[22] It is important to get comfortable with your personal assertiveness when it is easy, so you are ready later on when the pressure increases and the stakes are high.

To be clear, when we advise you to get comfortable saying no, we are not talking about legitimate requests from your boss or client. What we are actually referencing are requests of your time and energy that are out of scope, above and beyond, or simply not part of your job description. Being approached to head up a committee at your child's school. Your neighbor asking you to feed their cats while they are on vacation. Or a coworker asking you to read their unfinished novel. All of these requests, if you accept them, will make demands on you and consume large chunks of your time. As Steve Jobs once advised, "It's only by saying 'no' that you can concentrate on the things that are really important."[23]

Here are some tips to become more comfortable saying no:

Analyze the audience and the request

Start by making sure you understand clearly who is making the request and why they are making it. If the request is coming from a senior leader, consider your answer carefully. Is the request reasonable? Is it even within my job responsibilities? Is the deadline to make it happen even feasible with my current work-load and responsibilities? Ask yourself: Do I even want to do this?

Set boundaries and stick to them

If you are a compulsive people-pleaser, chances are you don't set boundaries. By failing to establish clear boundaries, you devalue your time and effort and people end up taking advantage of you or you end up feeling resentful or overworked. Clear boundaries that have been clearly communicated will keep everyone on the same page.

Take time to reflect before answering

A big trap people fall into is committing to a request immediately or before they have taken the time to give it careful consideration. Tell the person making the request you will review your schedule and get back to them with an answer. This takes the pressure off in the moment and buys you some time to consider all of the moving parts.

Understand what happens if you say yes

If you say yes to this proposal or commitment, actions and effort will flow from that decision. It will require your time, energy, and focus. Take a piece of paper and write down exactly what this commitment will mean to you if you answer yes. Create pro and con columns to help you sketch out an honest roadmap of what will happen if you agree to the project or request.

Be firm and don't waver

Once you say no, make your answer firm. Don't apologize or give excuses. Resist the impulse to defend your decision and don't let anyone make you feel guilty for turning down their request. It can also be helpful to use phrases that allow you to say no without saying no, such as "My schedule is simply too packed right now to take on additional jobs," or "This isn't something I am able to help you with at this time," or "I can't commit to this right now."

Know your personal limits

By taking the time to understand how you work under pressure, how much time you generally need to complete a request, and how you prefer to collaborate, you will be better able to know how to respond to a request. If the answer is no, don't apologize or express regret as this will communicate uncertainty in your answer and provide the person making the request with an opening to keep asking.

CHOOSE YOUR WORDS CAREFULLY

"Letters, syllables, words—these are the musical notes of speech," said Constantin Stanislavski, "Out of which to fashion measures, arias, whole symphonies."[24] The words you choose have the power to elicit specific emotional responses in your audience. For example, research has shown that complimenting or positively reinforcing the decisions of customers often results in larger tips, better evaluations for products, and higher sales commissions.[25] Andrew M. Carton addressed the power of language in the *Harvard Business Review*, writing, "Leaders must communicate strategies for growth that employees can clearly envision. Instead of invoking abstract ideals, the most effective leaders communicate their visions using image-based words."[26] Words like "daring," "hero," "unheard-of," and "stunning" make us feel something—specifically, something *positive*—when we hear them. Part of what made Steve Jobs a compelling speaker was the language he used. Jobs frequently peppered his presentations and product launches with words like "amazing," "unbelievable," and "boom." When delivering information to larger, more diverse crowds, simple language is the key for a leader to get their message across in a clear and compelling manner. According to Jon Favreau, former speechwriter for Barack Obama, "A leader's job isn't to educate the public—it's to inspire and persuade them. That requires meeting people where they are, and speaking in words that are easily accessible to the broadest possible audience."[27] And a message with image-based words has been shown to enhance performance significantly over messages with abstract statements. One study found that hospital workers who used image-based words when communicating with patients triggered better outcomes than those who communicated ideas more abstractly.[28]

Sensory language can be a powerful tool for a communicator because it is simple and relatable to anyone hearing it. "Talk to customers the way you would friends," advised *Rework* authors Jason Fried and David Heinemeier Hansson. "Explain things as if you were sitting next to them. Avoid jargon or any sort of corporate-speak. Stay away from buzzwords when normal words will do just fine. Don't talk about 'monetization' or being 'transparent'; talk about making money and being honest. Don't use seven words when four will do."[29] As author Herman Melville once observed: "A man thinks that by mouthing hard words he understands hard things."[30] When attempting to persuade or influence someone, you won't be successful if they are bored or confused with the information you are presenting. A great leader will use words that help them communicate passion and vision to drive their teams.

For anyone presenting information that is meant to influence others, words like "value" and "opportunity" can spark a fire in the mind of your listener and quickly capture their attention. Winston Churchill loved words, specifically their musical quality. "There is no more important element in the technique of rhetoric," Churchill once said. "Than the continued employment of the best possible word."[31] Salespeople are taught to use the word "you" and are encouraged to use a person's first name to help them build trust and rapport with a potential customer.

Another way to persuade someone is to demonstrate that you have things in common and that you are both part of the same in-group. By showing you share common traits or interests, you create a bond and build rapport. Simply using words like "we" or "us" will help reinforce the idea that you have commonality in the way you think and act: "We will have to go out and celebrate when this contract gets signed," or "This is going to create some exciting new opportunities for us," or "We've come a long way since this project first began."

> *Influence is like a savings account. The less you use it, the more you've got.*
>
> —ANDREW YOUNG

These are all examples of how you can use words to create a feeling of inclusion with a client or team member. Research has shown that including pronouns when delivering a pitch or proposal like this can actually create a feeling of pleasure for the other person because your words have conveyed to them a sense of commonality.[32]

Sensory language influences the emotions of a listener because it makes them see, taste, hear, smell, and feel something. According to neuroscience, when someone hears a sensory phrase like "cracking the code," "mean as a snake," or "stinking to high heaven," it actually lights up the parts of their brain that control sensation.[33] And since emotional reactions are driven by sensory information, strategically choosing and employing sensory words can wield great power. One study from Purdue University looked at the speeches of U.S. presidents and found that the ones who used more image-based words when they spoke were considered more charismatic than those who didn't.[34] Churchill frequently used powerful imagery and sensory language in his speeches to elicit emotional responses, including phrases like "blood, toil, tears, and sweat." For another example, take note of the imagery in this passage from Churchill's 1940 address to the House of Commons:

> We shall defend our Island, whatever the cost may be; we shall fight on the beaches, we shall fight on the landing grounds, we shall fight in the fields and in the streets, we shall fight in the hills; we shall never surrender. . . .[35]

According to Churchill's biographer, William Manchester, "Churchill's feeling for the English tongue was sensual, almost erotic. When he coined a phrase he would suck it, rolling it around in his palate to extract its full flavor."[36] By the way, if you are still on the fence regarding the power and benefit of using sensory language, try reading that last quote again out loud.

PUTTING IT ALL TOGETHER

If you have ever seen a great actor such as Daniel Day-Lewis or Meryl Streep perform or seen an expert such as Tony Robbins or Kelly McGonigal deliver a TED Talk, you will notice how it seems effortless, like they were born to be doing what they were doing. They are relaxed, present, and dynamic. What you are witnessing is a performer in *flow*, a term coined by University of Chicago psychologist Mihaly Csikszentmihalyi. In the 1980s and 1990s, Csikszentmihalyi studied artists in Italy and observed many of these performers in this state of total immersion. Flow has been described as "a state of effortless concentration so deep that [people] lose their sense of time, of themselves, of their problems."[37] Someone in flow will become so engrossed in the task of the moment that nothing outside of that particular task seems to matter. Athletes refer to this state as being in "the zone"—finding themselves at peak performance in the exact moment when they need to excel.

Actors, musicians, and leaders experience flow as well. Watch clips of Martin Luther King, Jr. delivering his "I Have a Dream" speech at the foot of the Lincoln Memorial or John F. Kennedy's inaugural address and you will see more examples of leaders in flow. With all of these examples we see professionals who are present in the moment, fully prepared, delivering their very best performance for the benefit of others. The feeling generated as a result of seeing someone in a state of flow is immediate and joyful. It fully engages us and demands our complete attention and focus. It makes us sit up and lean in. Flow is not a magical quality that is only attainable for a gifted few. It can occur for any of us, whether our task is playing music, delivering a presentation or interviewing for a job. The goal with flow is to make the exceptional seem ordinary and the difficult seem effortless.

For anyone wanting to experience flow, there are certain aspects of your work that can help you facilitate this state. First, choose work you are passionate about. People who love their job and are passionate about the daily interactions they have with their coworkers exude a positive feeling that is contagious. Finding work that offers you intrinsic motivation (a sense of personal accomplishment or feeling you are making a difference) will make you happier than one that offers only extrinsic motivation (a paycheck or the fear of getting fired). Choose tasks that are not too difficult but not too easy. If a task is too easy or fails to challenge us, we become bored or disengaged and flow won't happen. Conversely, if a task it too daunting or beyond our abilities, flow is disrupted by anxiety. Also, choose the right time to complete your task and be aware of your focus and the amount of time dedicated to the task so you are setting yourself up for success. It will be difficult to achieve flow if you are distracted by a chaotic environment or

> *The more I practice, the luckier I get.*
>
> —GARY PLAYER

attempting a task when you are exhausted after a full day of work. By clearing distractions, you will create an environment where flow can be achieved and you can perform at your best.

Preparation is also key to achieve the state of flow. The more prepared you are, the more you know your material, the less mental energy you will need to waste worrying about your content. This frees up capacity to give all of your effort and energy to the task at hand: accomplishing your objective and satisfying the needs of your audience. To achieve a state of flow as a communicator, return to The Pinnacle

Method. These three simple steps offer you a framework that will ensure you are prepared and able to deliver your message with passion and purpose, whether that communication takes place in a meeting, presentation, or interview setting.

1. *Analyze* your audience
2. *Understand* the reaction your message should elicit
3. *Modify* your delivery to achieve that result

Because you are prepared and ready, you will be able to deliver your message in a clear, concise, and compelling way that will influence emotion and motivate action. This is the process of effective communication and this is how you will achieve a state of flow—in your next meeting, during your next presentation, or when you interview for your next job. As Amelia Earhart once said, "The most difficult thing is the decision to act, the rest is merely tenacity."[38] You now have the tools to influence and inspire others with your communication. How you choose to employ them as a leader is up to you. The journey to becoming a more effective communicate begins now. Enjoy every step.

Blueprint to Bullseye—Chapter 10

Preparation Guide for Presentations

1. What topic are you presenting?

2. Who is your audience?
   a. Demographic analysis

   b. Psychographic analysis

   c. Situational analysis

3. What challenges could you face with this audience and this topic? (List three.)

4. What difficult questions might you be asked by this audience? (List three.)

5. What is the objective you hope to accomplish as a result of your audience hearing your message? (Be specific.)

6. What intentions will best help you accomplish your objective? (Choose from: excite, persuade, challenge, reassure, inspire, motivate, empower, etc.)

Notes

Introduction

1. John Brandon, "You Touch This Gadget 2,617 Times Per Day. Here's How to Stop," inc.com, January 13, 2017.
2. Cindy Perman, "Hate Meetings? Why Most Are Complete Failures," cnbc.com, September 6, 2012.
3. Victor Lipman, "65% of Employees Want More Feedback (So Why Don't They Get It?)," forbes.com, August 8, 2016.
4. Valerie Strauss, "The surprising thing Google learned about its employees—and what it means for today's students," Washington Post, December 20, 2017.
5. Kate Davidson, "Employers Find 'Soft Skills' Like Critical Thinking in Short Supply," wsj.com, April 30, 2016.
6. Ibid.
7. Scott Jaschik, "Well-Prepared in Their Own Eyes," *Inside Higher Ed*, January 20, 2015.
8. Ibid.
9. Carmine Gallo, "Richard Branson: 'Communication Is The Most Important Skill Any Leader Can Possess,'" forbes.com, July 7, 2015.
10. Carmine Gallo, "Billionaire Warren Buffett Says This 1 Skill Will Boost Your Career Value by 50 Percent," inc.com, January 5, 2017.
11. Ken Howard, *Act Natural: How to Speak to Any Audience* (New York: Random House, 2003), p. 189.

12. Ilya Pozin, "How Transparent Is Too Transparent in Business?" forbes .com, April 2, 2014.

13. Meghan Casserly, "Majority of Americans Would Rather Fire Their Boss Than Get a Raise," forbes.com, October 17, 2012.

14. Kavi Guppta, "Gallup: American Workers Are Unengaged and Looking Elsewhere," forbes.com, March 8, 2017.

15. Jim Clifton, "The World's Broken Workplace," news.gallup.com, June 13, 2017.

16. Susan Sorenson and Keri Garman, "How to Tackle U.S. Employees' Stagnating Engagement," news.gallup.com, June 11, 2013.

17. Constantin Stanislavski, *An Actor's Handbook: An Alphabetical Arrangement of Concise Statements of Acting* (New York: Theatre Arts Books, 1963), p. 27.

18. Lee Odden and Joe Pulizzi, "Building an Audience Development Strategy for Content Marketing," *Content Marketing Institute*, www .contentmarketinginstitute.com, September 8, 2014.

19. Ken Howard, *Act Natural: How to Speak to Any Audience* (New York: Random House, 2003), p. 47.

20. Declan Donnellan, *The Actor and the Target,* Theatre Communications Group (2006), p. 2.

21. Daniel Goleman, *Emotional Intelligence: Why It Can Matter More Than IQ* (London: Bloomsbury Publishing, 1995), p. 119.

22. James J. Murphy, "Demosthenes: Greek Statesman and Orator," *Encyclopedia Britannica*, www.britannica.com, July 20, 1998.

23. Charlotte Higgins, "Gordon Brown Invokes Demosthenes and Cicero— Badly," theguardian.com, May 4, 2010.

24. Constantin Stanislavski, *An Actor's Handbook: An Alphabetical Arrangement of Concise Statements of Acting* (New York: Theatre Arts Books, 1963), p. 53.

25. Bourree Lam, "What It Was Like to Write Speeches for Apple Executives," *The Atlantic,* June 10, 2016.

Chapter 1

1. Interview with G. Riley Mills, June 22, 2017.

2. A. Javier Trevino, *Goffman's Legacy* (New York: Rowman & Littlefield, 2003), p. 18.

3. Stephen Harold Riggins, *Beyond Goffman: Studies on Communication, Institution, and Social Interaction* (New York: Mouton de Gruyter, 1990), p. 77.

4. William Egginton, *How the World Became a Stage: Presence, Theatricality, and the Question of Modernity* (New York: SUNY Press, 2002), p. 21.

5. Allan and Barbara Pease, "The Definitive Book of Body Language," *New York Times,* September 24, 2006, p. 18.
6. Daniel J. O'Keefe, *Persuasion: Theory and Research* (Los Angeles: Sage Publications, 2016), p. 17.
7. Hillary Busis, "New York Comedy Festival: An interview with Patton Oswalt," *Entertainment Weekly,* November 7, 2012.
8. Jessica Lahey, "Teaching: Just Like Performing Magic," *The Atlantic,* January 21, 2016.
9. Lea Winerman, "E-mails and Egos," *Monitor on Psychology* 37, no. 2 (February 2006).
10. Emma Seppala and Kim Cameron, "Proof That Positive Work Cultures Are More Productive," *Harvard Business Review,* December 1, 2015.
11. Loulla-Mae Eleftheriou-Smith, "Dutch Teenager Vera Mol Died Bungee Jumping Due to Spanish Instructor's 'Poor English,'" *The Independent,* June 27, 2017.
12. Bitange Ndemo, "The Hidden Cost of Poor Communication in Health-care," *Daily Nation,* October 17, 2016.
13. Linda T. Kohn, Janet M. Corrigan, and Molla S. Donaldson, "To Err Is Human: Building a Safer Health System," *Institute of Medicine* (2000).
14. Amy J. Starmer, "Changes in Medical Errors after Implementation of a Handoff Program," *The New England Journal of Medicine,* November 6, 2014.
15. Interview and e-mail with G. Riley Mills, July 20, 2017.
16. Ibid.
17. *American Heritage Dictionary of the English Language, Fifth Edition* (2011).
18. Emma Hardman, *Griffith Review 31: Ways of Seeing* (Melbourne, Australia: The Text Publishing Company, 2011).
19. James Clear, "Achieve Your Goals: Research Reveals a Simple Trick That Doubles Your Chances for Success," *Huffington Post,* January 19, 2016.
20. Lynne McTaggart, *The Intention Experiment: Using Your Thoughts to Change Your Life and the World* (New York: Atria Books, 2008), p. 47.
21. Ibid., p. 80.
22. Stanislavski, *An Actor's Handbook,* p. 39.
23. Tracy Cochran, "Intention," parabola.org, August 17, 2015.
24. Hardman, *Griffith Review 31.*
25. Robert Dickman and Richard Maxwell, *The Elements of Persuasion* (New York: Harper Business, 2007), p. 134.
26. Constantin Stanislavski, *An Actor Prepares* (New York: Theatre Arts, 1936), p. 334.

27. Ann Latham, "Why You Should Outlaw Informational Meetings," forbes. com, September 4, 2016.

28. Stanislavski, *An Actor Prepares*, p. 137.

29. Declan Donnelan, *The Actor and the Targe*, (London: Theatre Communications Group, 2006), p. 18.

30. Simon Sinek, *Leaders Eat Last: Why Some Teams Pull Together and Others Don't* (New York: Portfolio/Penguin, 2014), p. 95.

Chapter 2

1. James Clear, "Martha Graham on the Hidden Danger of Comparing Yourself to Others," *Huffington Post*, December 6, 2017.

2. Shea Driscoll, "Eight Lessons for a Successful Career (and Life) from Jack Ma at Alibaba's Gateway '17,'" *South China Morning Post*, June 28, 2017.

3. Lucinda Shen, "China's Richest Man Says He Doesn't Have Time to Spend His Money," *Money*, September 20, 2017.

4. Tom Peters, "The Brand Called You," *Fast Company*, August 31, 1997.

5. Glenn Llopis, "Personal Branding Is a Leadership Requirement, Not a Self-Promotion Campaign," forbes.com, April 8, 2013.

6. Hal Gregersen, "The One Skill That Made Amazon's CEO Wildly Successful," fortune.com, November 19, 2015.

7. Matt Rosoff, "The only reason the Mac looks like it does is because Steve Jobs dropped in on a course taught by this former monk," businessinsider .com, March 8, 2016.

8. Scott Edinger, "Three Elements of Great Communication, According to Aristotle," *Harvard Business Review*, January 17, 2013.

9. Lori Nordstrom, *Maximizing Profits: A Practical Guide for Portrait Photographers* (Buffalo, NY: Amhert Media, 2015), p. 14.

10. Meghan Casserly, "Beyoncé's $50 Million Pepsi Deal Takes Creative Cues from Jay Z," forbes.com, December 10, 2012.

11. Sammy Said, "George Clooney Earns $40 Million from Nespresso Deal," therichest.com, September 17, 2013.

12. Darren Rovell, "Foreman's Grill Deal: Best in Sports Marketing History?" cnbc.com, August 11, 2010.

13. Dara Khosrowshahi, *Time Magazine*, October 9, 2017, p. 6.

14. Dave Zangaro, "Jim Schwartz on Nigel Bradham: 'You're Going to Be Labeled as a Dumbass,'" nbcsports.com, October 6, 2016.

15. "The Frontline Interview: Roger Stone," PBS, September 27, 2016, Jason M. Breslow, Digital Editor.

16. Sean Illing, "Trump Biographer: 'He's an Actor Who's Been Playing Himself for His Entire Life,'" vox.com, January 25, 2017.

17. Joe Klein, "What Comes Next with President Trump," time.com, November 10, 2016.

18. Nicholas Confessore and Karen Yourish, "$2 Billion Worth of Free Media for Donald Trump," *New York Times*, March 15, 2016.

19. Jemma Johnson, "Donald Trump: They Say I Could 'Shoot Somebody' and Still Have Support," *Washington Post*, January 23, 2016.

20. Glenn Thrush, "10 Crucial Decisions That Reshaped America," *Politico*, December 9, 2016.

21. Chris Jones, "In 'Trump Card,' Mike Daisey Explains Unlikely, Undeniable Pull of The Donald," *Chicago Tribune*, October 16, 2016.

22. Rebecca Shambaugh, "How Important Is Executive Presence to Executive Success?" *Huffington Post*, November 6, 2012.

23. Lauren Franze, "Ambition and Gender at Work," *Institute of Leadership and Management*, February 20, 2011.

24. Ibid.

25. Jenna Goudreau, "Do You Have 'Executive Presence'?" forbes.com, October 29, 2012.

26. Meredith Lepore, "10 Unexpected Body-Language Adjustments That Will Boost Your Career," fastcompany.com, January 21, 2015.

27. Max A. Eggert, *Body Language for Business* (New York: Skyhorse Publishing, 2012), p. 35.

28. Sandra Blakeslee, "Mind Games: Sometimes a White Coat Isn't Just a White Coat," *New York Times*, April 2, 2012.

29. Ibid.

30. Travis Bradberry, "12 Mind Tricks That Make You Likable and Help You Get Ahead," *Inc.*, January 13, 2016.

31. Katherine Schreiber and Heather Hausenblas, "What Eye Contact Can Do to You," *Psychology Today*, September 20, 2016.

32. Gretchen Rubin, "Eight Ways to Tell Whether You're Being Boring," *Slate*, December 2, 2009.

33. W. Ross Winterowd, *The English Department: A Personal and Institutional History* (Southern Illinois University Press, 1998), p. 37.

34. Melinda Wenner, "Smile! It Could Make You Happier," *Scientific American*, September 1, 2009.

35. Michael Kraus, "Voice-Only Communication Enhances Empathic Accuracy," *American Psychologist*, published online Oct. 10, 2017.

36. Constantin Stanislavski, *An Actor's Handbook: An Alphabetical Arrange-
     ment of Concise Statements of Acting* (New York: Theatre Arts Books,
     1963), p. 128.

37. Tom Rogan, "Why Thatcher was the 'Iron Lady,'" cnn.com, April 9,
     2013.

38. Polly Dunbar, "How Laurence Olivier gave Margaret Thatcher the voice
     that went down in history," *Daily Mail*, October 29, 2011.

39. Robin A. Smith, "'Caveman Instincts' May Favor Baritone Politicians,"
     Duke Today, August 7, 2015.

40. Ed Mazza, "Edward 'Tiger Mike' Davis, the World's Meanest Boss, Dead
     at 85," *Huffington Post*, September 27, 2016.

41. Geoff Beattie, "The Psychology behind Trump's Awkward Handshake . . .
     and How to Beat Him at His Own Game," *The Conversation*, February 20,
     2017.

42. Chris Cillizza, "The Merkel-Trump Handshake Heard "Round the
     World," cnn.com, July 6, 2017.

43. Stephanie Ruhle, "Try This Simple Trick to Unburden Yourself From an
     Over-Stuffed Schedule," nbcnews.com, January 28, 2018.

44. Alice G. Walton, "7 Ways Meditation Can Actually Change the Brain,"
     forbes.com, February 9, 2015.

45. Paula Kay Glass, "Be Mentally Aware," *Huffington Post*, April 16,
     2017.

46. Marla Paul, "Rhythm of Breathing Affects Memory and Fear," *Neuro-
     science News*, December 7, 2016.

47. Travis Bradberry, "6 Ways Nice People Can Master Conflict," *Huffington
     Post*, May 14, 2016.

48. Adrienne A. Taren, Peter J Gianaros, et al., "Mindfulness Meditation
     Training Alters Stress-Related Amygdala Resting State Functional Con-
     nectivity: A Randomized Controlled Trial," *Social Cognitive and Affective
     Neuroscience*, 2015, 1–11, September 13, 2015.

49. Nikki Waller, "How Men and Women See the Workplace Differently,"
     Wall Street Journal, September 27, 2016.

50. Tony Schwartz and Christine Porath, "Why You Hate Work," *New York
     Times*, May 30, 2015.

51. Christine Allen, "Are You an Authentic Leader? Here's Why You Should
     Be," forbes.com, September 5, 2017.

52. Modeline Fenelon, "Millennials: 'We Are More Than Working
     Machines, We Are Driven by More Than Money,'" linkedin.com,
     January 19, 2015.

Chapter 3

1. Adam Bryant, "Walt Bettinger of Charles Schwab: You've Got to Open Up to Move Up," *New York Times,* February 4, 2016.
2. Rebecca Lerner, "Business Lessons from Malcolm Gladwell, Samantha Bee and The Stars of OZY Fest," forbes.com, July 25, 2017.
3. Jennifer Grasz, "Employers Tell All: The Most Unusual Interview Mishaps and Biggest Body Language Mistakes," careerbuilder.com, January 15, 2015.
4. Sam Rega, "Shake Shack's Millionaire Founder Danny Meyer Looks for These 2 Things When Hiring People," businessinsider.com, September 12, 2016.
5. Alex Hern, "How Do You Answer Facebook's Hiring Question about Your Very Best Day at Work?" *The Guardian,* February 24, 2016.
6. Nicholas Carlson, "Answers to 15 Google Interview Questions That Will Make You Feel Stupid," businessinsider.com, November 5, 2009.
7. Ibid.
8. Barbara Mikkelson, "Salted Food Test," snopes.com, April 21, 2011.
9. Jonathan Horn, "Why Americans Fear the Job Interview" *The San Diego Union-Tribune,* August 20, 2013.
10. Gena-mour Barrett, "21 Of the Most Embarrassing Things People Have Done in Job Interviews," *Buzzfeed,* July 6, 2015.
11. Daniel B. Morgan, *Last Stage Manager Standing* (New York: Page Publishing, 2014).
12. Brad Zomick, "10 Great Examples of Interview Horror Stories," *Graffiti Recruitment,* October 27, 2016.
13. Jessica Stillman, "The Casanova's Guide to Job Interview Success," cbsnews.com, November 28, 2011.
14. Linda Kuehn and Jen Robinson, "Change Agents Get Personal on 'Inspire<GO>,'" *Bloomberg Media Forum,* March 17, 2017.
15. Shana Lebowitz, "21 Psychological Tricks That Will Help You Ace a Job Interview," businessinsider.com, March 19, 2017.
16. Richard Feloni, "LinkedIn's Head of Recruiting Explains Why the First Thing He Does in Every Job Interview Is Hand over a Marker," businessinsider.com, January 11, 2017.
17. Jeff Haden, "Do You Think You're Smart? Then the CEO of Burger King Definitely Won't Hire You", inc.com, February 8, 2018.
18. Leslie Kwoh and Lauren Weber, "The Receptionist Is Watching You," *The Wall Street Journal,* September 21, 2012.
19. Peter Harris, "Who Gets Hired: Why Employers Select One Candidate Over Another," workopolis.com, August 28, 2013.

20. Facebook post and interview with G. Riley Mills, June 23, 2017.

21. Adam Gordon, "Win First Seconds of a Job Interview and Ride Tailwind of Confirmation Bias," forbes.com, February 17, 2017.

22. Ibid.

23. Laura Vanderkam, "Why It's So Hard to Change a Bad First Impression," *Fast Company*, August 9, 2016.

24. Mark Shrayber, "These Catastrophic Job Application Stories Will Make You Nervous About Your Next Interview," *Uproxx*, March 5, 2016.

25. Maureen Dempsey, "5 Things Job Candidates Obsess Over That Hiring Managers Don't Care About," *Fast Company*, December 17, 2014.

26. Ursula K. Le Guin, *The Wave in the Mind: Talks and Essays on the Writer, the Reader and the Imagination* (Boston: Shambhala, 2004), p. 199.

27. David Givens, *Love Signals: A Practical Field Guide to the Body Language of Courtship* (New York: St. Martin's Press, 2005), p. 57.

28. Chris Whipple, "Ted Kennedy: The Day the Presidency Was Lost," abcnews.go.com, August 31, 2009.

29. Dina Bair, "Posture Can Affect Your Mood: Northwestern University study," *wgntv.com*, February 10, 2016.

30. Aneri Pattani, "Smiling May Hinder Outcome of Interviews," *The Huntington News*, December 4, 2014.

31. Mollie A. Ruben, Judith A. Hall, and Marianne Schmid Mast, "Smiling in a Job Interview: When Less Is More," researchgate.net, January 1, 2015.

32. Cari Romm, "How to Say 'Um' and 'Like' and Also Sound Smart," *New York Magazine*, July 26, 2016.

33. Michael Saul, "Caroline Kennedy No Whiz with Words," *New York Daily News*, December 29, 2008.

34. Carol Kinsey Goman, "The Art and Science of Mirroring," forbes.com, May 31, 2011.

Chapter 4

1. Doris Kearns Goodwin, *People of the Century* (New York: Simon & Schuster), p. 113.

2. Kathleen Dalton, *Theodore Roosevelt: A Strenuous Life* (New York: Random House, 2004), p. 202.

3. Christopher Klein, "When Teddy Roosevelt Was Shot in 1912, a Speech May Have Saved His Life," history.com, October 12, 2012.

4. Maria Popova, "What Makes People Compelling," *Brain Pickings*, January 28, 2014.

5. Sue Ashford, "Why Everyone Should Think of Themselves as a Leader," *Harvard Business Review*, August 31, 2017.

6. Beth Comstock, "Jeff Immelt: 'To Be a Better Leader, Lose the Distractions and Focus on What's Really Important,'" linkedin.com, August 4, 2017.

7. Thom Shanker, "Snowflakes," *New York Times*, December 24, 2006.

8. Lisa Quast, "Why Grit Is More Important Than IQ," *Seattle Times*, December 26, 2016.

9. Filippo Di Giovanni, "The Art of Leadership: What Makes a Great Leader," linkedin.com, January 13, 2015.

10. David Horsager, *The Trust Edge: How Top Leaders Gain Faster Results, Deeper Relationships, and a Stronger Bottom Line* (New York: Free Press, 2009), p. 103.

11. Katie Zezima, "Trump: My Strongest Asset 'Is My Temperament,'" *The Washington Post*, September 27, 2016.

12. Nikki Waller, "How Men & Women See the Workplace Differently," *The Wall Street Journal*, September 27, 2016.

13. American Psychological Association, "When the Boss Is a Woman," apa .org, March 22, 2006.

14. Barry Reece, *Effective Human Relations: Interpersonal and Organizational Applications* (Mason, OH: South-Western College Publishing, 2013), p. 26.

15. Adam Taylor, "Polish Politician Says Women Should Earn Less because 'They Are Weaker, They Are Smaller, They Are Less Intelligent,'" *The Washington Post*, March 3, 2017.

16. Eleanor Barkhorn, "Are Successful Women Really Less Likable Than Successful Men?" *The Atlantic*, March 14, 2013.

17. Gerald H. Graham, Jeanne Unruh, Paul Jennings, "The Impact of Nonverbal Communication in Organizations: A Survey of Perceptions," *The Journal of Business Communication* 28, no. 1 (Winter 1991), p. 48.

18. Julia Belluz, "Want to Save 32,000 Lives a Year? Get Male Doctors to Practice More Like Women," vox.com, December 19, 2016.

19. Ibid.

20. Maggie Fox, "Female Doctors Outperform Male Doctors, According to Study," nbcnews.com, December 19, 2016.

21. Katty Kay and Claire Shipman, *The Confidence Code* (New York: HarperBusiness, 2014), p. 8.

22. Tacy M. Byham and Richard S. Wellins, "Should a Woman Act More Like a Man to Succeed at Work?" success.com, March 8, 2016.

23. Kimberly Fitch and Sangeeta Agrawal, "Female Bosses Are More Engaging Than Male Bosses," gallup.com, May 7, 2015.

24. Christina Baldassarre, "Five Ways Employees Can Thrive Under Female Leadership," forbes.com, July 31, 2017.

25. Crosby Burns, Kimberly Barton, and Sophia Kerby, "The State of Diversity in Today's Workforce" *Center for American Progress*, July 12, 2012.

26. Rebecca Riffkin, "Americans Still Prefer a Male Boss to a Female Boss" gallup.com, October 14, 2014.

27. Adam Hetrick, "For Girls, You Have to See It to Be It—" The Historic and Powerful *Fun Home* Tony Acceptance Speeches You Didn't See on TV," playbill.com, June 8, 2015.

28. Susan Adams, "10 Things Sheryl Sandberg Gets Exactly Right In 'Lean In,'" forbes.com, March 4, 2013.

29. Lydia O'Connor, "Sheryl Sandberg Says We Have a Problem 'Telling Little Girls Not to Lead,'" huffingtonpost.com, July 30, 2017.

30. Matt Bonesteel, "Jameis Winston Tells a Crowd of Little Kids That Women Should Be 'Silent, Polite, Gentle,'" *The Washington Post*, February 23, 2017.

31. Emily Crockett, "Hillary Clinton: 'I Had to Learn as a Young Woman to Control My Emotions,'" vox.com, September 8, 2016.

32. Sylvie Woolf, "7 Workplace Collaboration Statistics and Advice That Will Have You Knocking Down Cubicles + How to Make It Happen in YOUR workplace," clearcompany.com, September 3, 2017.

33. Robert Stribley, "Why I Talk Politics on Social Media," huffingtonpost. com, January 16, 2017.

34. Constantin Stanislavski, *Building a Character* (New York: Routledge/Theatre Arts Books, 1949), p. 140.

35. Art Markman, "What Do (Linguistic) Hedges Do?" *Psychology Today*, October 30, 2012.

36. Chris Cillizza, "Why Mitt Romney's '47 Percent' Comment Was So Bad," *The Washington Post*, March 4, 2013.

37. Amy Chozick, "Hillary Clinton Calls Many Trump Backers 'Deplorables,' and G.O.P. Pounces," *New York Times*, September 10, 2016.

38. Janell Ross, "From Mexican Rapists to Bad Hombres, the Trump Campaign in Two Moments," *Washington Post*, October 20, 2016.

39. Alasdair Nairn, *Engines That Move Markets: Technology Investing from Railroads to the Internet and Beyond* (Hoboken, NJ: John Wiley & Sons, 2002), p. 449.

40. John Maeda, *The Laws of Simplicity* (Boston: MIT Press, 2006), p. 89.

41. nationalchurchillmuseum.org.
42. American Psychological Association, "When the Boss Is a Woman," apa .org, March 22, 2006.
43. Ronald Reagan. *An American Life* (New York: Simon & Schuster, 1990), p. 161.
44. Max Weber, "The Theory of Social and Economic Organization," Translated by A. M. Henderson & Talcott Parsons. (New York: The Free Press, 1947).
45. "A Review of Workplace Leadership Styles: Men vs. Women," helioshr .com.
46. Alice Eagly and Linda L. Carli, "Women and the Labyrinth of Leadership," *Harvard Business Review,* September 2007 issue.
47. Robyn Benincasa, "6 Leadership Styles and When You Should Use Them," *Fast Company,* May 29, 2012.

Chapter 5

1. Maya Oppenheim, "Barack Obama Electrifies Crowd with Anecdote on How He Got his Election Slogan 'Fired Up, Ready to Go,'" *The Independent,* November 8, 2016.
2. Dan Fipphen and Elyse Kelly (video), "The Story of the Iconic Obama Campaign Chant, Animated," *The Atlantic,* January 19, 2017.
3. Travis Bradberry, "8 Mistakes that Make Good Employees Leave," forbes. com, September 7, 2016.
4. Richard Fry, "Millennials Surpass Gen Xers as the Largest Generation in U.S. Labor force," *Pew Research Center,* May 11, 2015.
5. "The 2016 Deloitte Millennial Survey: Winning Over the Next Generation of Leaders," www2.deloitte.com.
6. Alicia Jerome, Michael Scales, Cliff Whithem, and Bill Quain. "Millennials in the Workforce: Gen Y Workplace Strategies for the Next Century," *Journal of Social & Behavioral Research in Business,* 2014.
7. Rebecca Ray and Evan Sinar, "What Skills Will Leaders Need in the Future?," *Chief Learning Officer,* March 23, 2017.
8. Alison Hillhouse, "Consumer Insights: MTV's 'No Collar Workers,'" blog.viacom.com, October 4, 2012.
9. Dan Schawbel, "Millennials vs. Baby Boomers: Who Would You Rather Hire?" *Time,* March 29, 2012.
10. Rodd Wagner, "The End of 'Employee Engagement,'" forbes.com, May 11, 2015.
11. Ibid.

12. Ankit P. Patel, *The International Journal of Indian Psychology* 4, issue 1, no. 77 (2016) 184.

13. Kenneth Allan, *Contemporary Social and Sociological Theory: Visualizing Social Worlds* (Los Angeles: Sage Publications, 2012), p. 75.

14. Megan Cole, "The Case for Developing Communication Skills in Managers: More Engagement, More Profits," *Association for Talent Management,* March 15, 2016.

15. Jack Zenger and Joseph Folkman, "How Damaging Is a Bad Boss, Exactly?" *Harvard Business Review,* July 16, 2012.

16. Gretchen Spreitzer and Christine Porath, "Creating Sustainable Performance," *Harvard Business Review,* January–February 2012 issue.

17. Gianluca Biggio and Claudio G. Cortese, "Well-being in the Workplace through Interaction between Individual Characteristics and Organizational Context," *National Center for Biotechnology Information,* February 18, 2013.

18. Jodi L. Berg, "The Role of Personal Purpose and Personal Goals in Symbiotic Visions," *National Center for Biotechnology Information,* April 14, 2015.

19. John Hilton, "Employees Yearn for a 'Sense of Purpose': Survey," *Human Resources Director,* October 21, 2016.

20. Coeli Carr, "How to Sell Employees on Noncash Bonuses," *Inc. Magazine,* November 2016.

21. Bill Hettler and Human Kinetics Organization, *Health and Wellness for Life* (Champaign, IL: Human Kinetics, 2009), p. 447.

22. Drake Baer, "The 10 Things High Engagement Does for You," *Fast Company,* July 10, 2013.

23. Ryan Fuller and Nina Shikaloff, "What Great Managers Do Daily," *Harvard Business Review,* December 14, 2016.

24. Ibid.

25. Ibid.

26. Benjamin Snyder, "Half of Us Have Quit Our Job because of a Bad Boss," *Fortune,* April 2, 2015.

27. Sabrina Son. "The Power of Employee Appreciation [Infographic]," tinypulse.com, October 30, 2015.

28. Joyce Maroney, "The Top Three Factors Driving Employee Burnout," forbes.com, February 1, 2017.

29. Travis Bradberry, "6 Stupid Things Managers Do to Kill Morale," forbes.com, November 30, 2016.

30. Declan Donnellan, *The Actor and the Target* (London: Theatre Communications Group, 2006), p. 50.

31. Interview and e-mail exchange with G. Riley Mills, October 30, 2017.

32. Victor Lipman, "Why Does Organizational Change Usually Fail? New Study Provides Simple Answer," forbes.com, February 8, 2016.

33. Ibid.

34. Interview with David Lewis, February 2017.

35. Sandra M. Oliver, *A Handbook of Corporate Communication and Public Relations* (New York: Routledge, 2004), p. 21.

36. Ed Catmull and Amy Wallace, "'If You Think, You Stink': From 'Toy Story' to 'Inside Out,' How the Creative Geniuses at Pixar Bring New Things into Being" *Salon,* June 21, 2015.

37. Randall Beck and Jim Harter, "Managers Account for 70% of Variance in Employee Engagement," *Gallup,* April 21, 2015.

38. Amy Jen Su, "How New Managers Can Send the Right Leadership Signals," *Harvard Business Review,* August 8, 2017.

39. Society for Human Resource Management, "SHRM Survey Shows Jump in Employees' Satisfaction with Work," shrm.com, April 28, 2015.

40. Christine Porath, "Half of Employees Don't Feel Respected by Their Bosses," *Harvard Business Review,* November 19. 2014.

41. Mark Murphy, "All Great Leadership Styles Begin by Spending Time with Employees," *Leadership IQ,* June 22, 2015.45.

42. Monte Burke, "At Age 25 Mark Cuban Learned Lessons about Leadership That Changed His Life," forbes.com, March 28, 2013.

43. Peter Guber, *Tell to Win: Connect, Persuade and Triumph with the Hidden Power of Story* (New York: Crown Business, 2011), p. 203.

44. Juliet Eilperin, "White House Women Want to Be in the Room Where It Happens," *The Washington Post,* September 13, 2016.

45. Jim Harter and Amy Adkins, "Employees Want a Lot More from Their Managers," *Gallup,* April 8, 2015.

46. Maren Hogan, "5 Employee Feedback Stats That You Need to See," linkedin.com, February 8, 2016.

47. Eric Barker, "New Neuroscience Reveals 4 Rituals That Will Make You Happy," *The Week,* February 28, 2016.

48. Towers Watson, "'Turbocharging' Employee Engagement: The Power of Recognition from Managers—Part 1," *willistowerswatson.com,* 2009.

49. Dan Ariely, Uri Gneezy, George Loewenstein, and Nina Mazar, "Large Stakes and Big Mistakes," *The Review of Economic Studies,* April 1, 2009.

50. Coeli Carr, "How to Give Out Bonuses That Really Motivate Your Employees," *Inc. Magazine,* November 2016.

51. Kristen Frasch, "Just How Bad Are We at Engagement?" *Human Resource Executive Online,* October 17, 2016.

52. Simon Sinek, "When We Tell People to Do Their Jobs, We Get Workers. When We Trust People to Get the Job Done, We Get Leaders," linkedin. com, September 10, 2016.

53. Interview and e-mail exchange with G. Riley Mills. October 11, 2017.

54. Anisa Purbasari, "I Followed Benjamin Franklin's Daily Schedule for a Week, and the Most Rewarding Part Was Also the Most Difficult," businessinsider.com, August 24, 2016.

55. Jenna Goudreau, "Google HR Boss Explains the Only 2 Ways to Keep Your Best People from Quitting," businessinsider.com, April 8, 2015.

56. Daniel McGinn, "The Science of Pep Talks," *Harvard Business Review,* July–August.

57. Gwen Moran, "The Science behind Why Inspirational Quotes Motivate Us," *Fast Company,* September 25, 2015.

58. McGinn, "The Science of Pep Talks."

Chapter 6

1. John C. Maxwell, *Maxwell Daily Reader: 365 Days of Insight to Develop the Leader Within You* (Nashville, TN: Thomas Nelson, 2007), p. 360.

2. barrypopik.com, March 18, 2014.

3. Napoleon Hill, *Think and Grow Rich* (New York: Armchair Millionaire, 2005), p. 60.

4. Dick Wirthlin, *The Greatest Communicator: What Ronald Reagan Taught Me About Politics, Leadership, and Life* (Hoboken, NJ: John Wiley & Sons, 2004), p. 12.

5. Edmund Morris, "Five Myths about Ronald Reagan," washingtonpost. com, February 4, 2011.

6. Margot Morrell, *Reagan's Journey: Lessons from a Remarkable Career* (New York: Simon and Schuster, 2011).

7. Mallie Jane Kim, "Ronald Reagan's Leadership Lessons," *U.S. News and World Reports,* May 26, 2011.

8. Tim Bell, *Right or Wrong: The Memoirs of Lord Bell* (London: Bloomsbury Publishing, 2015), p. 72.

9. Pamela Regan, "When It Comes to Relationships, the Little Things Count," *Psychology Today,* September 3, 2012.

10. Emily Esfahani Smith, "Masters of Love," *The Atlantic,* June 12, 2014.

11. Daniel Goleman. *Emotional Intelligence: Why It Can Matter More Than IQ* (New York: Bantam Books, 2005), p. 114.

12. Smith, "Masters of Love."
13. Karen Bridbord, "Respond and Engage," gottman.com, September 30, 2015.
14. Ernest J. Wilson III, "Empathy Is Still Lacking in the Leaders Who Need It Most," *Harvard Business Review,* September 21, 2015.
15. Constantin Stanislavski, *An Actor's Handbook: An Alphabetical Arrangement of Concise Statements on Aspects of Acting* (New York: Theatre Arts Books, 1963), p. 96.
16. Travis Bradberry and Jean Greaves, *Emotional Intelligence 2.0* (San Diego, CA: Talent Smart, 2009), p. 169.
17. Ezra Klein (video). vox.com, September 8, 2016.
18. Daniel Goleman, *Emotional Intelligence: Why It Can Matter More Than IQ* (London: Bloomsbury Publishing, 1995), p. 104.
19. Mandy Oaklander, "The Science of Crying," *Time Magazine,* March 16, 2016.
20. Travis Bradberry, "Seven Small Things People Use to Decide If They Like You," forbes.com, January 10, 2017.
21. David Wallis, "Will Michael Strahan Go from Locker Room Leader to Leader of the Free World?" *The Observer,* June 16, 2016.
22. Adam Bryant, "Walt Bettinger of Charles Schwab: You've Got to Open Up to Move Up," *New York Times,* February 4, 2016.
23. Ekaterina Walter, "5 Myths of Leadership," forbes.com, October 8, 2013.
24. Travis Bradberry, "12 Habits of Genuine People," *Huffington Post,* June 10, 2017.
25. Olga Khazan, "What Is Social Anxiety?" *The Atlantic,* October 22, 2015.
26. Markham Heid, "We Need to Talk About Kids and Smartphones," *Time Magazine,* October 10, 2017.
27. Julie Lythcott-Haims, "Former Stanford Dean Shares the 8 Skills Everyone Should Have by Age 18," businessinsider.com, April 17, 2016.
28. Adam Boult, "The Two Key Things People Judge You on When They First Meet You," *The Telegraph,* January 19, 2016.
29. Ezra Klein (video). vox.com, September 8, 2016.
30. *The Roosevelts: An Intimate History* by Ken Burns, *PBS* (2014).
31. Ibid.
32. Daniel L. Everett, *Don't Sleep, There Are Snakes: Life and Language in the Amazonian Jungle* (New York: Random House, 2008), p. 11.
33. David G. Myers, *Psychology in Everyday Life* (Holland, MI: Worth Publishers, 2009), p. 394.
34. Ed Yong, "The Incredible Thing We Do During Conversations," *The Atlantic,* January 4, 2016.

35. Melissa Dahl, "People Will Like You More If You Ask Them Questions," *New York Magazine,* June 14, 2017.

36. Nikki Sapp, "How Negative Thoughts and Complaining Affect Your Brain," fractalenlightenment.com, October 9, 2016.

37. Daniel Goleman, *Emotional Intelligence: Why It Can Matter More Than IQ* (London: Bloomsbury, 1995), p. 116.

38. Chris Weller, "A Neuroscientist Who Studies Decision-Making Reveals the Most Important Choice You Can Make," businessinsider.com, July 28, 2017.

39. Caroline Beaton, "Millennials, This Is Why You Haven't Been Promoted," forbes.com, May 12, 2016.

40. Monte Burke, "At Age 25 Mark Cuban Learned Lessons about Leadership That Changed his Life," forbes.com, March 28, 2013.

41. Shana Lebowitz, "Harness the Power of the 'Ben Franklin Effect' to Get Someone to Like You," businessinsider.com, December 2, 2016.

42. Constantin Stanislavski, *An Actor's Handbook: An Alphabetical Arrangement of Concise Statements on Aspects of Acting* (New York: Theatre Arts Books, 1963), p. 59.

43. Melissa Dahl, "People Will Like You More If You Ask Them Questions," *New York Magazine,* June 14, 2017.

44. Adrian F. Ward, "The Neuroscience of Everybody's Favorite Topic," *Scientific American*, July 16, 2013.

45. Valerian J. Derlaga and John H. Berg, *Self-Disclosure: Theory, Research, and Therapy* (New York: Springer, 1987), p. 307.

Chapter 7

1. *The Kid Stays in the Picture,* USA Films, 2002.

2. Carolyn O'Hara, "How to Tell a Great Story," *Harvard Business Review,* July 30, 2014.

3. Interview with G. Riley Mills, October 2, 2017.

4. Franc Chamberlain, *Michael Chekov* (London: Routledge, 2004), p. 59.

5. Daniel Kahneman, *Thinking, Fast and Slow* (New York: Farrar, Straus and Giroux, 2011), p. 199.

6. Kristi Hedges, "Seven Types of Stories Every Leader Should Tell," forbes.com, January 30, 2015.

7. Richard Branson, "Storytelling Is as Old as the Campfire," virgin.com, March 27, 2017.

8. Frank Addante, "5 Storytelling Secrets That Can Transform Your Company," inc.com, May 18, 2016.

9. Jonathan Gottschall, "Infecting an Audience: Why Great Stories Spread," *Fast Company,* October 20, 2013.

10. Carmine Gallo, "An Analysis of 700 presentations revealed that adopting one speaking skill can make you more persuasive," inc.com, March 25, 2017.

11. Quora, "More Great Stories About People Meeting Steve Jobs," forbes. com, September 12, 2013.

12. Ed Catmull, *Creativity, Inc.* (New York: Random House, 2014), p. 305.

13. Eddie Merla, "Storytelling Is for Kids—and Project Managers," *Project Management Institute,* 2009.

14. Lars Schmidt, "Three Unexpected Brands That Are Turning to Story-telling to Drive Recruiting," forbes.com, September 17, 2016.

15. Interview with G. Riley Mills, October 1, 2017.

16. Michele Weldon, "Your Brain on Story: Why Narratives Win Our Hearts and Minds," *Pacific Standard,* April 22, 2014.

17. Shana Lebowitz, "Scientists Say Men with One Intriguing Characteristic Are More Attractive to Women," businessinsider.com, May 25, 2016.

18. Elyane Youssef, "This Quote on Mistakes from Louis C.K. Should Be Required Reading for Life," *Elephant Journal,* July 25, 2017.

19. Maria Popova, "The Psychology of What Makes a Great Story," brainpickings.com, January 20, 2016.

20. TED: Ideas Worth Spreading, "Helen Fisher Tells Us Why We Love + Cheat," February 2006.

21. Ewan Spence, "Five of the Greatest 'One More Thing . . . ' Moments from Steve Jobs and Apple," forbes.com, October 19, 2013.

22. Taryn Hillin, "Science Explains Why Surprise Brings Us Pleasure," splinter.com, April 1, 2015.

23. Ibid.

24. Ibid.

25. Ibid.

26. Joe Winston and Miles Tandy, *Beginning Drama 4–11,* third ed. (London: Routledge, 1998), p. 3.

27. David Hackett, "What Former McDonald's Global Marketing Officer David Green Has Learned," 941ceo.com, June 23, 2017.

28. Christian Conte, "Nordstrom customer service tales not just legend," Jacksonville Business Journal, September 7, 2012.

29. Paul Smith, *Lead with a Story: A Guide to Crafting Business Narratives That Captivate, Convince, and Inspire* (AMACOM, 2012), p. 74.

30. Mark McKinnon, "It's Storytelling, Stupid: What Made Donald Trump Smarter Than Hillary Clinton," *The Daily Beast,* November 24, 2016.

31. Ibid.

32. Harrison Monarth, "The Irresistible Power of Storytelling as a Strategic Business Tool," *Harvard Business Review,* May 11, 2014.

33. The Churchill Project, "Exploring the Official Biography: Churchill's 'The Scaffolding of Rhetoric,' "*The Churchill Project,* April 29, 2016.

Chapter 8

1.   Thomas Maier, *When Lions Roar: The Churchills and the Kennedys* (New York: Crown, 2014), p. 490.

2.   Michael McKinney, "5 Leadership Lessons: What Is Your Intention?" leadershipnow.com, January 14, 2008.

3.   Susanna Schrobsdorff, "Teen Depression and Anxiety: Why the Kids Are Not Alright," *Time Magazine,* October 27, 2016.

4.   Simon Sinek, "The Video on Millennials in the Workplace That Everyone Must Watch," *New York Post,* September 30, 2017.

5.   Thomas Gilovich and Kenneth Savitsky, "The Spotlight Effect and the Illusion of Transparency," *Sage Journals,* December 1, 1999.

6.   Matt Burns, "Meg Whitman Details Layoffs to HP Employees in Internal Video, Thinks HP Is 'Rebuilding Credibility,'" TechCrunch, May 23, 2012.

7.   JT Genter, "United CEO Mishandles Earnings Call, Stock Price Tumbles 12%," the pointsguy.com, October 19, 2017.

8.   Eliza Barclay, "A Buddhist Monk Explains Mindfulness for Times of Conflict," vox.com, January 28, 2017.

9.   Chris Weller, "A Harvard Psychologist's Advice on How to Argue When You Know You're Right," businessinsider.com, February 4, 2016.

10. Constantin Stanislavski, *An Actor's Handbook: An Alphabetical Arrangement of Concise Statements of Acting* (New York: Theatre Arts Books, 1963), p. 17.

11. Matthew Hutson, "Why You Trust Email Way More Than You Should," *New York Magazine,* April 17, 2017.

12. Noah J. Goldstein, Steve J. Martin, and Robert Cialdini, *Yes!: 50 Scientifically Proven Ways to Be Persuasive* (New York: Free Press, 2008), p. 202.

13. Matthew Hutson, "Why You Trust Email Way More Than You Should," *New York Magazine,* April 17, 2017.

14. Jennifer Parlamis and Daniel Ames, "Face-to-Face and Email Negotiations: A Comparison of Emotions, Perceptions and Outcomes." Paper presented at the International Association of Conflict Management Conference, Boston, MA, June 24, 2010.

15. Jean W. Rioux, *Ethics: Collected Readings: Collected Readings* (Eugene, OR: Wipf and Stock Publishers, 2005), p. 25.

16. Mike Berardino, "Mike Tyson Explains One of His Most Famous Quotes," *Sun Sentinel,* November 9, 2012.

17. Tim Webb, "BP Boss Admits Job on the Line over Gulf Oil Spill," *The Guardian,* May 13, 2010.

18. Richard Wray, "Deepwater Horizon Oil Spill: BP Gaffes in Full," *The Guardian,* July 27, 2010.

19. Ibid.

20. Bianca Bosker, "Mark Zuckerberg Sweats on Privacy Hot Seat at All Things Digital (video)," *Huffington Post,* June 3, 2010.

21. Dan Nosowitz, "Mark Zuckerberg Gives Awkward, Sweaty Interview at D8: Touches on Privacy and Scandal," *Fast Company,* June 3, 2010.

22. Constance Staley, *Focus on College Success* (Boston: Wadsworth, 2014), p. 69.

23. Richard E. Petty, John T. Cacioppo, and Martin Heesacker, "Effects of Rhetorical Questions on Persuasion: A Cognitive Response Analysis," *Journal of Personality and Social Psychology* 40, no. 3 (1981): 432–440.

24. Mark Murphy, "Fewer Than Half of Employees Know If They're Doing a Good Job," forbes.com, September 4, 2016.

25. Judith V. Jordan, *Women's Growth in Connection: Writings from the Stone Center* (New York: Guilford Press, 1991), p. 82.

26. Ibid.

27. Andrea Christensen, "Delivering Bad News? Don't Beat around the Bush," *Science Daily,* October 5, 2017.

28. Justin Bariso, "It took Sheryl Sandberg Exactly 2 Sentences to Give the Best Career Advice You'll Hear Today," inc.com, October 31, 2016.

29. Roy Larson, "Listening from the Heart," linkedin.com, March 12, 2015.

30. Kathryn Dill, "3 Body-Language Tricks for Giving Employees Feedback," cnbc.com, March 21, 2017.

31. Michael McKinney, "5 Leadership Lessons: What Is Your Intention?" leadershipnow.com, January 14, 2008.

32. Eric Barker, "Neuroscience Reveals 4 Rituals That Will Make You Happy," *The Week,* February 28, 2016.

Chapter 9

1. Leslie A. Perlow, Constance Noonan Hadley and Eunice Eun, "Stop the Meeting Madness," *Harvard Business Review,* July–August 2017 issue.

2. Ibid.

3. Microsoft, "Survey Finds Workers Average Only Three Productive Days per Week," microsoft.com, March 15, 2005.

4. Eric Matson, "The Seven Sins of Deadly Meetings," fastcompany.com, April 30, 1996.

5. Laura Montini, "What Unproductive Meetings Are Costing You (Infographic)," inc.com, June 13, 2014.

6. Michael Mankins, Chris Brahm, and Greg Caimi, "Your Scarcest Resource," *Harvard Business Journal,* May 2014.

7. Kevan Hall and Alan Hall, "Bad Meetings: Analyzing the Cost to Business," trainingjournal.com, September 21, 2017.

8. Drake Baer, "$37 Billion Is Lost Every Year on These 12 Meeting Mistakes," businessinsider.com, April 9, 2014.

9. Geoff Pugh, "20 Funniest Quotes about Office Life," *The Telegraph,* March 1, 2016.

10. Drake Baer and Jenna Goudreau, "13 Tricks Steve Jobs, Jeff Bezos, and Other Famous Executives Have Used to Run Effective Meetings," businessinsider.com, October 13, 2015.

11. Adam Lashinsky, "Amazon's Jeff Bezos: The Ultimate Disrupter," *Fortune,* November 16, 2012.

12. Aine Cain, "Jeff Bezos's Productivity Tip? The '2 Pizza Rule,' "inc.com, June 7, 2017.

13. Baer and Goudreau, "13 Tricks."

14. Ibid.

15. Abby Jackson, "Elon Musk Has Reportedly Used a Brutal Tactic to Keep from Wasting Time in Meetings," businessinsider.com, October 3, 2017.

16. Baer and Goudreau, "13 Tricks."

17. Laura Montini, "What Unproductive Meetings Are Costing You (Infographic)," inc.com, June 13, 2014.

18. Wrike, "Wrike Releases 2015 Work Management Survey," wrike.com, October 7, 2015.

19. Lucy MacDonald, *You Can Manage Your Time Better: Change Your Thinking, Change Your Life* (London: Duncan Baird, 2006), p. 108.

20. John G. Miller, "Hold Yourself Accountable—You'll Be Happier," *Time Magazine,* November 17, 2016.

21. Donald Spoto, *The Redgraves: A Family Epic* (Robson Press, 2012), p. 307.

22. Jenna Goudreau, "So Begins a Quiet Revolution of the 50 Percent," forbes.com, January 30, 2012.

23. Geoff Ho, "Office Meetings Can Be a Black Hole for Time, Says Geoff Ho," *Express,* April 30, 2017.

24. Jason Fried and David Heinemeier Hansson, *Rework* (Crown Business, 2010), p. 109.

25. Northcote Parkinson, "Parkinson's Law," *The Economist,* November 19, 1955.

26. Corey Wainwright, "You're Going to Waste 31 Hours in Meetings This Month," blog.hubspot.com, June 12, 2014.

27. Sue Shellenbarger, "A Manifesto to End Boring Meetings," *The Wall Street Journal,* December 20, 2016.

28. Laura Montini, "What Unproductive Meetings Are Costing You (Infographic)," inc.com, June 13, 2014.

29. Constantin Stanislavski, *Building a Character* (New York: Routledge/ Theatre Arts Books, 1949), p. 278.

30. Bruce Davis, "There Are 50,000 Thoughts Standing between You and Your Partner Every Day!" *Huffington Post,* May 23, 2013.

31. Anne Fisher, "Giving a Speech? Conquer the Five-Minute Attention Span," *Fortune,* July 10, 2013.

32. Kermit Pattison, "Worker, Interrupted: The Cost of Task Switching," *Fast Company,* July 28, 2008.

33. Bob Sullivan, "Brain, Interrupted," *New York Times,* May 3, 2013.

34. Lindsay Abrams, "Study: A 3 Second Interruption Doubles Your Odds of Messing Up," *The Atlantic,* January 10, 2013.

35. Kim Tong-hyung, "Kim Jong-Un Executes Vice Premier for 'Disrespectful' Sitting Position at Meeting, South Korea Says," *National Post,* August 31, 2016.

36. Adam Bryant, "How to Run a More Effective Meeting," *New York Times,* May 9, 2017.

37. Don Yaeger, "Four Ways to Make Your Team Meetings Matter," forbes .com, February 15, 2017.

38. Adam Bryant, "How to Run a More Effective Meeting," *New York Times,* May 9, 2017.

39. Stephanie Wood, "Scientists Reveal How Smartphones Make Us Dumber," eartheasy.com, August 9, 2017.

40. Nancy F. Clark, "Gal Interrupted, Why Men Interrupt Women and How to Avert This in the Workplace," positivitydaily.com, January 2, 2017.

41. Lolly Daskal, "9 Things Enormously Productive People Refuse to Do," inc.com, April 22, 2016.

42. Kristi Hedges, "How to Get People Off Their Phones in Meetings without Being a Jerk," forbes.com, July 5, 2014.

Chapter 10

1. Kathy Maher, *The Barnum Museum,* Bridgeport, CT, barnum-museum. org, October 13, 2017.

2. Bob Cullen, "Two Weeks at Camp David," *Smithsonian Magazine,* September 2003.

3. Andrew S. Rancer and Theodore A. Avtgis, *Argumentative and Aggressive Communication: Theory, Research, and Application* (Thousand Oaks, CA: Sage Publications, 2006), p. 177.

4. Tali Sharot, "How Our Desires Shape Our Beliefs," *The Guardian,* August 27, 2017.

5. Ibid.

6. Robert Lee Hotz, "Science Reveals Why We Brag So Much," *The Wall Street Journal,* May 7, 2012.

7. Sharot, "How Our Desires Shape Our Beliefs."

8. Bourree Lam, "What It Was Like to Write Speeches for Apple Executives," *The Atlantic,* June 10, 2016.

9. Ananth Pandian, "Bazemore, Riley Curry Helped Steph Choose Under Armour over Nike," cbssports.com, March 24, 2016.

10. George A. Miller, "The Magic Number Seven, Plus or Minus Two: Some Limits on Our Capacity for Processing Information," *Psychological Review* 63, no. 2 (1956): 81–97.

11. Jacquelyn Smith, "10 Public Speaking Habits to Avoid at All Costs," businessinsider.com, June 9, 2014.

12. Megan Bruneau, "5 Hacks for Overcoming Social Anxiety and Networking Like a Pro," forbes.com, May 28, 2016.

13. "Dorothy Raymond Sarnoff Obituary,"*New York Times,* December 23, 2008.

14. Jaruwan Sakulku and James Alexander, "The Imposter Phenomenon," *International Journal of Behavioral Science* 6, no. 1 (2011): 73.

15. Malcolm Gladwell, "Complexity and the Ten-Thousand-Hour Rule," *The New Yorker,* August 21, 2013.

16. Daniel Goleman, "Why The 10,000 Hour Rule Is a Myth," huffingtonpost.com, October 7, 2013.

17. Kimberly Weisul, "Mark Cuban's Top 3 Rules for Business Success . . . and 1 Secret," inc.com, May 20, 2015.

18. Amie M. Gordon, "Have You Fallen Prey to the 'Spotlight Effect?'" *Psychology Today,* November 21, 2013.

19. Travis Bradberry, "How Successful People Quash Stress," forbes.com, December 9, 2014.

20. Greg McKeown, "The Difference Between Successful and Very Successful People," *Entrepreneur,* January 6, 2015.

21. Jenna Goudreau, "Why It's Harder for Women to Say 'No' to Extra Work," businessinsider.com, December 17, 2014.

22. Kevin Kruse, "Overcome 'The Disease to Please,'" huffingtonpost.com, December 30, 2016.

23. Mark Milian, "The spiritual side of Steve Jobs," cnn.com, October 7, 2011.

24. Robert Lewis, *Method—or Madness?* (New York: Samuel French, 1958), p. 60.

25. Nick Kolenda, *Methods of Persuasion* (Kolenda Entertainment, 2013), p. 89.

26. Andrew M. Carton, "People Remember What You Say When You Paint a Picture," *Harvard Business Review,* June 12, 2015.

27. Jack Holmes, "Donald Trump Woos Republicans by Speaking at a 4th Grade Level," *Esquire,* October 21, 2015.

28. Andrew M. Carton, "People Remember What You Say When You Paint a Picture," *Harvard Business Review,* June 12, 2015.

29. Jason Fried and David Heinemeier Hansson, *Rework* (Crown Business, 2010), p. 262.

30. Herman Melville, *The Poetry of Herman Melville—Volume 3* (Portable Poetry, 2013).

31. "Exploring the Official Biography: Churchill's 'The Scaffolding of Rhetoric,'" The Churchill Project, April 29, 2016.

32. Nick Kolenda, *Methods of Persuasion* (Kolenda Entertainment, 2013), p. 98.

33. Leo Widrich, "The Science of Storytelling: Why Telling a Story Is the Most Powerful Way to Activate Our Brains," *lifehacker.com,* December 5, 2012.

34. Cynthia G. Emrich, *Administrative Science Quarterly,* September 2001 issue.

35. Winston Churchill, "We Shall Fight on the Beaches," *International Churchill Society,* June 4, 1940.

36. William Manchester, *The Last Lion, Winston Spencer Churchill,* Volume 1 (New York: Bantam Books, 1988), p. 30.

37. Eric Ramsay, "Blog Post: Thinking, Fast and Slow by Daniel Kahneman: Parallels with Player Development in Football," www.linkedin.com, November 11, 2016.

38. Richard Branson, "The Fears Are Paper Tigers," virgin.com, November 6, 2015.

Acknowledgments

1. Lawrence Senelick, *Theatre Arts on Acting* (New York: Routledge, 2008), p. 248.

Glossary of Terms

Active Listening—Concept pioneered by psychologists Carl R. Rogers and Richard E. Farson that puts forward the idea that listening is not a passive activity but requires energy and effort

Amplification—The technique of spotlighting the ideas or contributions of others in a meeting

Articulation—The formation of clear and distinct sounds in speech

Attention Span—The length of time a person can devote to an activity before their mind wanders

Benefit—Something advantageous or positive that an audience will achieve or receive as a result of hearing your message

Body Language—Nonverbal communication such as gestures, postures, and facial expressions that help support a person's intention

Civil Inattention—The process whereby strangers who are in close proximity demonstrate that they are aware of one another, without imposing on each other

Climax—The highest point of tension in a story; the major turning point in the plot

Close-ended Question—A question that can be answered with a simple yes or no answer, or with one specific piece of information

Cognitive Nervousness—Anxiety relating to or involving thinking, reasoning, or remembering

Communication—The process of sending and receiving messages with attached meaning

Confirmation Bias—A tendency to search for, interpret, favor, and recall information in a way that confirms one's preexisting beliefs

Congruence—The state when all aspects of voice and body language perfectly support a communicator's intention

Convergent Questions (*closed-ended questions*)—Questions that can be answered with a simple yes or no or a specific bit of information

Core Breathing—The low belly breath used by actors and singers for maximum support; also called *diaphragmatic breathing*

Critical Inner Voice—Any negative thoughts or insecurities that can distract or cause anxiousness in a speaker

Developmental Change—Organizational changes you make to improve current business procedures

Diffusion of Responsibility—The idea that a person is less likely to take responsibility for action or inaction when others are present

Distress—Negative stress; threat stress that causes strain, anxiety, or suffering

Divergent Questions (*open-ended questions*)—Exploratory questions that can have more than one possible answer and are designed to elicit expanded thinking

Dopamine—A neurotransmitter that helps control the brain's reward and pleasure centers

Empathy—The ability to understand and share the feelings of another

Empathic Attunement—The ability to comprehend the momentary psychological state of another person

Employee Engagement—The emotional commitment an employee has to the organization and its goals

Engagement—A connection with an audience that finds them in a willing state of attentiveness during your communication

Eustress—Positive stress; challenge stress that is healthy or provides fulfillment

Exposition—The basic information (who, what, when, where) an audience needs to know to be able to follow a story

Exposure Effect—The idea that the more you are exposed to an experience, the easier and less daunting it becomes

Falling Action—The short series of events in a story immediately following the climax and just before the final resolution is reached

Flow—A state of total immersion and focus, a concept first coined by Mihaly Csikszentmihalyi

Gesture—Any movement of the hand, arm, body, head, or face that communicates a specific idea, opinion, or emotion

Glossophobia—Greek term for stage fright or speech anxiety

Gravitas—The serious, dignified manner we associate with strong leaders

Ground Rules—Guidelines for individual and team behavior

Halo Effect—A cognitive bias in which the overall impression you create with another person then influences how they feel and think about your character and abilities.

Home Base Position—The relaxed, open body position that serves as a communicator's physical neutral when not moving or gesturing

Illusion of Transparency—Phenomenon whereby individuals often believe their internal states are more apparent to others than is actually the case

Imposter Syndrome—An inability to internalize accomplishments and a persistent fear of being exposed as a fraud despite possessing accomplishments and achievements to the contrary

Impromptu Speaking—A delivery mode where someone is called upon to speak without preparation or notes

Inciting Incident—The event in a story that serves as a trigger to set the initial events or action in motion

Incongruence—The state of someone's delivery where mixed messages are being communicated, a result of an intention not being properly supported

Inflection—The specific pitch in the voice (up or down) used at the end of a word or phrase

Intention—An aim that guides action, informing all aspects of a person's physical and vocal delivery

Intention Cues—Any aspect of a person's vocal or physical communication that conveys meaning to an audience or listener

Isopraxism—The idea that an audience will mirror back whatever emotion or behavior a speaker projects; *see also* mirror theory

Jargon—Words or expressions that are used by a particular profession or group and are difficult for others to understand

Listening—The process of receiving, constructing meaning from, and responding to spoken and/or nonverbal messages

Meeting Assets—Action items, consensus, or decisions made as a result of a meeting occurring

Micro Expressions—The involuntary facial movements and physical tics that occur without our even being aware of them

Mirror Theory—The idea that people pick up on whatever emotion or intention a speaker projects and both feel and project back that emotion; *see also* isopraxism

Monotone—A succession of sounds or words that is unchanging in pitch

Motivating Language Theory—Idea that an inspiring speech can have a direct, positive effect on critical employee outcomes associated with motivation

Mutuality—The sharing of a feeling, action, or relationship

Nonverbal Communication—Any aspects of communication—aside from the actual words spoken—that send messages or convey meaning to a listener

Norm of Reciprocity—Expectation that people will respond favorably to one another by returning benefits for benefits, and responding with either indifference or hostility to slights or harms.

Objective—A goal you hope to accomplish with your communication

Open-ended Question—A question that cannot be answered with a single word or a yes or no and requires more information or detail

Oxytocin—A chemical that encourages empathy in the receiver of the story

Pace—The rate, based on words per minute spoken, at which a person speaks

Pacifier—Any nervous behavior or activity displayed by a speaker that communicates discomfort or nervousness

Parkinson's Law—Adage that says work will always expand to fill the time available for its completion

Pattern Interrupt—Any action or behavior that breaks a pattern in an effort to maintain the attention of an audience

Personal Brand—The way you project yourself to the world and, consequently, how you are seen by others

Personal Branding Statement—A one- to two-sentence statement answering what you are best at, who you serve, and how you do it uniquely

Phatic Communication—Communication that has a social function, such as to start a conversation, greet someone, or say goodbye

Physiological Pause—A silence during your communication that requires you to stop speaking so you can take a breath or take sip of water

Pitch—The highness or lowness in the voice determined by the rate of vibration in the vocal cords

Posture—The position of a person's body when standing or sitting

Psychological Pause—A silence during your communication used to evoke or provoke an emotional response from your audience

Resolution—The final element of a story where all loose ends are tied up and any outstanding questions are answered

Resonation—The prolongation and intensification of sound produced by transmission of its vibrations in the various body cavities (chest, mouth, nasal cavity, skull, throat)

Rhetorical Questions—Questions that are asked to make a point rather than elicit an answer.

Rising Action—The events in a story that follow the inciting incident and build to the climax

Social Awareness—The ability to pick up on the emotions and intentions of others with whom we interact

Social Loafing—An idea that posits that the larger the meeting, the less accountable meeting attendees will feel toward making contributions of ideas or efforts

Spatiality—The way in which a speaker uses space, movement, and distance when communicating a message to others

Spotlight Effect—Phenomenon in which people tend to believe they are being noticed more than they really are

Street Intimacy—Fleeting connections with strangers, usually in public settings

Transformational Change—A shift in the business culture of an organization resulting from a change in the underlying strategy or processes that the organization has used in the past

Transitional Change—A shift in the way a process within an organization is completed, designed to increase efficiency

Treadmill Verb—An intention that lacks the ability to influence emotion or motivate action

Verbal Virus—Verbal fillers (such as *ah, um,* or *I mean*) that show up in speech and communicate uncertainty to an audience or listener

Vocal Dynamics—The ways in which you use the various qualities of the voice (pitch, tone, resonation, inflection, articulation, volume, and pace)

Vocal Variety—Effective variation of vocal qualities achieved through combining and varying pitch, tone, resonation, inflection

Acknowledgments

Everything has to come to an end, sometime.
—L. Frank Baum

Recently the Pinnacle team climbed the three highest mountains in the United Kingdom as part of a charity event to raise funds for Pinnacle Performance Academy, our program to teach leadership and communication skills to underprivileged and underserved youth. Gathering at the base of the first mountain, as we assigned roles and responsibilities, it became apparent that everyone would play a crucial role in the success of the team being able to complete these hikes. And as we ascended the mountain and the weather abruptly shifted from hot and dry to cold and wet, it became even more obvious how much we would need each member of the team. We shared food, bandaged our blisters, and entertained each other with stories to make the grueling hours pass.

The research and writing that is brought together in *The Bullseye Principle* is not that far removed from what happened on those mountain climbs. We could not have written this book without the contributions and generosity of every member of the Pinnacle family. To paraphrase Viola Spolin, they were the spokes in the wheel that made this project roll. Every topic or idea discussed in these pages was developed and refined over time in various Pinnacle trainings and workshops across the globe. We would like to gratefully acknowledge the contributions of our core group of Pinnacle team members, many of whom have been with us from the beginning: Vicky Albertelli, Cheryl Avery, Spencer Baculi, Stephanie Baculi, Yvonne Blackwell, Richard Bradford and Disquiet Dog, Anu Bhatt, Mitchell Chaban, Jason Denuszek, Kevin Douglas, Minita Gandhi, John Garnett, Chris Gausselin, Regan Gausselin, Tina Gluschenko, Aarti Gupta, Clare Hallinan, Valda Henry, Erica Hernandez, Frey Hoffman, Francesca Hutchings, Jessica Kadish, Tim Kasper, Tom LaMere, Brad Lawrence, Gerri Leon, Rob Lynch, James Mackey, Connor McNamara, Brian McNeany, Heidi McNeany, Claudio Medeiros, Eliza Jane Morris, Christian Mortensen, Naomi Ouellette, Ben Osbun, Blair Robertson, Adrian Romanski, Jay Schwartz, Laura Shatkus, Kaelan Strouse, Craig Tafel, Cindy Tegtmeyer, DawnMarie Vestevich, Kern Wasan, Andrew Weir, Jonathan Weis, Jason Wong, and Lizzie Yirrell. We'd also like to acknowledge Israel Antonio, an inspiring and amazing athlete whom we have proudly sponsored for the past eight years, and the great Phil Davison, who has been so generous with his time, talent, and passion. To everyone mentioned above, your commitment, dedication, and input have been invaluable in the process of developing and writing this book.

To our families—especially our wives, Jo and Celeste, our children, Sadie, Sawyer, Rider, and Hunter, and our parents and in-laws—thank you for the support and understanding you have allowed us as we shaped and formed this book, often spending extended periods of time working out of town or overseas.

To our network of friends and supporters—specifically Jacob Alexander, Hassan Al Juaidi, Steve Bertrand, Daniel Bird, John Bowden, Julie Bowden, Leo Bustamante, Darren Callahan, Sam Conjardi, Kim Conjardi, Melissa Farley, Steve Farley, Ja'Mal Green, Mike Heneghan, Elvia Heneghan, Benjamin Host, Chuck Huber, Bob Hudson, Zubin Kammula, Ryan Lance, James Lynch, Ryan Mecum, Rob Nelson,

Treshan Weerasooriya Pereira, Kurt Rolle, Morgan Rowe, Gernot Schulz, Matt Sullivan, Adam Szewc and Lucy Szewc—thank you for being a part of this adventure. We'd also like to thank our agent, the great Eric Lupfer at Fletcher & Company, for seeing the potential of this project from the start, as well as our editors Kelly Martin, Shannon Vargo, Deborah Schindlar, Marketing Manager Peter Knox and the entire staff at John Wiley & Sons. We are humbled by the invaluable guidance you have provided in shaping this book throughout the entire process. We are thrilled to call Wiley home.

We'd also like to thank those who provided us with interviews and stories for the book, especially Jay Bonansinga, Phil Davison, William "Andy" Freels, Ramesh Kaushik, Angela Kenyatta, David O'Connor, Albert Robinson, and Pat Wadors. Thank you for your time and generosity.

Finally, we wish to thank our various clients across the globe, specifically Ruth Almen, Cori Aluli-Chott, Paola Alvarez, Marc Bartolone, Elizabeth Bayee, Tiffany Berrecloth, Nancy Blonski, David Bowden, Aaron Boyle, Patrick Boyle, Owen Callahan, Keith Chan, Remi Chau, Marcia Childers, Therese Dickerson, Karen Dubiel, Marie Dumas, Nanette Fairley, Rich Fendrych, Gina Fernandes, Rachel Fichter, David First, Mindy Geisser, Amy Governale, Doris "Pippi" Guilfoyle, Candace Gunderson, Brian Hackerson, Steven Hamilton, Jonathan Hart, Theresa Haskins, Eloise Haverland, Kate Hay, Rob Hill, Bob Hilt, Matthew Hunter, Christina Itzkowitz, Bill Joiner, Regina Kaufman, Wade Kretman, Heather Lawrence, Marc Letendre, Sha-Ron Low, Matt Luke, Karen Jaw-Madson Nikki Magistro, Dana Mayhew, David McCulloch, Simon McGoran, Matthew McGrattan, Mark McNitt, Michelle Nikodem, Vikki Powell, Krysta Van Ranst, Craig Robbins, Susan St. Amant, Patricia Santini, Courtney Scheffler, Peter Sepessy, Thomas Shirley, David Small, Katherine Steen, Sal Venegas, Pat Wadors, Samuel Wang, Holly Whitcomb, Greg Willmore, and the numerous trusted partners at Capgemini and Infosys. We are grateful for the privilege you have given us to work with you. We could not have accomplished any of this without the trust and belief you have shown toward us and it has been a distinct honor to watch your employees blossom and grow as a result of the work we have done together.

For everyone who has read this book, we hope the principles and insights we have shared serve you well as you advance in your career and develop as a leader. Put these tools and concepts into your communicator's tool belt and carry them with you. If you keep them sharp, they will serve you well. Keep pushing yourself, put in the time, and strive for mastery as a communicator. Aspire. Believe. Commit. Because, as Stanislavski often reminded his actors "Talent without work is nothing more than raw unfinished material."[1]

We wish you the best of luck. Get out there and be amazing.

About the Authors

David Lewis is cofounder and CEO of Pinnacle Performance Company, a global intention-based training firm that has revolutionized presentation and communication skills training. He is also coinventor of The Pinnacle Method™; a unique and innovative learning system that meshes time-tested acting techniques with contemporary business skills (Intention-Based Communication®) to teach professionals how to clearly and concisely influence their audience through the delivery of their message. Prior to launching Pinnacle, his corporate track record stretched from Wall Street to Silicon Valley, generally performing in executive level sales and marketing leadership positions at both Fortune 500 companies and hi-tech/Internet start-ups.

In 2004, Mr. Lewis cofounded LastLine Endeavors, a film development and production company that produced the award-winning feature film, *Brothers Three: An American Gothic.* He is a member of the Screen Actors Guild with a number of stage, film, and TV commercial credits and is a graduate of Cornell University with a Bachelors' Degree in Business and Communications.

David lives in Chicago where he proudly serves on the Board of Directors for Ronald McDonald House Charities.

G. Riley Mills is the cofounder and COO of Pinnacle Performance Company and coauthor of *The Pin Drop Principle*. He was named one of Inc. Magazine's "Top 100 Leadership Speakers of 2018" and has served as an elite coach to some of the world's top executives and leaders in over 30 countries across the globe. Mills has guest-lectured or delivered keynotes at such events and institutions as Columbia University, NASSCOMM Conference (India), CIPD Conference (London and Manchester), ATD International Conference and Exposition, London Chamber of Commerce, New York University, Young Presidents' Organization, MENA Conference (Saudi Arabia), Cox School of Business, Southern Methodist University, University of Liverpool, London, The Cornell Club, Learning and Skills Conference (London), SHRM Annual Conference & Exposition, Purdue University, Singapore Management University, and Manchester United.

As a writer, Mills has twice been awarded the Joseph Jefferson Award (Chicago's Tony Award) for Best New Work and is also the recipient of a 2007 NAPPA Honor Award. He has twice been nominated for the Distinguished Play Award from the American Alliance for Theatre & Education. Most recently his acclaimed musical, *The Hundred Dresses* (written with Grammy-nominated musician Ralph Covert) premiered Off-Broadway at The Atlantic Theatre Company in New York City. His writing has also been featured in *Fast Company* and he is a frequent contributor to *Forbes*. He is a member of the Screen Actors Guild and his acting resume features many notable stage, television, and film appearances.

Mills is also the cofounder of The Bookwallah Organization, a charitable association whose mission is to collect storybooks and set up libraries in orphanages around the world (www.bookwallah.org).

ABOUT PINNACLE PERORMANCE COMPANY

Pinnacle Performance Company delivers its intention-based communication skills training to business professionals on six continents in nearly 50 countries around the world, meshing time-honored performance-delivery techniques with the essential business communication skills needed to succeed and influence at every level of the corporate arena. Building on its award-winning methodology (The Pinnacle Method), Pinnacle uses customized, experiential simulations and a detailed focus on delivery to help participants become more confident, credible, and compelling communicators. For more information about our company and offerings, please log on to www.pinper.com.

For additional material and bonus content not included in *The Bullseye Principle,* go to pinper.com/resources.

Index